MULTICULTURALISM AND THE HISTORY OF CANADIAN DIVERSITY

Is Canada a country of equal and peacefully coexisting identities, working towards what Charles Taylor has called a 'post-industrial *Sittlichkeit*'? In this analysis of the history of Canadian diversity, Richard Day argues that no degree or style of state intervention can ever bring an end to tensions related to ethnocultural relations of power.

Using Foucault's method of genealogical analysis and a theory of the state form derived from the works of Deleuze and Guattari, Day creates a framework for his exploration of the construction of human difference and its management over the years. He argues that Canada's multicultural policies are propelled by a fantasy of unity based on the nation-state model. Our legislation, policies, and practices do not move us towards equality and reciprocity, he reveals, because they are rooted in a European drive to manage and control diversity.

Day challenges the notion that Canadian multiculturalism represents either progress beyond a history of assimilation and genocide or a betrayal of that very history that supports the dominance of Anglo-Canadians. Only when English Canada is able to abandon its fantasy of unity, Day concludes, can the radical potential of multiculturalism politics be realized.

RICHARD DAY is an assistant professor in the Department of Sociology, Queen's University.

Multiculturalism and the History of Canadian Diversity

RICHARD J.F. DAY

UNIVERSITY OF TORONTO PRESS
Toronto Buffalo London

© University of Toronto Press Incorporated 2000
Toronto Buffalo London
Printed in Canada

Reprinted 2002

ISBN 0-8020-4231-7 (cloth)
ISBN 0-8020-8075-8 (paper)

∞

Printed on acid-free paper

Canadian Cataloguing in Publication Data

Day, Richard J.F.
'Multiculturalism and the history of Canadian diversity

ISBN 0-8020-4231-7 (bound)   ISBN 0-8020-8075-8 (pbk.)

1. Multiculturalism – Canada – History.   2. Canada – Ethnic
relations – History.   I. Title

FC105.M8D39 1999   971'.004   C99-932435-7
F1035.A1D39 1999

Fig 1.1 is reprinted from Standing Committee on Multiculturalism, *Multiculturalism: Building the Canadian Mosaic* (Ottawa: Supply and Services Canada, 1987). Fig. 1.2 is reprinted from Dept. of the Secretary of State, *Multiculturalism: Being Canadian* (Ottawa: Supply and Services Canada, 1987). Figs. 1.1 and 1.2 are reproduced with the permission of the Minister of Public Works and Government Services (1999) and the Minister of Canadian Heritage. Fig. 6.3 is reprinted with permission of the publisher from J.S. Woodsworth, *My Neighbor* (University of Toronto Press, 1972).

This book has been published with the help of a grant from the Humanities and Social Sciences Federation of Canada, using funds provided by the Social Sciences and Humanities Research Council of Canada.

University of Toronto Press acknowledges the financial assistance to its publishing program of the Canada Council for the Arts and the Ontario Arts Council.

University of Toronto Press acknowledges the financial support for its publishing activities of the Government of Canada through the Book Publishing Industry Development Program (BPIDP).

Canadä

To my parents

Contents

Figures

Acknowledgments

The Department of Sociology and Anthropology at Simon Fraser University provided funding for the research upon which this book is based. The many-faceted support of my dissertation supervisors, Ian Angus and Dany Lacombe, has been particularly valuable to me, as has the help and advice of Ellen Gee, who was Chair of the sociology department during my time at SFU. I would also like to acknowledge the contributions made to my thinking on these issues by Lori Barkley, David Firman, Marilyn Gates, Krista Henriksen, David Howarth, Kieran Keohane, Ernesto Laclau, Guy-Kirby Letts, Yannis Stavrakakis, Richard Toews, and Jerald Zaslove. Finally, I must thank Alison Gowan for sticking with me through the absurdly difficult process of pursuing an academic career while raising two young children. It is only because of her commitment to our family life that I have been able to spend so much time worrying about nations, states, and ethnocultural groups.

Abbreviations

B & B Report   Canada. Royal Commission on Bilingualism and Biculturalism. *Report of the Royal Commission on Bilingualism and Biculturalism*. Ottawa: Supply and Services Canada, 1969.

Bagot Report   'Report on the Affairs of the Indians in Canada, Laid before the Legislative Assembly, March 20 1845.' *Journals of the Legislative Assembly of Canada* 8 (Victoria 1844–5), Appendix EEE.

CIHM   Canadian Institute for Historical Microreproductions.

CSY   Canada. Dept. of Agriculture. *The Statistical Year-Book of Canada*. Ottawa: Government of Canada, 1886–1905. Continued as: Canada. Statistics Canada. *The Canada Year Book*. Ottawa: Statistics Canada, 1906–.

DC & I   Department of Citizenship and Immigration.

DHC   Canada. Parliament. House of Commons. *Official Report of Debates*. Ottawa: Government of Canada, 1867–.

DRCHC   A. Shortt and G. Doughty, eds. *Documents Relating to the Constitutional History of Canada*. Ottawa: King's Printer, 1907.

HBRSS   Hudson's Bay Record Society. *Hudson's Bay Record Society Series*. London: The Champlain Society, 1938–.

JHC   Canada. Parliament. House of Commons. *Journals of the House of Commons of the Dominion of Canada*. Ottawa: Government of Canada, 1867–.

MCBC   Canada. Dept. of the Secretary of State. *Multiculturalism: Being Canadian.* Ottawa: Supply and Services Canada, 1987.

MCBCM   Canada. Standing Committee on Multiculturalism. *Multiculturalism: Building the Canadian Mosaic.* Ottawa: Supply and Services Canada, 1987.

MCWR   Canada. Ministry of State for Multiculturalism and Citizenship. *Multiculturalism: What Is It Really About?* Ottawa: Supply and Services Canada, 1991.

NAC   National Archives of Canada.

PC   Privy Council

PD-NYCD   Paris Documents I. In *Documents Relating to the Colonial History of New York.* Vol. IX, CIHM 53992.

Relations   R.G. Thwaites. *The Jesuit Relations and Allied Documents.* Cleveland: Burrows Brothers, 1897–.

RSC   Canada. *Revised Statutes of Canada.* Ottawa: Government of Canada, 1985.

SPHC   Canada. Parliament. *Sessional Papers of the Dominion of Canada.* Ottawa: Government of Canada, 1868–1925.

StatsCan   Canada. Statistics Canada.

MULTICULTURALISM AND THE HISTORY OF CANADIAN DIVERSITY

Chapter One

Introduction

The Problem of the Problem of Diversity

In this book, I set out to show how contemporary Canadian multi-culturalism has emerged out of an older and broader discourse on diversity that can be traced back to Herodotus. The central chapters follow the continuities and ruptures in this tradition as they appear in colonial and state policy, philosophical-theoretical analyses, and popular culture. Based on this evidence, I ask whether the current state policy of multiculturalism, as Charles Taylor has suggested, is a stage on the way to a 'post-industrial *Sittlichkeit*' (1975: 461). The answer is clearly negative; relations of power found in the 'deficient' Hegelian forms of recognition, particularly those of the struggle to the death and the master-slave dialectic, have been the rule and norm, rather than the exception, in the history of Canadian diversity. Indeed, those forms of local autonomy and identity which currently exist have survived, not by virtue of a history of multiculturalist tolerance, but through determined *resistance* to a statist dream of a perfectly striated space of social order.

Thus, while Canadian multiculturalism presents itself as a new solution to an ancient problem of diversity, it is better seen as the most recent mode of *reproduction* and *proliferation* of that problem. Far from achieving its goal, this state-sponsored attempt to design a unified nation has paradoxically led to an increase in both the number of minority identities and in the amount of effort required to 'manage' them. This said, I want to be careful not to align myself with those

commentators who see multiculturalism as a form of 'dangerous fragmentation' that threatens a fragile 'Canadian unity.' My view is quite
different: as long as it retains the hope of reaching a position of fullness, reconciliation, and rest – even within a liberal-pluralist framework – I argue that multiculturalism will remain a slave to the history
of Canadian diversity. To escape the limitations of the modern-colonial
nation-state, those who would be Canadians must traverse the fantasy
of unity which underlies both the problem of diversity and its solution
via state 'recognition' of a system of official identity categories. Only
then can the potential of multiculturalism as radical imaginary, which
tends towards spontaneous emergence, be separated from multiculturalism as state policy, which tends towards management, discipline,
and uniformity.

There are, of course, many 'dividing practices' operating upon the
Canadian population, each of which has created its own form of diversity.[1] In this book I will focus on differentiation by 'ethnocultural
origin,' a term defined within state policy discourse as including 'cultural, national, or racial origin of a person' (Standing Committee on
Multiculturalism, *Multiculturalism: Building the Canadian Mosaic* [1987]:
87; hereafter cited as *MCBCM*). Inasmuch as culture, nation, and race
are assumed to be conditioned by climate, genetics, and history, Canadian ethnocultural diversity appears as an 'objective,' 'natural' phenomenon which is inscribed on certain bodies. 'Diversity is a fact of life
in this country,' a government pamphlet declares (Ministry of State for
Multiculturalism and Citizenship, *Multiculturalism: What Is It Really
About?* [1991]: 11; hereafter cited as *MCWR*). A newspaper photograph
showing a White woman enjoying a tea party with a Chinese woman,
an orthodox Jew, and a Rastafarian is overlain with the headline: 'Multiculturalism: Has diversity gone too far?' (*Globe and Mail*, 15 March
1997: D1). Not wishing to be left out, social scientists have eagerly
joined in the circular dance of definition: 'Canada is a multiethnic
nation with a variety of ethnic, racial, religious, and political identities.
Some societies have more diverse populations than others; Canada is
among the most polyethnic' (Driedger 1996: 2).

With all of this semiotic activity, it is very difficult to spend even a
short time in Canada without becoming acutely aware that Canadian
diversity not only exists, but poses a serious *problem*. This problem, like
the diversity that 'causes' it, must be constantly reproduced for, as
Joseph Gusfield points out, 'human problems do not spring up, full-
blown and announced, into the consciousness of bystanders. Even to

recognize a situation as painful requires a system for categorizing and defining events' (Gusfield 1981: 3). The *public* character of public problems must be created, as well, since 'all social problems do not necessarily become public ones' (5). The eligibility of a given social problem for attempts at public solution tends to be a matter of ongoing debate, especially in the current context of neo-liberal attacks on the welfare state and the consequent pressure to 'privatize' both problems and their solutions. In general, though, once a problem has been successfully classified as within the public realm, the way has been cleared for the operation of *government*, for attempts to 'structure the possible field of action of others' (Foucault 1982: 221). Newspaper articles declare a crisis situation, royal commissions are struck, a ministry is created, legislation is drafted, buildings are erected and staffed, as the bodies and minds of concerned citizens are swept up in a whirl of rational-bureaucratic activity. Out of this chaos a consensus emerges: there is a crisis, but it is being addressed and all will soon be well again. The problem of the problem of diversity, then, is that *the assumption of an objectively existing and problematic ethnocultural diversity covers over the work of differentiation itself.* Because it is a discursive construct with no basis in an empirical reality – not a 'thing' of any sort at all – Canadian diversity 'does not exist.' However, as a discursive formation with certain regularities, the field of Canadian diversity most certainly conditions the possibilities of life for those who are trying to 'be Canadian.'

While some suggest that the problem of Canadian diversity should not be given public status (Bissoondath 1994; Brotz 1980; Clifton and Roberts 1982), this is to argue against a long history of attempts at governmental management of ethnocultural identities within the territory now claimed by the Canadian state. As I will show, the problem of Canadian diversity *has always been public*, it has always involved state-sponsored attempts to define, know, and structure the actions of a field of problematic Others (Savages, Québécois, Half-breeds, Immigrants) who have been distinguished from unproblematic Selves (French, British, British-Canadian, European) through a variety of means (civilization, humanity, race, culture, ethnicity, ethnocultural origin).[2] It must also be noted that these acts of government have always provoked *resistance*: for almost five hundred years, first the French and then the British have been trying to 'civilize' the 'Savages'; for over two hundred years, the British have not been able to eliminate or accommodate the French; and over the past century, the list of problematic Others has been continually expanding as the state and corporations have sought to increase the size of the population and the economy via immigration. Even the most cursory scan of the mass media and academic presses makes it clear that this struggle shows no signs of abating in the near future.

Yet, despite this history of proliferating rational-bureaucratic action and failure, multiculturalism policy documents produced by the Canadian state proudly declare that the problem of Canadian diversity has always already been solved, that multiculturalism has 'been a fact of Canadian life for centuries,' since 'the first European settlers arrived to join the Aboriginal peoples in the northern half of a vast continent' (Department of the Secretary of State, *Multiculturalism: Being Canadian* [1987]: 3; hereafter cited as *MCBC*). In some documents, the history of Canadian diversity is extended back prior to the 'joining,' to times that literate, European minds see as prehistoric or primordial:

> Cultural diversity characterized the earliest societies to be seen through the mists of our history. Aboriginal peoples speaking a diversity of Algonkian tongues were spread across the breadth of North America. (*MCBCM*: 13)

While this claim is hard to support if 'multiculturalism' is taken to mean 'the recognition of the cultural and racial diversity of Canada and of the equality of Canadians of all origins' (*MCBC*: 3), it does make sense if it refers only to the 'recognition of cultural and racial diversity.' Here one needs to distinguish among three prevalent usages of 'multiculturalism': to *describe* (construct) a sociological *fact* of Canadian diversity; to *prescribe* a social ideal; and to *describe and prescribe* a government policy or *act* as a response to the fact and an implementation of the ideal (Angus 1997: 139; Kallen 1982: 51). By paying close attention to these resonances, we can see that the Canadian government is attempting to confound the descriptive and prescriptive senses of multiculturalism in order to provide its policy with an unearned history and reality. This effort has created a fourth meaning of multiculturalism, as an *already achieved ideal*.

While I follow the policy documents in locating the emergence of this history, or multiculturalism as fact, at the time of the arrival of the Europeans, I do not agree that multiculturalism as act or social ideal existed at this time. These came later, as products of the methods of constructing and managing human difference that were brought by the

Europeans. In chapter 2, I provide a theoretical-methodological justification for analysing this work of construction and management as the 'field of Canadian diversity,' and show how it cuts across the three sub-fields of state policy, academic analysis, and popular culture representations. I then argue that this field provides a starting point for a genealogical analysis of Canadian multiculturalism which would critically assess the claim that the discourse on Canadian diversity is in the process of achieving its own ideal. A reading of the concept of recognition from the point of view of Lacanian theory provides a guiding thread for this analysis, which is the concern of the central chapters of the book.

Chapter 3 sets out the ancient antecedents of the discourse on Canadian diversity through an examination of texts of Herodotus, Plato, and Aristotle. These characteristics – the division of human individuals into groupable 'types,' the arrangement of these types into a hierarchy, the naming of some types as presenting a 'problem,' and the attempt to provide 'solutions' to the problem so constructed – act as a metastructure which has reproduced itself throughout many changes in its form and content. Of course, the reader might wonder why I reach back to the beginnings of Western civilization in a discussion of Canadian multiculturalism. First, the degree of continuity is quite striking, once one becomes aware of it, and I believe that this continuity should be directly addressed by current policy and theory that purports to make a break with Canada's colonial past. Second, the age, depth, and subtle interconnections of this highly adaptable 'problem' suggest that its 'solution' will be no simple matter, not something a royal commission or a piece of legislation can hope to achieve with one blow, or even a series of blows. Indeed, the system has survived precisely by turning such shocks to its advantage.

The task of chapters 4 through 8 is to show how Canadian multiculturalism as state policy is descended from these ancient forms, not in a line of simple repetition, but as a complex process of adaptation and proliferation. In each discursive situation, through an examination of what I consider to be epitomal texts, I look at the nature of the categories and the hierarchical order established, the problems constructed, and the solutions proposed and implemented. In chapter 4, I discuss how the ancient Western discourse on diversity was adapted, by the British and French, to the circumstances of European colonization of that portion of the New World that has come to be known as Canada. Here the figure of the Savage provided the crucial negative pole to the

New World European identities. With the conquest of New France, addressed in chapter 5, the French became internal Others to the British, and were subjected to a series of failed attempts at elimination via transportation, extermination, assimilation, and, ultimately, integration. With the addition of a 'European' Other, the system of diversity in British colonial Canada became more complex, and the basis for construction of problematic difference began to shift from humanity and civilization to race and religion; the French were obviously 'people,' but they were just as obviously not the same *kind* of 'people' as the British.

Chapter 6 shows how the Dominion of Canada imitatively reproduced the British discourse on diversity in a self-conscious quest to rise from the status of 'colony' to that of a 'nation' with colonies of its own. The Canadian expansion into the Red River region is taken as the archetype here, involving violent displacement of the existing population, seductive integration through the offer of provincial status, followed by assimilation through massive inward movement of people who occupied higher positions on what had become a Great Chain of Race (White, Yellow, Black, Red). The acquisition – through immigration – of these apparently more 'desirable' person-types only exacerbated the problem it set out to solve, however, as it led to a proliferation of problematic identities within the category of White itself. The Canadian state began a series of attempts at physical elimination of these bodies, such as *rejection* of Immigrants based on racial criteria, *exclusion* via selective immigration policies, and *ejection* via individual deportation and group transportation. All of this was in keeping with the ideology of 'Anglo-conformity,' which held that all 'new Canadians' must be assimilated, or at least *assimilable*, to an English-Canadian model.

In the early 1900s, what I consider to be the key texts in the twentieth-century Canadian discourse on diversity appeared: Kate Foster's *Our Canadian Mosaic* (1926); and Robert England's *The Central European Immigrant in Canada* (1929). These texts, in their creative reproduction of earlier forms epitomized by J.S. Woodsworth's *Strangers within Our Gates* (1907), established a set of generic characteristics that have come to dominate thought, writing, and practice regarding the problem of Canadian diversity. The 'Mosaic' metaphor for Canadian society is one well-known example, but there are many others: the 'Flood' metaphor for incoming diversity; the tabular arrangement of racial groups versus numbers arriving over some given time period; and the catalogue display of a variety of human types considered to be different from some unmentioned canonical type. Chapter 7 addresses these texts in detail, showing how they are descended from previous formulations, and how current government policy and many academic analyses are descended from them. Two critical shifts occurred during this period: a decline in Anglo-conformist, *design theories* of Canadian identity, in favour of what I refer to as a *constrained emergence theory* symbolized by the Mosaic metaphor; and, concomitantly with this, a movement away from coercive assimilation and exclusion of races to *seductive integration of cultures*. This shift began to be officialized with the advent of the Second World War and the Nationalities Branch of the Department of National War Services, which provided the bureaucratic conditions necessary for the emergence of multiculturalism as state policy.

It has been argued that with its shift to an official policy of multiculturalism during the 1970s, the Canadian state finally began to solve the problem of diversity through granting 'recognition' to non-canonical identities (Kymlicka 1995; Taylor 1992). Other commentators have seen this development as a 'dangerous' form of 'fragmentation' (Bibby 1990; Bissoondath 1994). However, from the perspective developed in chapter 8, Canadian multiculturalism appears as neither a generous gift of liberal democracy, nor a divisive practice threatening to destroy the enjoyment of Canadianness for all. Rather, it is a reproduction of an ethnocultural economy which takes as its raw material the 'objective contents' of Canadian diversity and hopes to produce out of it a simulacrum of Canadian unity. The reality of Canadian diversity is symbiotically dependent upon this fantasy of unity – without it, a diversity simply could not exist, and certainly could not be a problem. The rhetoric of multiculturalism says that Canada is attempting to become, not a nation-state, but a self-consciously multinational state, in which all nations can seek their enjoyment in possession of a national Thing (Zizek 1991a: 165). This Thing is universal, it is every Thing. But, as *every*thing it is also *no*thing at all. This paradoxical object is tellingly represented in an image that I call the National Jewel: a disembodied Mosaic floating in an empty space, as seen on the cover of the government policy document *Multiculturalism: Being Canadian* (Department of the Secretary of State 1987), and reproduced here as figure 1.2 (see p. 11). I argue that multiculturalism as state policy may well be 'post-industrial,' but only in the sense that it marks a shift in attention from controlling difference to controlling *différance*; it is more modern than

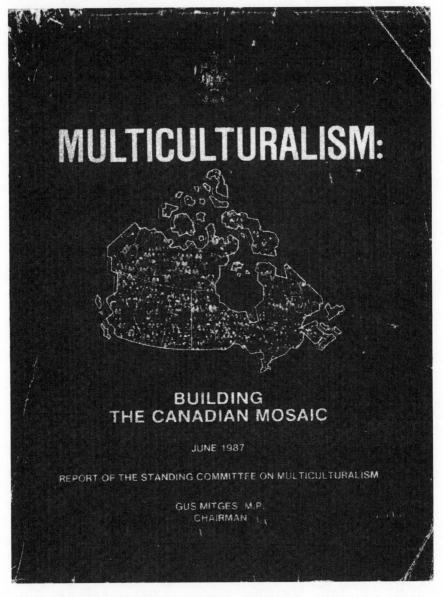

Fig. 1.1. The problem? A full container

Fig. 1.2. The solution? The National Jewel

ever in its unwillingness to accept diversity in the social, political, and linguistic forms that bind the ever-absent Canadian nation to the all-too-present Canadian state.

Guarding the National Jewel is necessary because the discourse on Canadian diversity also contains, as its continually repressed Other, the possibility of abandoning the formation of designed, singular identities through mass Self-acceptance and Other-exclusion (culture), in favour of an emergent and multiple (post-cultural) experience of subjectivity. Staying within the discourse on Canadian diversity, we might refer to this as a *free emergence* theory of identity. In the final chapter, I argue that multiculturalist theory and practice must traverse the fantasy of fullness associated with the modern nation-state. It must see that, while the history of Canadian diversity does contain what is necessary for its own overcoming, this is not to be found in an already achieved ideal. On the contrary, precisely where diversity has seemed most problematic, where the symptoms of lack of unity have been most intense, we can see the outlines of three necessary affirmations. Canadian multiculturalism must: (i) openly admit and orient to the impossibility of full identity; (ii) affirm the value of difference and the Other as such; and (iii) recognize the necessity of a negotiation of *all* universal horizons, including that of the nation-state. Only by *abandoning* the dream of unity, Canada may, after all, lead the way towards a future that will be shared by many other nation-states; it may, in its failure to achieve a universal mass identity, or even a universal mass of identities, inadvertently come closer to its goal of mutual and equal recognition amongst all who have chanced to find themselves within its borders.

Terminological Issues

In examining and commenting upon the problem of Canadian diversity, I will be obliged to use certain terms that would be better left behind. Among these I would include all terms that ascribe group membership to an individual based on some means of differentiation from other groups; for example, on the basis of humanity, civilization, nation, ethnicity, culture, region. Some of these words have gained so much notoriety that approaching them brings on an intense struggle. Race is perhaps the best example, leading to such stategies as the following:

I have followed philosophical convention in italicizing reference to the concept of *race* and in placing between single quotation marks the word 'race' when mentioning (referring to) it. (Goldberg 1993: ix)

In addition to creating a typographical nightmare, the problem is that there is no *single* 'concept' (signified) to which the 'word' (signifier) *race* 'refers.' Relationships between this signifier and signified, as in all semiosis, are worked out through perpetual negotiation, and thus it cannot be said that '*the* concept of race' exists at all, except as a fuzzy set within certain discursive constraints of space, time, and enunciation. A related difficulty is highlighted when one attempts to separate the 'unscientific'-everyday from the biological-expert resonances of the signifier 'race.' Here, the narrative of genetics is given a privilege that it does not deserve, and the ability of scientific intervention to *multiply* rather than delimit the resonance of a term is completely overlooked. Finally, if race is flagged more often than, say, 'civilization' or 'humanity,' this is only because European ears are at present more sensitive to the atrocities of Nazism than to those of European colonialism. Acts carried out in the name of civilization and culture have caused at least as much death and despair as those deriving their motivation from race, and therefore deserve to be treated with equal caution.

How to handle these problems? The English language, in its everyday usage, provides a clue. Already, references to 'peoples' considered to be differentiable along various lines are capitalized, as in Canada ('nation,' 'society,' 'state'), Mongol ('race'), Jew ('religion,' 'ethnicity,' 'culture'), Maritime Provinces ('region' within 'Canada'). In current English usage, however, the bases for these differentiations are *not* marked, and this is what causes philosophers, semioticians, and social scientists so much grief. The simplest answer would be to flag not only the names of the particular groups that are supposed to provide the content of human diversity, but also the terms that *enable* their differentiation. The Canadian reader is likely to have only a little difficulty in coping with Race, as these days 'everyone knows' that it is a construct. Reading Culture may not be quite so easy, though, and Region, with its attachments to 'solid ground' may be extremely difficult to set free from its discursive foundation. Also, once this process is set in motion, it is very difficult to stop. If culture is a construct, then so is language ... and so is every word ever uttered. Clearly it is not possible to mark each instance of a contested term in any text. And yet, certain words are so offensive – as a result of a spreading awareness of their lack of any concrete referent and of the power of words to consecrate horrible acts – that something must be done with them. Savage, a distinction based on a presumed lack of humanity and civilization, deserves the same sort of attention as French, which has been variously created out of presumed possession of superior civilizational, geographical, cultural, and racial attributes. I will capitalize Pagan and Barbarian for similar reasons, along with Discover, Conquer, Explore, and their cognates and, in the context of Canadian immigration policy, Immigrant, Useful, Desirable, Visible, and Invisible.

This does not solve all of the problems, as it is very difficult to avoid constructs like 'the British' when referring to the speech and acts of certain individuals who see themselves as representing or participating in a group, which they define in exclusion of another group, such as 'the French.' I will use terms like 'the British' and 'the French' to denote spatio-temporally delimited *discursive positions,* and not physical bodies, a transcendental Folk Spirit, or even a 'gene pool.' Similar difficulties arise when using 'they' or 'them' to refer to such positions, as an 'us' is always implied. In these cases, I hope the reader will grant the possibility of taking a position that is Other to the system of Otherness in question, and treat 'them' and 'they' as 'mere' references to constructs that have already been marked as problematic. Similarly, references to the possibility of discerning human 'groups' or 'types,' and any discussion of the 'problem,' 'solution,' 'recognition,' or 'toleration' of the 'fact' of Canadian 'diversity,' 'unity,' or 'identity' are always to be treated with caution, as I will not continue to mark them, except when rhetorical considerations make it absolutely necessary to do so. Also in the interest of readability, all references to an unqualified 'multiculturalism' can be assumed to refer to 'Canadian multiculturalism,' and where 'diversity' appears unqualified, please read 'ethnocultural diversity.'

As I will make use of the term 'hybridity' throughout this book, I should point out how I will be using it. With regard to the Canadian Half-breed and Métis identities, this term will appear as a description of what was then seen as a 'mixing of races' that produced new – and generally 'inferior' – *human types*.[3] Both here and elsewhere, though, I will also be playing off of the current meaning of hybridity within postcolonial theory, as a *semiotic process* through which new *poles of identification* are constructed. On this theme, Homi Bhabha suggests that the 'wider significance of the postmodern condition' lies not in the philosophical deconstruction of Western metaphysics, but in 'the awareness that the epistemological "limits" of those ethnocentric ideas are also the enunciative boundaries of a range of other dissonant, even dissident, histories and voices – women, the colonized, minority groups, the bearers of policed sexualities' (Bhabha 1994: 4-5). For Bhabha, the in-between spaces of fixed identities 'open up the possibility of a cultural hybridity that entertains difference without an assumed or imposed hierarchy' (4). While this 'entertaining' of difference could be construed as an 'overcoming' of European colonialism, I do not want to give the impression that hybridity points the way towards a 'solution' of the problem of Canadian diversity through a 'recognition' or 'acceptance' of postmodern fragmentation. As Bhabha notes, 'the social articulation of difference ... is a complex, on-going negotiation that seeks to *authorize* cultural hybridities that emerge in moments of historical transformation' (2, emphasis added). States can, have, and always will be able to authorize 'hybrid' identities by nominating them as 'pure,' and then using the resulting category as a means of mass articulation with an administrated population.[4]

Finally, I should also point out that within the constraints of a racist, capitalist, patriarchal, anti-nature, mass state society, I think that multiculturalism is preferable to fascism or imperialistic forms of ethnic nationalism. I don't agree with the Canadian Reform party, or certain American 'liberals,' that questions of race, sex, and sexuality are, or should be, 'merely private' concerns. I have no doubt that it is 'better' to be seductively integrated than coercively assimilated or exterminated, and I have great respect for those whose calling it is to risk their own destruction – emotional, financial, physical – in the name of ameliorating the violent excesses of mass state societies. But I shall leave it to others to fight and die for the question of who is or is not Canadian. My object is not to contribute to the expansion of the discourse on Canadian unity and diversity, but to help *dissipate* it.

Chapter Two

The Field of Canadian Diversity

Some Methodological Concerns

In approaching the field of Canadian diversity, I follow Pierre Bourdieu, who argues that the term 'field' does not name an analytic object, but is rather a 'shorthand' for *a mode of construction of analytic objects* (Bourdieu 1992: 228). A field has regularities and rules, which an investigator must identify; it is a 'space,' in both the physical and semiotic senses, the margins of which can be traced; and, finally, it is a space of *play*, of competition and cooperation involving objects within the field, and over the boundaries of the field itself (97). Thus, rather than suggesting that the discourse on Canadian diversity is 'inscribed' into multiculturalism policy, and then 'written' onto Canadian bodies, I would hold that this discourse and the individuals who are its subjects and objects *condition each other* in a complex, non-linear interaction that is never adequately captured in any theory of 'coding' or 'inscription.' 'Those who dominate in a given field,' Bourdieu writes, 'are in a position to make it function to their advantage but they must always contend with the resistance, the claims, the contention, "political" or otherwise, of the dominated' (Bourdieu 1992: 102).

While Bourdieu's work shows how the field of Canadian diversity can be specified as an object of analysis, his method must be supplemented in order to study *past configurations* of this field. For this I turn to genealogy, which includes, or rather *is*, an ongoing critique of proper historical analysis: 'It is necessary to master history so as to turn it to genealogical uses' (Foucault 1985: 93).[1] For Foucault, this involves three specific steps: genealogy is 'parodic, directed against reality, and opposes the theme of history as reminiscence or recognition'; it is 'dissociative, directed against identity, and opposes history given as continuity or representative of a tradition'; and finally, genealogy is 'sacrificial, directed against truth, and opposes history as knowledge' (93). Whereas history is devoted to the business of getting at truth, genealogy is a 'concerted carnival' which acknowledges itself to be simultaneously using and abusing the historical tradition out of which it emerges. This is not to say, however, that genealogy is not 'serious,' not capable of producing critical commentary on current social conditions. As Ernesto Laclau has pointed out, 'to reveal the original meaning of an act ... is to reveal the moment of its radical contingency – in other words, to reinsert it in the system of real historical options that were discarded ... by showing the terrain of the original violence, of the power relations through which that instituting act took place' (Laclau 1990: 34).[2] In the case at hand, it is the history of Canadian diversity that must be mastered and put to genealogical use in a critique of the power relations present in the instituting acts of Canadian multiculturalism.

As a first step in delimiting the field of Canadian diversity, I want to state precisely what will be considered as part of a particularly *Canadian* history. For the purposes of this study, I take as being Canadian that discourse which emerges out of the British and French invasion of the northeastern portion of what is now known as North America, starting with the voyages of Cabot in 1497 and Cartier in 1534. This choice is not arbitrary for, as we will see, certain regularities can be observed in the attempts that have been made to impose a hegemonic regime of signification upon this expanding geographic space, as well as in the self-identifications and other-ascriptions of the bodies that have inhabited the territories it has claimed. Obviously, the French colonizers of the sixteenth century did not think of themselves as Canadian, but they did send a 'Governor of Canada' as early as 1540. Over the years, the quality of being Canadian has been variously attributed to the Native inhabitants of New France, French *Canadiens*, British settlers only, British and French and people from western Europe but not Blacks or Asians, until, in the current situation, 'everyone' who lives within a certain territory is considered to be officially Canadian, or at least Canadianizable. Limiting the study to those geographical and semiotic spaces out of which the current 'Canada' has emerged provides some sense of containment, a realm of structure within which the freedom of narrative might be exercised.[3]

Within this realm, I will focus on three subfields: government policy and practice; philosophical / social scientific analysis; and popular culture representations. As a focus of activity in the modern Eurocolonial domain, the state form is of crucial importance in analysing the discourse on Canadian diversity as a technology of governance. Social science and philosophy are important for their ongoing contributions of empirical data and moral justifications to this cause. Finally, no mass identity can exist without a population that is prepared to identify, to play the game of inclusion and exclusion, obedience and resistance. Within the history of Canadian diversity, activity in all of these fields has aided in the proliferation of ethnocultural identities, and each of them can be shown to observe similar rules in the construction of its objects, statements, and practices. In the following sections, I will show in detail how these regularities are displayed, and how they work in relation to the broader field of Canadian diversity that structures and is structured by all of them.[4]

Canadian Diversity in State Policy

In its current configuration, the field of Canadian diversity is deeply conditioned by the activities of several levels of government. With all the means of modern coercion and postmodern seduction at their disposal, legislators and bureaucrats have set out to bolster the reality of Canadian multiculturalism as fact and act, problem and solution, distopia and social ideal. The effects of this activity are a matter of current debate. Has diversity gone too far? Can tolerance be legislated? Is multiculturalism policy 'working'? One is tempted to interject: of course, it is – it is signification on a mass scale. More important and interesting questions, though, would be to ask *how* it is working, and *what* it is working to do. And we must not forget that the answers to these questions might be only accidentally related to any 'goals' or 'objectives' of the policy-makers, their constituents, and the philosophers and social scientists who set out to inform them.

The rules of the current official discourse on diversity can be derived from policy documents produced by the Canadian government since the 1960s. I have chosen to look at three of these texts, which cover various policy regimes and address different audiences. The first is the multi-volume *Report of the Royal Commission on Bilingualism and Biculturalism (B & B Report)*, which was published from 1963 to 1967, and remains the most in-depth and wide-ranging document of its type, appealing to academics, legislators, and the general public. The next is *Multiculturalism: Building the Canadian Mosaic (MCBCM)*, which was produced in 1987 as a product of the new policy of 'multiculturalism in a bilingual framework.' This document, which is specifically addressed to legislators and lobbyists, more clearly defined the goals and approaches of official multiculturalism, and provided a basis for the Canadian Multiculturalism Act of 1988. The other document of interest here is *Multiculturalism: Being Canadian (MCBC)*, which describes itself as a 'background paper' addressed to 'all Canadians' (2). The purpose of this document was to 'spread the word' that multiculturalism was an official government policy and was being enshrined in a legal statute, and so it is best seen as a report of a policy rather than a policy report.

All three of these documents display similarities in the content they address and the ways in which this content is presented. Most importantly, they all make constant reference to Canadian ethnocultural diversity as a public problem that needs a bureaucratic solution, using constructs that appear to have been passed along from one generation of reports to the next. One example is the strategy of normalizing the problem of ethnocultural diversity by providing it with a natural/historical basis. This strategy can be seen at work in the table of contents of volume 4 of the *B & B Report*, chapter 1 of which is entitled 'The Historical Background.' The title presumably refers to the historical background of 'Immigration,' which immediately precedes it as the title of part 1. In a subsection entitled 'Early Ethnic Diversity,' it is suggested that 'the population of what is now Canada has always been ethnically diverse' (18). In order that the reader may know what 'ethnic diversity' is, succeeding subtitles make reference to the many 'types of immigrants' that have come to Canada. These include 'Early German Immigration,' 'The Dutch and Scandinavians,' 'Other Europeans,' 'Negro Immigration,' and 'Asians on the West Coast,' and so on. The arrival of these person-types is described in the *B & B Report* with the help of a naturalistic metaphor of inundation that I call the Flood metaphor. On page 18 of volume 4, immigrants to Canada are depicted as part of a 'flow' or 'influx.' On page 21, the metaphor is used more strongly, to liken the arrival of people to Canada to a 'vast tide.' Significantly, the Flood metaphor is not used to describe the earlier arrival of British and French immigrants, thus silently balancing these naturally problematic Others with naturally unproblematic Selves.

The writers of *MCBCM* drew heavily from the work of the *B & B*

Report in their presentation of the problem of Canadian diversity, but also added some innovations of their own. The idea that Canadian diversity is a natural / historical object is deployed in section 1.0, 'A Primordial Cultural Diversity.' Here Canadian diversity is seen as originating 'in the mists of our history' and as being 'inevitably intensified' over time (13). This diversity 'continued to grow' until it became a 'massive flow.' In the Executive Summary,' a different and contrasting set of metaphors is invoked to give the problem a firm foundation:

> Regardless of where they [immigrants] came from ... depending on where they settled in Canada they developed differences and formed their own distinctive cultures in adapting to the particular geography and prevailing social and economic conditions of the different regions of the country where they made their homes. (pages not numbered)

In the next paragraph, however, the economic and social connections are lost, leaving only the 'natural' forces of 'geography' as a cause: 'Canada needs to come to terms with these many differences *which will always prevail due to the very nature of its geography*' (emphasis added).

MCBC also makes good use of the historical approach, complete with the Aboriginal peoples connection, in its chapter 1, 'A Tradition of Diversity':

> Cultural and racial diversity have existed in Canada since long before the 16th century, when the first European settlers arrived to join the Aboriginal peoples in the northern half of a vast continent. Aboriginal society was multicultural as well as multilingual. (3)

Through these devices, Canadian diversity appears as a natural-historical phenomenon that has always existed, and will continue to exist in the future. The term 'multiculturalism' is often used, in a *descriptive* mode, to denote this *fact* of diversity.

But Canadian multiculturalism is not just a fact – it is a problematic fact, a call to action. Each document, in its own way, suggests that the problem of Canadian diversity has reached crisis proportions, and that dire consequences will result if steps are not taken soon. In volume 1 of the *B & B Report*, the commission quotes its own preliminary report in order to reinforce the critical nature of the problem faced by the Canadian nation-state:

It was our conviction that ... 'Canada was facing a national crisis, a time when decisions must be taken and developments must occur leading either to its break-up or to a new set of conditions for its future existence.' This is still the situation. (xvii)

The writers of the report go on to assure their readers that they shall 'examine various aspects of the crisis and shall propose some remedies' (xvii). These remedies involve changes in documents that will presumably lead to changes in institutions and practices. As can be seen from the table of contents of volume 1 of the report, such changes include 'An Extension of Section 93 of the BNA Act,' 'A New Section 133 of the BNA Act,' and a 'Federal Official Languages Act.' Thus the *B & B Report*, concentrating on the 'British/French' problem, took on the task of suggesting how to modify certain words on certain pages so as to achieve the effect of preventing the Canadian nation-state from 'breaking up.'

Just as official bilingualism and biculturalism were the solutions proposed to prevent an imminent binary fission of the Canadian nation-state, multiculturalism appeared as the name for the bureaucratic work that sought to avoid a multiple fracture. From the 'Executive Summary' of *MCBC*:

Since one third of the Canadian population is from minority ethnocultural communities, and this diversity continues to grow, there is an obligation on the part of the Canadian Parliament and Government to respond ... Therefore, the Standing Committee ... submits various recommendations pertaining to a Multiculturalism Policy, Act, and Department.

Whereas the policy reports work on the fears of policy-makers by heightening the sense of crisis, the report of the policy gives the impression that the state has solved its problems, and now hopes that the people will do their part as well. The following passages from *MCBC* display the complete cycle of problem creation, bureaucratic solution, and, finally, request for the adherence of all good citizens to the sorts of behaviour that have been legally codified and deemed appropriate. First, the problem:

Analysis of current population trends suggests that the country will have to rely on immigration, if it intends to maintain or increase its population. Moreover, most future immigrants are expected to come from non-

European roots. This will mean that the size of Canada's racial minority communities, now roughly 1.9 million or seven percent of the population, will increase during the next several decades. (25)

The state's role in providing a solution:

The government is confident that Canadians, their institutions and the country's existing communities will make the necessary adaptations in a spirit of generosity and understanding. Still, it recognizes that changes of any kind make some persons uneasy, so it accepts its responsibility to provide active leadership in fostering among all Citizens a heightened appreciation and understanding of multiculturalism. (25)

And the citizen's role in conducting his or her life according to the appropriate legislation:

By maintaining Canadian citizenship values, by observing the provisions of an amended and strengthened *Official Languages Act*, and by following the principles and policies of multiculturalism, the government believes that Canada will always be a country where all groups can thrive and contribute.

Within the constraints imposed by the necessity of communicating effectively with their intended audiences, the policy reports and the report of the policy are commonly concerned with creating a problem of Canadian diversity that can be solved through rational-bureaucratic intervention. However, at the same time as the fact of multiculturalism (Canadian diversity) is seen as primordial, so is the act of multiculturalism as recognition and tolerance of diversity. If 'aboriginal society was multicultural as well as multilingual,' and if multiculturalism means both fact of problem and act of solution, does this not mean that the problem has also always been solved? Sometimes it seems that the policy documents would like this to be the case. *MCBC* takes a step in this direction: 'The Standing Committee believes that it is time to further the recognition of the multicultural reality of Canada by giving this reality its own legislative base' (18). This is obviously not much of a reality, if it can't stand unaided on its own two feet. Perhaps it is just too young? Indeed, we see its maturation into tautology a few paragraphs later:

[T]o say that multiculturalism is for all Canadians is to say that Canadians from the majority communities can also, and should also, participate in multiculturalism ... It recognizes that *all* Canadians have a cultural background which forms the essence of Canada's cultural diversity, that is multiculturalism. (19)

Here the bumps in the language and thought process have been smoothed out, allowing the text to move smoothly back and forth between fact and act: 'Having been a fact of Canadian life for centuries, multiculturalism has been official policy in Canada since 1971' (*MCBC*: 3). Through this rhetorically compelling confusion between a non-existent history of harmonious coexistence and a package of toothless legislation, the reader is led to believe that the Canadian government is on the high road to achieving unity within an ancient and problematic diversity. It is quite possible, of course, that this state-sponsored definition of the problem and its solution is merely a figment of the bureaucratic imagination. That is, one might want to know what effects these moves in the subfield of state policy have had in other subfields. It is to this question that we now must turn.

Canadian Diversity in Popular Culture

Since the stated goal of the policy documents is to further belief in, and acceptance of, the fact and act of multiculturalism, public opinion on these matters might give some indication of the degree to which they have succeeded. Government-funded surveys and studies abound which purport to show that multiculturalism is indeed 'working.' One of these was conducted in 1988, by Thompson Lightstone, and the findings were presented in a report by Optima Consultants. Two thousand adults were asked a series of questions designed to elicit their 'attitudes towards multiculturalism' (Optima 1988: 1). Of those surveyed, 86 per cent 'agreed' with the statement that 'Canadians have come from just about every country in the world'; 83 per cent thought that 'Canadians of all backgrounds have the freedom to maintain their cultures and languages'; and 76 per cent felt that multiculturalism 'makes Canada a better country to live in' (2). While its results might have been encouraging to the Department of the Secretary of State, the survey suffers from a methodological problem: all of the questions are as positively slanted and highly leading as the examples given above. This fact was not lost on the consultants from

Optima, who suggested in the 'Conclusion' that 'it would be useful to repeat a more comprehensive range of questions to track public attitudes in a more definitive manner. These questions should cover both the "hopeful" and "apprehensive" aspects of public attitudes regarding multiculturalism' (12).

A similar study was conducted in 1991 by the Angus Reid Group. This study was much more extensive, involving both quantitative telephone survey research and focus groups. The questions in the telephone survey were not as obviously loaded to produce desired responses, although the section on 'Credibility of Statements concerning Multiculturalism' shows great similarity to the work done in 1988. The statement of highest credibility, weighing in at 95 per cent, was 'You can be proud of being Canadian and proud of your ancestry at the same time.' This was closely followed, at 94 per cent, by 'Canadian citizenship is a two-way street ... it means everyone in Canada has both rights and responsibilities.' The lowest rate of credibility achieved was still impressive, at 83 per cent, for 'Multiculturalism is about equality for Canadians of all origins' (Angus Reid 1991: 20).

Based on these findings, it would seem that all is well in the world of Canadian multiculturalism. However, a quick glance at what is going on in the mass media suggests that the situation is not so cut and dried. It seems that the confusion fostered by government policy has taken firm root – indeed, many see multiculturalism policy as part of the problem of Canadian diversity rather than a solution to it. A recent issue of the *Vancouver Courier* carried an article under the headline 'Zulu woman condemns divisive, stigmatizing multiculturalism,' with the subhead 'Integration impossible' (27 Nov. 1996: 17). Here a 'black South African' is quoted as saying that 'multicultural idealism keeps Canada from being a united country.' A month before this, the *Globe and Mail* ran the headline 'Ottawa fails to sell multiculturalism: Report for Heritage Canada points to growing backlash against federal policy that aids ethnic groups' (18 Oct. 1996: A8). In both articles, the theme is the same: allowing people to be different is dangerous, and threatens the existing social order.

In the *Globe* article, Hedy Fry, Secretary of State for Multiculturalism, took the blame for this failure of the Act, admitting that 'in the past we have not done a good enough job in getting the message out.' Again, the curious necessity of 'selling' an objective reality appears. Despite public acknowledgment of its failure, though, nothing seems to have changed in the world of official multiculturalism. Witness the March

1996 edition of *What's New in Multiculturalism*, produced by Canadian Heritage and bearing the name of the Honourable Hedy Fry:

> Since assuming the office of Secretary of State (Multiculturalism) ... I have been meeting with Canadians from all walks of life and listening to their views on multiculturalism. Canada has been built by people of diverse backgrounds who together have created a unique country governed by respect for differences. As we face the challenges of a new millennium to improve on what we have built together, we will continue to be a role model to the world.

Nowhere in this press release is there any indication of what Canadians from all walks of life have been saying to the Secretary of State, but there is no doubt that her writers are well versed and able to pound the old platitudes without a twinge of bad faith.

In addition to the occasional act of individual rebellion, there are also more organized and influential discourses of resistance to multiculturalism policy. These must be considered as they are a great aid in locating the (fluid) boundaries of the field, and because they bring out relevant speech that simply cannot be found anywhere else. It is important to note that these movements of resistance are in many cases themselves interventions in the field; that is, they accept the terms of the discourse, and are oriented primarily to improving the position of some particular identity. An example of an attempt to alter the configuration of the field would be the lobbying by organizations purporting to represent 'the other ethnic groups' that helped to change the policy of 'bilingualism and biculturalism' into 'multiculturalism in a bilingual framework.' This sort of activity is ongoing, as various groups jockey for position in the Canadian ethnocultural hierarchy, and it most certainly forms part of the field of Canadian diversity.

Examples of discourses that are more of a challenge to the existing economy can be found in the various sovereignty movements (Québécois, Métis, Native Nations, Western provinces) that seek to break the connection between the Canadian state and part of its territory. Again, while these discourses challenge the system of Canadian identity and diversity in its current form, they generally seek to replace this system with another based on the same principle of geographical-ethnocultural power. The working out of relations between Quebec's *pur laine* families and those who arrived before or after them shows this effect very well. These interventions will also be discussed, at least inasmuch as they appear within the federal field of power, which means, as much as they appear in the English language, in the context of British social, political, and legal institutions. I do not claim to adequately discuss, or even fully comprehend, the complexities of the various sovereignty movements within their own languages and contexts. The crucial point for my analysis is that, although there is disagreement within and without the halls of Ottawa on the value of the act of multiculturalism, there is almost complete acceptance of multiculturalism as a problematic fact. Thus, despite the hand-wringing and public confessions of failure, the Canadian government has made an important contribution to the tradition of diversity through its perpetuation of the belief that this diversity exists, poses a public problem, and requires an immediate and ongoing rational-bureaucratic response.

Canadian Diversity and the Academy

Social scientists have often been employed by the state to conduct demographic analyses and survey research addressing the problem of Canadian diversity. Indeed, without sociology, there could be no sociological fact of diversity. As I will show in chapter 7, Canadian academics have also been involved at the highest levels of policy analysis and construction throughout the twentieth century. Starting with the work of Robert England and Watson Kirkconnell, professional social scientists began to engage Canadian multiculturalism as a social ideal, and entered into debates about what Canada *should* be. Thus the Canadian academic tradition has played an important role in the construction and management of the problem of Canadian diversity. However, to be included in the analytic field that is emerging in this chapter, it would be necessary for the academic discourse to display the same regularities as are found in state policy and popular culture. That is, we must see the fact of diversity being naturalized, historicized, and problematized, along with the assumption that state intervention can solve, and is already solving, this problem. In this section I will show that, despite its own lack of unity, these criteria are met by the dominant stream of the academic discourse on Canadian diversity.

While texts in the academic field are rarely so naïve as to totally reproduce the discourse on Canadian diversity, most accept several of the major axes while taking issue with one or two others. The aspect of the field that is most often left in place is the problematic natural-sociological fact of Canadian diversity. Old-time demography is perhaps the greatest culprit here, with its focus on ethnicity as 'an amalgam of objective factors ... that characterize the individual' (Hiller 1996: 196; see also Halli et al. 1990). In blithely setting out to quantify difference, demography has been a major contributor to the proliferation of ethnocultural subject-positions, as well as conjuring up further distinctions, such as those between visible and invisible minorities, single and multiple origin ethnicities, and so on. According to Elliot and Fleras, however, this tendency is on the wane: 'Emphasis on objective features and cultural content has weakened in recent years, replaced to some extent by an interest in the subjective experiences and symbolic boundaries that define and encircle an ethnic group' (1992: 134). While this may appear to be a step in the right direction, the 'social identity' approach does not bring into question the enabling constraints that make ethnocultural identifications possible in the first place.

Scholarly writing has also contributed to the origin myth of Canadian multiculturalism as an already achieved ideal, through its invocation of a history of diversity and tolerance marred only by occasional 'exceptional' events which, upon reflection, are seen as rationally motivated and therefore 'understandable.' In his *History of Canada*, first published in 1887, William Kingsford referred to the expulsion of the Acadians as a 'painful episode' that, 'whatever its character ... must be fully placed on the record' (502). In his account, the 'ignorance' of the 'primitive' and 'illiterate' population of Acadia was played upon by unscrupulous Roman Catholic priests who opposed British interests. The Acadians also 'precipitated the adoption of active measures against them' by sending an 'insolently written' petition to the governor, who was then forced to do his duty 'without an eye to sentiment' (505). Writing on the same topic in 1912, J.C. Hopkins also defended Governor Lawrence's actions on the ground of self-protection from dangerous internal Others, and attempted to downplay the severity of those actions, offering up his own version of a 'fairly reasonable explanation' (Hopkins 1912: 104). As well, Hopkins provided the story with a happy ending, claiming that 'as time passed on ... the Acadians were allowed to wander back to their old homes and to rebuild the altars of their sires, until, by the census of 1891 ... there were more than a hundred thousand loyal, light-hearted and prosperous British subjects of Acadian descent' (104).

These texts are, of course, products of a previous era. But the traditional version of Canadian history has also infiltrated much current work that is otherwise very critical and careful. Again, while few texts reproduce the official narrative entirely, many rationalize and displace the operation of the Canadian discourse on diversity by 'excusing' the state-people for its actions. Valerie Knowles, whose study of the history of Canadian immigration policy is thorough, concise, and very valuable in its attention to the repressed side of this history, also succumbs, on occasion, to the powerful desire to maintain at least a few fragments of the canon:

> Shortly after the outbreak of the [First World] war the federal government took upon itself unprecedented authority with the passage of the draconian War Measures Act, designed to give Ottawa emergency powers to deal with real or apprehended war, invasion, or insurrection. Nowhere was the blanket character of the act revealed more clearly than in the provisions of clause 6 ... Before the war's end this provision was invoked in the internment of some 8,579 enemy aliens, *a relatively small number however*, when it is realized that over 80,000 such individuals had been registered. The *insignificant number* of enemy aliens incarcerated during the war in no way reflects, though, the depth of anti-alien sentiment felt by much of the Canadian population. (Knowles 1997: 99–100, emphasis added)

Within the space of this passage, the internment of Enemy Aliens moves from a 'draconian' act to something involving a 'relatively small,' and then an 'insignificant,' number of people. The final return to a discussion of 'anti-alien sentiment' shows the Canadian state rising above the feelings of the masses through its 'limited' use of concentration camps.

John Herd Thompson, in *Ethnic Minorities during Two World Wars*, avoids falling for the justification for internment provided by the War Measures Act – 'nightmares about enemy aliens were groundless,' he declares (Thompson 1991: 5) – only to reproduce the economic emergency trope: 'The Great Depression further exacerbated ethnic relations. Massive unemployment *forced* the Bennett government to shut off immigration in 1930 and it remained restricted thereafter' (11, emphasis added). Even without an emergency, fear and hatred can be justified for no particular reason except that the Other has been so impertinent as to exist. D.J. Hall, in a biography of Clifford Sifton, explains away Canadian nativism by noting that 'the hostility, though deeply regrettable, was understandable,' because of 'the rising tide of western settlement' (D.J. Hall 1981: 262).

The most subtle work of the multiculturalist origin myth can be found in texts that follow Kingsford's *History of Canada* in attempting a public confession of Canada's less than glorious past. As an epitome of this genre, let us consider *Cultures in Canada: Strength in Diversity* (Buchignani and Engel 1983), which appears to be aimed at high-school-age readers and/or adult readers who are recent immigrants.[5] This text very quickly sets up Canadian diversity as a problem that has already been solved:

> As you study Cultures in Canada you will begin to understand how Canadians have met the challenge of living and working together. You will see examples of Canadians from varied backgrounds working side by side in harmony. (4)

But it is relatively sophisticated in that it immediately attempts to cover for the covering it has put in place: 'You will also find that we have not always respected the rights of our neighbours. Our history contains examples of our failure to live up to the ideal of treating one another as we ourselves would like to be treated' (4). Buchignani and Engel go on to note that the Beothuck 'died out' (25), but provide a happy ending to the story by noting that 'elsewhere in Canada, the experience of the Native people with the Europeans was different from that of the Beothuck. Instead of a culture becoming extinct, a new and distinct culture emerged' (26). Through this transition, the text introduces the Métis and acknowledges their desire to be seen as a people, but does not mention their successive displacements, the theft of their land through the scrip system, and the necessity of sending in troops to force them to become Canadians. Another happy ending is presented instead: 'Riel asked that the Red River area be made a province, and that the Metis land, French language rights and religion be protected. Many of these terms were met. A new province, called Manitoba, was created in 1870' (49). Later, the text notes that the Acadians were transported by the British, but again a pleasant gloss is placed on the story in the final line of the section: 'Although the British had uprooted them, the Acadians managed to preserve their way of life' (30). While it is significant that all of these stories are given happy endings, it is much more important to note that the text *does not connect any of these events together*, except to say that all of them are unfortunate exceptions to a general – yet historically unsupported – rule of harmonious co-existence. In this way, the representation of Canadian multiculturalism as an already achieved ideal, which plays a crucial role in the state discourse, is unwittingly reproduced.

The official history of Canadian diversity has been under fire for some time, of course, beginning with a number of studies that were published in the late 1960s and 1970s. Ken Adachi's work on the Japanese, *The Enemy That Never Was* (1976), contributed to a movement for recognition of, and compensation for, their dispossession, internment, and displacement during the Second World War. Robin Winks's *The Blacks in Canada* (1971), Myrna Kostash's *All of Baba's Children* (1977), and George Woodcock's *The Doukhobors* (1968) all contributed to the historical visibility of non-canonical peoples in Canada, and thereby challenged the multiculturalist origin myth. Peter Ward made an explicit attempt, in *White Canada Forever*, to contest the 'belief that the nation has evolved more or less harmoniously as a multicultural society' (Ward 1978: x). But this text focused on a single issue and group, namely anti-Oriental attitudes and policies that prevailed in British Columbia between the mid-nineteenth and mid-twentieth centuries.[6] Other than the work of Donald Avery (1995; 1979) and Howard Palmer (1991; 1982a; 1973) there have been few attempts to draw out the commonalities and regularities across these groups and across time. And no one, to my knowledge, has undertaken a genealogical study of the history of Canadian diversity in its broadest form.

In the Canadian academic literature, much critical attention has been devoted to an 'ideology critique' of multiculturalism as state policy. In this approach, multiculturalism as an achieved social ideal is confronted with an analysis of unequal relations of power between various racial and ethnic groups and found to be a 'false' representation. The classic text here is *The Vertical Mosaic*, in which John Porter began to take apart Canadian multiculturalism before it had even been put together: 'Segregation in social structure, to which the concept of the mosaic or multiculturalism must ultimately lead, can become an important aspect of social control by the charter group' (Porter 1965: 73–4). Karl Peter, writing after the official adoption of multiculturalism in a bilingual framework, called multiculturalism a 'myth ... based on high-sounding liberal ideals, not on the empirical reality of Canadian society' (Peter 1981: 65). Peter ended this piece with a call for a 'true multiculturalism' which would be 'put into the service of revitalizing and reconstructing a Canada for the twenty-first century – a Canada that is built by all for the benefit of all' (66). Kogila Moodley has very subtly and sharply attacked the 'superficial nature' and 'depoliticization' of Canadian multiculturalism policy (Moodley 1983: 324), which 'trivializes, neutralizes and absorbs social and economic inequalities' (326). She also makes reference to a 'true multiculturalism' which, in her case, 'presupposes official multilingualism' (324). The 'multiculturalism as ideology' debate is still going strong into the 1990s, with Laverne Lewycky trying to move beyond false consciousness and into a Mannheimian conception of ideology and utopia (Lewycky 1992).

Inasmuch as Lewycky's approach does not posit a 'true' multiculturalism to hold up against its actually existing manifestation, it begins to pass over from ideology critique into relational discourse analysis (Jackson and Nielsen 1991; Jenson 1993). To see this approach at work, we must move towards the margins of the academic literature, arriving at those Canadian writers who have challenged the existence of multiculturalism as a sociological fact. Roman Onufrijchuk, in an insightful essay written in 1988, held that 'ethnicity is already a construct – an edifice. It is the product of history and discourse. This ethnicity emerges from the official discourse of Canadian federal multicultural policy' (Onufrijchuk 1988: 3). Further steps have been taken by Evelyn I. Légaré, in a piece that adopts and maintains a relational distance to the discourse of Canadian multiculturalism, and shows how culture, like race before it, serves as a means of producing problematic Others:

> Canadian discursive practices position culturally defined identities as exclusive categories. These categories are not defined using the rigid grammar of race or biology. Nevertheless, this discourse shares many similarities with nineteenth and early twentieth century constructions of race, in that 'culture' is invoked to signify ethnic identities as Other than the normatively defined Canadian identity. (Légaré 1995: 347)

Légaré's work is also important in that it moves towards the deconstruction of the problematic character of Canadian diversity, placing the 'blame,' not on the arrival of different person-types, but on Canadian nationalism. 'Full inclusion within the nation demands "sameness,"' she notes. 'Thus, difference is always problematic, even when it is recognized' (351).

The 'naturalness' of the discourse on Canadian diversity has been most effectively challenged by Himani Bannerji. In her essay 'On the Dark Side of the Nation: Politics of Multiculturalism and the State of "Canada"' (1996), she suggests that multiculturalist ethnicities are 'officially constructed identities' (105) arising out of individual and group acceptance of a 'machinery of state that has us impaled against its spikes' (104). Rather than a happy history of harmonious coexistence, she sees a tradition in which 'Europeans continue the same solidarity of ruling and repression, blended with competitive manipulations, that they practised from the dawn of their conquests and state formations' (107). With regard to the social ideal, she ironically notes that 'some among us ["immigrants," "ethnics," "visible minorities"] even demanded the end of racist capitalism – and instead we got "multiculturalism"' (105). Bannerji plainly rejects Canadian multiculturalism as natural-historical fact, rational-bureaucratic act, and social-philosophical ideal, choosing to locate its emergence in a history of difference 'measured or constructed in terms of distance from civilizing European cultures' (117). The approach Bannerji sketches in her article is close to what I have set out to achieve, except that my focus will be limited to modes of differentiation based on humanity, civilization, race, culture, and ethnicity, and will only peripherally engage the other axes.

Identity, Identification, and the Desire for Recognition

Just as diversity is naturalized and problematized, so is identity, at the individual, ethnocultural, and national levels. As I have shown in the preceding discussion of state policy documents, the supposition that individuals can 'have' or 'achieve' stable ethnocultural identities is essential to multiculturalism in all of its modes. Multiculturalism also assumes that a proper, full, Canadian *national* identity is possible, but is being 'blocked' by a diversity of more 'successful' individual-ethnocultural identifications. In this section, I want to show how Lacanian social and political theory provides insights that challenge this prevailing wisdom.

With regard to the question of the necessity of *seeking* an identity or identities, Lacanian theory would not deviate from the sort of functional social-psychological perspective that dominates the Canadian field, and can be found in the influential 'social identity' theory of Henri Tajfel: 'Social identity' of an individual can be conceived as consisting of those aspects of his self-image, positively or negatively valued, which derive from his membership [in] various social groups ... (Tajfel 1978: 443). However, Lacanian theory does take issue with the possibility of actually *achieving* a full identity, of halting the search, of reaching the point of unproblematic 'membership.' There are two crucial differences between the Lacanian subject and the Tajfelian individual that must be addressed in the context of the problem of the search for identity.

First, for Lacanian theory, there is no entity such as an 'individual' who can take on an 'identity.' Rather, the individual – we had better say the *subject* – is afflicted by a constitutive alienation at the imaginary level via the experience of the 'mirror stage':

> This erotic relationship in which the human individual fixes upon himself an image which alienates him from himself, is the energy and the form from which there originates that passionate organization which he calls his *moi*. (Lacan, 'Aggresivité en psychanalyse,' cited in Wilden 1968: 173)

The *moi*, hoping to heal the wound dealt to it by this failed imaginary identification with itself, tries to identify with *others* through the register of the symbolic. This gives rise to the *je*, the subject of language (Lacan 1981: 199). The Lacanian subject, as both *moi* and *je*, emerges out of, yet is always within, both the imaginary and symbolic registers. Thus, there are no 'aspects' of one's 'self-image' which are *not* social, that is, not constructed in and through discourse; there is no 'core' of 'individual identity' that could be extracted or excluded. For Lacan, the subject is 'barred,' split, a subject of a constitutive *lack* that cannot be remedied through identifications at any level. In Ernesto Laclau's formulation, which deals explicitly with the social-political context, 'the structure of the identificatory act preserves, without superseding, the constitutive nothing of the subject' (Laclau and Zac 1994: 14).

Second, even though there is no escape from the social, the social itself also necessarily fails to exist. There will always be a constitutive outside, an exclusion, remainder, supplement, that cannot and *must not* be absorbed by the system:

> Therein consists the fundamental paradox of the 'logic of the signifier': ... we constitute a Totality not by adding something to it, but by subtracting something from it, namely the excessive 'besides' which opens up the totality of 'all things possible.' A totality without exception serving as its boundary remains an inconsistent, flawed set which 'doesn't hold together' ... (Zizek 1991b: 111)

This necessarily excluded element, which signifies only through its absence, is the moment of the *real* in the tripartite Lacanian schema. For Zizek, the real is 'the unfathomable fold which prevents it [language] from achieving its identity' (112). The existence of the social, then, is predicated not upon its centre, but upon its *margins*. As Ernesto Laclau has argued, '... only if the beyond becomes the signi- fier of pure threat, of pure negativity, of the simply excluded, can there be limits and system (that is an objective order)' (1996: 38). Para- doxically, the perennially problematic and excluded Other is in fact *required* in order to create a simulation of wholeness for the Self. In the Canadian context, this means that multiculturalism as problem of diversity not only 'prohibits' multiculturalism as social ideal, it also provides its condition of possibility, through the very failure of its attempts at a hegemonic suture of the social space which would achieve 'full' inclusion.

Of course, the ongoing failure of these attempts to constitute society as an all-inclusive totality also maintains it as a system of exclu- sions. Those who desire a full national identity thus tend to see multiculturalism as 'fact of diversity' as the source of a *prohibition* of multiculturalism as ideal of unity and identity, blaming 'Savages' or 'Immigrants' for what is in fact constitutive of all identities, that is, their incompleteness. It is belief in this prohibition that enables both the representation of the problematic Other as the symptom of a lack of unity, and the staging of a fantasy of harmonious recovery of this unity by bringing *all* others within the boundaries of the nation. In the con- temporary Canadian context – and throughout its history, as I will show – the search for identity and unity can be understood through a critical appropriation of the notion of *recognition*.

Within the Canadian discourse on diversity, recognition is often invoked as a kind of incantation whose mere utterance will ward off social antagonisms. This function can be seen most clearly in state policy documents. For example, the Canadian Multiculturalism Act of 1988 (35–36–37 Elizabeth II) sets out the government's commitment to:

3.(1)(a) *recognize and promote the understanding* that multiculturalism reflects the cultural and racial diversity of Canadian society;

3.(1)(b) *recognize and promote the understanding* that multiculturalism is a fundamental characteristic of Canadian heritage and identity;
...

3.(1)(d) *recognize the existence* of communities whose members share a common origin and their historic contribution to Canadian society, and enhance their development ...

Charles Taylor has given greater substance and specificity to the concept of recognition by according it a central role in his theory of identity.[7] For Taylor, in modern societies, 'our identities are formed in dialogue with others, in agreement or struggle with their recognition of us' (1991: 45–6). The achievement of identity through recognition is closely related to a 'developing ideal of authenticity' (46). That is, in order to acquire an identity, we must be recognized for 'what defines us as human agents,' as 'who we are.' 'The recognition I am talking about,' writes Taylor, 'is the acceptance of ourselves by others in our identity' (1993: 190). Thus, while he tries to stress its dialogical character, recognition for Taylor ultimately depends upon correct outward perception of a pre-existing inner being or essence. It is, in this sense, in keeping with modern essentialist theories of identity.

Taylor's emphasis on 'correct' recognition is related to his desire to achieve Canadian unity. He hopes for 'reconciliation' on two levels: that of the individual and his or her people; and of a multiplicity of peoples and their state. Each of these reconciliations involves the recovery of something supposed to have been lost. On the individual level, Taylor argues in his *Hegel* that 'the problem of ... recovering a set of institutions and practices with which men can identify, is with us in an acute way in the apathy and alienation of modern society' (1975: 460). Throughout his work, he has considered the same theme on the level of groups, suggesting, to take the most pertinent example, that 'we' English Canadians – as a state people – should recognize 'them' – French Canadians as a conquered people – in order to 'reconcile the solitudes' in which Canada's two largest ethnocultural identities exist. Reconciliation would constitute a return of the pleasurable articulation of a single nation with a single state, supposedly found in modernity, but now in the postmodern, plural form of a *multiplicity* of nations within a single state. This would be the achievement of a working, functional, *ethical community.* 'We need at once freedom and a post-industrial *Sittlichkeit*' (461). Taylor thus stages a fantasy of a dual recovery: of the subject supposed to be lost, the Canadian; and the country supposed to be lost, Canada.

At the close of his book on Hegel, Taylor states his feeling that 'any serious attempt' to restore the good society 'must incorporate the language and insights of those which [*sic*] have gone before. Among these Hegel is a giant' (461). Chief among Hegel's insights relevant to this discussion was his use of the concept of recognition to show how an ethical community can arise out of individual self-consciousness. So, I will now turn to what Taylor calls 'the most influential early treatment' of this topic (Taylor 1991: 49), that is, chapter 4 of Hegel's *Phenomenology of Spirit* (Hegel 1977). The relevant sections of the *Phenomenology* appear in the second major division, which is concerned with the passage from consciousness to self-consciousness, from the sensation, perception, and understanding of inanimate objects to the mutual recognition of oneself in another human being. It is important to note that, for Hegel, the Self's appropriation of objects – both material and human – is by its nature destructive in intent; the Self seeks to *negate* (eat, know, incorporate) its others as a means of gaining certainty of its own existence. This quest for *satisfaction* is constitutive of self-consciousness: 'self-consciousness *is* Desire' (109). Desire is, however, always frustrated, since objects resist their negation: 'self-consciousness, by its negative relation to the object, is unable to supersede it; it is really because of that relation that it produces the object again, and the desire as well' (109).

Now, while the attempt to assimilate objects is futile on the biological level, Hegel believes that self-consciousness *can* achieve satisfaction 'when the object ... effects the negation within itself' (109). This service can be provided only by *another* self-consciousness. 'Self-consciousness exists in and for itself when, and by the fact that, it so exists for another; that is, it exists only in being acknowledged' (111). This quest for acknowledgment occurs in the field of what Kojeve has called 'anthropogenetic desire,' through which the drama of the dialectic of recognition is played out (Kojeve 1969). The first act is the encounter that leads to the *struggle to the death*, which I will now quickly outline.[8]

1. Two consciousnesses meet. They are objects to each other.
2. Each tries to negate the other; each threatens the life of the other in order to see if it is subject rather than object. This means, at the same time, that each stakes its own life, and shows its humanity in its willingness to die for an idea.
3. What are the possible outcomes? If one self-consciousness kills the other, the winner has achieved nothing since a dead body cannot provide recognition.
4. Thus, a more productive arrangement is struck: one self-consciousness chooses to negate itself by *submitting* to the other; it becomes a slave, recognizing and dependent, while the other becomes a master, recognized and independent. To the slave falls the endless task of wrestling objects into forms fit for human consumption; while the

enjoyment of *consuming* these objects falls to the master, who is thereby relieved of the necessity of struggle, and might be said to have achieved 'pure' satisfaction.

We should note that Kojeve's reading of Hegel 'stopped' here, as he saw *all* intersubjective relations as variations upon the theme of master and slave. A number of contemporary writers have been trying to rescue Hegel from this highly influential Kojevian reading. Habermas has argued that in the early Hegel there is a concept of recognition through labour, symbolization, and interaction that is not predicated upon the master-slave relationship and is not swept away by a breath of *Geist* (Habermas 1996). In *The Struggle for Recognition* (1995), Axel Honneth has sought to de-idealize and 'reconstruct' the early Hegelian line of argument by giving it a social-scientific, rather than an idealist, basis. While I will not delve into these questions of interpretation, I think it is worth carrying on to the further 'stages' that Hegel envisions, because of the interesting results that can be achieved through their use in analysing concrete historical situations. To return to the play:

5. One might think that the master, with his or her 'pure' enjoyment, is now at a point of rest, but for Hegel 'the outcome is a recognition that is one-sided and unequal' (116). The master is recognized, not by another human being, but by a thing. It has proven itself to be a thing precisely by choosing material existence over spiritual integrity. It is of no more use than a dead body.
6. The master thus does not get what she or he wanted, but does not know this, nor ever becomes aware of this situation. Only the slave, through fear and discipline, arrives at the idea of freedom as a *possibility*.
7. This possibility realizes itself in several stages, which, of course, are deficient. The first is Stoicism, in which the slave simply *decides* that he or she is free, 'whether on the throne or in chains' (121). In this mode, slavery is constructed, or thought, as itself a form of freedom. This is the Notion of freedom, says Hegel, but not its actuality.
8. The next stage is Scepticism, which is the 'realization as a *negative* attitude' of the Notion of freedom. Scepticism means here nihilistic solipsism; it 'affirms the nullity' (126) of the world, yet continues to live in it. In this mode, one might say that slavery is seen as no more or less free than any other condition, since all conditions are equally meaningless and ungrounded.

9. The Sceptic position becomes the contradictory, Unhappy Consciousness, in which *both* master and slave are present.

This unhappy, inwardly disrupted consciousness 'must forever have present in the one consciousness the other also; and thus is it driven out of each in turn in the very moment when it imagines it has successfully attained to a peaceful unity' (126). The Unhappy Consciousness contains within itself both the changeable and the unchangeable; the finite and the infinite; the particular and the universal; but does not know how to *reconcile* these opposites, and so suffers.

There is a long road to travel before the Notion of freedom is *fully* actualized: all the way to the end of the *Phenomenology*, when Absolute Spirit starts foaming out of the chalice. But it is taken as far as needed for my purposes a little sooner than that, in the third division, where Hegel writes: 'It is in fact in the life of a people or nation that the *Notion* of self-conscious Reason's actualization – of beholding, in the independence of the 'other,' complete *unity* with it ... has its complete reality' (212). This unity 'speaks its universal language' in the 'customs and laws' of the nation; the individual finds 'in the actual world nothing but himself; he is as certain of the others as he is of himself' (213). 'There is nothing here which would not be reciprocal' (213); each individual is immersed in an 'ethical substance' (*Sittlichkeit*) (216), and 'this unity means happiness' (215). So, *through the nation the split in the Unhappy Consciousness is healed*. Such is the Hegelian fantasy of fullness through recognition, as a state that can be achieved by a thoroughly modern identification of the individual with his or her culture and nation. As I will show, it is this fantasy that provides support for multiculturalism as a state policy of recognition that would solve, once and for all, the problem of Canadian diversity.

Nation and State, Power and Resistance

Of course, nations existed, even in Hegel's day, not as monads but in a context of differences both internal and external. In order to ensure the survival and well-being of their particular form of ethical life, they required a connection with a state. In the *Phenomenology*, 'state power' is discussed only briefly, along with 'wealth,' as one moment in the 'world of self-alienated spirit,' or culture (301). For a fuller account of its role in Hegel's system, we must turn to the *Philosophy of Right*.[9] Here the state appears as 'the actuality of the ethical idea,' as 'absolutely rational inasmuch as it is the actuality of the substantial will which it possesses in the particular self-consciousness once that consciousness has been raised to consciousness of its universality' (Hegel 1952: 155–6). That is, to the extent that one has travelled along the Hegelian highway, one will 'find oneself' in the state as the actualization of the particular ethical ideal of one's nation, and will therefore see it as 'mind objectified' – mind here translating *Geist*, as a 'thorough-going unity of the universal and the single' (156). For Hegel, there is no question of a 'contract' between the individual and the state: such theories 'destroy the absolutely divine principle of the state, together with its majesty and absolute authority' (157). Rather, the state, as the 'final end,' has 'supreme right against the individual, whose supreme duty it is to be a member of the state' (156). The individual is *duty bound* to make the state her own, to find herself in it regardless of its specific content, and only on the basis of the universality and rationality which it is granted *through this act of submission itself.*

In his famous Preface to the *Philosophy of Right*, Hegel makes it clear that he is not out to prescribe any future ideal, but only to describe what has come before the moment of his own writing:

> This book, then, containing as it does the science of the state, is to be nothing other than the endeavour to apprehend and portray the state as something inherently rational. As a work of philosophy, it must be poles apart from an attempt to construct a state as it ought to be; it can only show how the state, the ethical universe, is to be understood. (11)

But surely this distinction is suspect as, in its dialectic structure, it posits the discovery of what it has itself hidden. More precisely, the state only appears 'rational' to those who take Hegel's description as a prescription – those who do not are summarily dismissed as irrational and suffering from their inability to move beyond a state of 'ignoble consciousness.' Certainly, many who have come after Hegel have seen the state form evolve into something much less easily apprehended as 'rational' in the sense he gives the term. From Marx to Habermas, from Weber to Bourdieu, and from Nietzsche to Foucault and Deleuze, unquestioned submission has been replaced by constant questioning: the state's universality has been reduced to the particularity of a ruling class; its rationality has been recast as rationalization; and its relation to the individual has been taken beyond either contract or duty, into the realm of the creation and management of *subjects as objects.*

Hegel's most immediate and profound critic was, of course, Karl Marx. In *The German Ideology*, while he agreed that 'only in the community ... is personal freedom possible' (Marx in Tucker 1978: 197), Marx directly attacked Hegel's claim that the state could embody or actualize this freedom in a universal form:

> In the previous substitutes for the community, in the State, etc., personal freedom has existed only for the individuals who developed within the relations of the ruling class, and only insofar as they were individuals of this class. The illusory community, in which individuals have up till now combined, always took on an independent existence in relation to them ... (197)

Thus – using Hegel's own terms, and on his own sacred ground – did Marx do away with the supreme right of the capitalist state and the supreme duty of the individual to immerse himself in it. Of course, Marx did not want to do away with the state as such, nor with the community as a site of achieved fullness, and reproduced Hegel's category of universal actor – albeit with a new particular content – as the proletariat.

Weber's critique of Marx's class reductionism was an important moment in the theorization of the modern state, as was his analysis of the characteristics of 'bureaucratic authority' and 'bureaucratic management' (Weber 1946: 196). The notion of bureaucracy as a form of rational domination has been picked up by many others, notably by Jürgen Habermas in his *Theory of Communicative Action* (1989). After a close critique of Weber's theory of rationalization, Habermas offers his own theory of the colonization of the everyday 'lifeworld' by a 'system' of 'purposive rational economic and administrative action' (2.154). An important cleavage in contemporary debates is that between the positions of Lyotard and Habermas, with the former offering little in the way of possibilities for what the latter refers to as the successful 'completion' of the 'project of modernity,' that is, for the possibility of a form of reason that could overcome rational-instrumental technique (cf. Rorty 1985).

The stream of thought with which I identify most strongly does not concern itself with providing a solution to the problem of Enlightenment, but rather tries to analyse how it has proceeded to do and undo its work. This leads us to the question of *power*, which figures prominently in the work of Bourdieu and Foucault. Bourdieu cautiously offers up a theory of the state, with a tip of the hat to Max Weber, as 'the ensemble of fields that are the site of struggles in which what is at stake is ... the power to constitute and to impose as *universal* and *universally applicable* ... within the boundaries of a given territory, a common set of coercive norms' (Bourdieu 1992: 112). The question of power is also a crucial moment of Foucault's genealogical method. In 'Two Lectures' (written in 1976), Foucault notes that 'the course of study I have been following until now ... has been concerned with the *how* of power' (1980: 92; italics in original). Later, in 'The Subject and Power' (written in 1982), he says that his purpose has *not* been to analyse power, but rather to 'create a history of the different modes by which, in our culture, human beings are made subjects' (1980: 208).

However, for Foucault, the most important effect of power is precisely to create human subjects. Thus, in order to understand how discursive formations enable and constrain human subjects, it is necessary to know how power operates. Foucault's polemic against 'the repressive hypothesis' is of relevance here, especially as it is developed in the first volume of *The History of Sexuality*, where it is articulated to a positive statement of some of the central features of his own methodology. Here he argues that modern discursive formations have not been out to 'repress' the objects and individuals that don't fit into their schemes, if by repression one means the attempt to cause an object to cease to exist or at least remain out of sight. Rather, Foucault says, the operation of modern power has caused a *proliferation* of non-canonical objects, subjects, and practices, the purpose of which is to provide evidence and justification for a complementary proliferation of normalizing management and disciplinary techniques. With regard to the discourses of sexuality, Foucault claims that

> the machinery of power that focused on this whole alien strain did not attempt to suppress it, but rather to give it an analytical, visible, and permanent reality ... not the exclusion of these thousand aberrant sexualities, but the specification of each one of them. (1978: 44)

For Foucault, the goal of modern discourses of power has been to create a series of *management problems* for which solutions must (obviously, urgently) be found. These solutions take the form of innumerable codifications of practice, daily regimens, compulsory exclusions and inclusions, and definitions of what is and isn't to be accepted as 'normal' behaviour. In the seventeenth and eighteenth centuries, Foucault says, a new form of power began to arise in Europe, which had to find ways to 'gain access to the bodies of individuals, to their acts, attitudes, and modes of everyday behaviour' (1980: 66–7). Thus, these various regimes have as their object, their focal point and final goal, the disciplining and conditioning of the human body itself. They provide the means by which structures of power come to permeate our bodies, allowing the operation of what Foucault has called 'bio-power,' which, as I will show in the Canadian context, has emerged as a specific form of governmentality as an ongoing attempt at *rational-bureaucratic domination*.

On this point, Deleuze and Guattari have established a useful distinction between 'state' and 'nomadic' forms of social organization. In their *Nomadology: The War Machine* (1986), they include ancient empires, modern nation-states, and postmodern disciplinary regimes as state forms, and also cut across the boundary that traditionally separates the Western and Eastern traditions:

> There is a unity of *composition* of all states, but states have neither the same *development* nor the same *organization*. In the Orient, the components are much more disconnected, disjointed, necessitating a great immutable Form to hold them together: 'despotic formations' ... In the West ... the interconnectedness of the components makes possible transformation of the state-form through revolution. (Deleuze and Guattari 1986: 58–9)

One thing that all of these forms have in common is the task they set for themselves: to *striate* the space over which they reign. States hope to 'capture flows of all kinds,' to make order where there is chaos, convert outside into inside, or utilize the smooth outside spaces as a means of communication in the service of the inside (59). State forms build fences, gates, and fortresses, survey the land, and develop systems of roads and highways. Whatever is outside and not part of the plan is to be brought in, reduced to the known, and thereby rendered manageable.

European civilization knows all too well what can happen when the war machine comes in off the steppes, sweeping away everything that matters: houses, walls, fields, property, lives, cultures. That China has fared no better is obvious in its monument to state insecurity, the Great Wall, the sedentary obstacle repeatedly breached and now a crumbling tourist attraction. Inside and outside are *interdependent*, each potentially giving rise to the other, each warding off the other, in an ongoing play of relations of power:

> It is not in terms of independence, but of coexistence and competition *in a perpetual field of interaction*, that we must conceive of exteriority and interiority, war machines of metamorphosis and state apparatuses of identity, bands and kingdoms, megamachines and empires. The same field circumscribes its interiority in states, but describes its exteriority in what escapes states or stands against states. (17)

The desired – but never fully achieved – effect of operations in the field of governmental power, then, is to striate or order physical, bodily, and semiotic spaces, and to protect these from external forces of disorder or smoothness.

Of course, these attempts can never be fully successful, as there will always be someone, something, or somewhere left out, or emerging from within, that offers *resistance* to their goals. Rather than 'determining' action or existence, discursive formations, in Foucault's formulation, 'mark out the dispersion of the points of choice, and define prior to any option ... a field of strategic possibilities' (Foucault 1972: 37). As with Bourdieu's notion of field, we are dealing with a system of rules that has conditioning, but not determining, effects on the possibilities of signification, material existence, and action. Thus power, for Foucault, 'includes strategies for self-development that both constrain – through objectifying techniques – and enable – through subjectifying techniques – agency' (Lacombe 1996: 334).

This line of theoretical questioning leads to a crucial observation: if all discourses of power multiply the subjects they attempt to objectively manipulate; if subjects always are capable of resistance; and if every boundary creates a sedentary interior which will be challenged by a nomadic exterior and vice versa, then *the likelihood of a discourse of power ever solving a problem it sets for itself is really quite low.* What we would expect to see is an endless series of failed attempts, perpetually renewed efforts, which might have some efficacy, but will in the end only *exacerbate* the problems they are intended to solve, thereby creating a justification for further attempts at regulating everyday life. In this regard, Lacanian theory is compatible with Foucault's and Bourdieu's emphasis on discourse as an enabling constraint, leading to a proliferation of subjects and resistances competing and cooperating within an ever-expanding and changing field. As I will show, this is precisely what we see in the history of Canadian diversity, as an *ongoing effort to use the state form as a tool to fashion a Canadian nation*. From the first colonial encounters up to the present day, various modes of the state form have been deployed to create the 'right' kind of space for unity and harmony. Even though the state form has never been able to rise to the challenge, its failures have simply led to its further, more concentrated application. In this endless quest, we see the evidence of a frustrated desire, of a partial traversal of a fantasy of wholeness which is being reduced to drive, the 'domain of the closed circular palpitation which finds satisfaction in endlessly repeating the same failed gesture' (Zizek 1997b: 30).

Delimiting the Field

In this cursory study of the field of Canadian diversity as it is displayed in state policy, popular culture, and academic discussions, I have argued that it observes the following regularities: (1) Canadian diversity is seen as a natural-historical, objective *fact*, resulting from innate differences in human types based on race, culture, ethnicity, geography, and climate; (2) this diversity is thought to represent a public problem meriting state intervention, or a series of rational-bureaucratic *acts*; (3) inasmuch as the fact of multiculturalism is conflated with the act, the problem of Canadian diversity is thought to contain its own solution, to be in the process of solving itself, of achieving its own *ideal*. Where these three criteria are met in the context of a battle for articulation with disciplinary regimes associated with territories that have come, or might have come, under the sway of the Canadian state, I will hold that the speech/event/text in question can be included in the field of Canadian diversity.

I have also outlined a theoretical-methodological justification for a genealogical analysis of the appearance of the policy of multiculturalism within the field of Canadian diversity; an investigation of how the discourse on diversity has shifted from object to object, method to method, in a futile quest to construct a Canadian nation which could be articulated with a Canadian state, and thereby achieve a full identity. In the following chapters, I will examine how this process of *recognition* has played itself out on the level of what might be called 'ethnogenetic desire,'[10] in the modalities of struggle to the death, master-slave relation, and stoic and sceptical notions of freedom. I will proceed by accepting the claim, under proposition (1) above, that the tradition of Canadian diversity extends back to the arrival of the Europeans in North America, and use this to examine the assumption, given in proposition (3), that the discourse on Canadian diversity is in the process of achieving its own ideal. My answer to this question will be given in chapters 8 and 9, after the evidence for it has been presented. At this point, I only wish to suggest that to see the limits of multiculturalism as a state policy of official recognition of difference requires seeing its fantasmatic basis in the desire for an end to the play of power between ethnocultural identities. The crucial lesson to learn from Lacanian theory is that if the achievement of a full identity – as an individual, society, or nation – is an impossible limit that can never be achieved, then *no individual, group, or sociological fact of diversity can be blocking it*, and no amount of rational-bureaucratic intervention will ever remove the (non-existent) blockage. With this thought in mind, we are now ready to proceed with a genealogy of the problem of Canadian diversity.

Chapter Three

European Antecedents to the Problem of Canadian Diversity

Wherever and whenever in Europe or around the Mediterranean the collection and description of the manners and customs of mankind have assumed considerable volume, or when new and astonishing types of human behaviour have been called to the attention of Europeans, there and then the arresting problem of cultural diversity, or some one of its subordinate problems, has emerged – not only for the Hebrews, the Greeks, and the Romans, not only for the amateur anthropologists of the sixteenth and seventeenth centuries, but also for the moderns.

– Margaret Hodgen, *Early Anthropology in the Sixteenthth and Seventeenth Centuries*, 481

How Difference Changes, How It Remains the Same

Staring into the mist. Straying into the mist. How far must we travel? Where and when did the problem of Canadian diversity emerge? The Canadian government claims that there is an origin to be found in a primordial diversity of pre-invasion cultures, but I have suggested that whatever differences were 'present' prior to the arrival of the Europeans, they could not have signified within the Western discourse on diversity. If Canadian diversity did not exist until Europeans arrived to 'discover' it, the conditions of possibility for its emergence must be sought in the work of those who first took on the task of creating, defining, and ranking the European Self and its Others: Herodotus, Plato, Augustine, Linnaeus, and the travellers, scientists, and Colonizers who followed in their wake. Configured in a line of descent, these constitute what one might call the discourse of Western political anthropology, which establishes a hierarchical order among human beings of various types and uses this order to justify certain relations of power. I will argue that it is out of this discourse, and not out of 'the land' or 'the people' of the New World, that the problem of Canadian diversity has emerged.

In recent years, many layers of the sediment left by the operation of Western political anthropology have been excavated, and its effects in both the early European and current Eurocolonial contexts have been traced (Dickason 1984; Friedman 1981; Goldberg 1993; Hodgen 1964; Todorov 1993, 1984). As the literature is large and growing exponentially, I do not propose to make an exhaustive study of it here. Instead, I will fashion a narrative that succinctly shows the nature and weight of the conceptual baggage that the European invaders brought with them to the New World, in general, and Canada, in particular. Between each turning point, I will discuss the nature of the categories and the hierarchical order established, the problems thereby created, and the solutions proposed.

I will also pay close attention to the matter of 'sign flow' between identities, which will be addressed through the terms *assimilation* and *integration*, defined as follows:

Identity A *assimilates* subject/identity B; or
B *is assimilated by* A:
B takes on signs that mark A, and may or may not give up signs of its own particularity. In the limit case, B *becomes* A, is indistinguishable from A. A will commonly be in a position of greater structural power (social, economic, political, cultural), and thus able to use both force and seduction to bring about the assimilation of B. B may attempt to resist the flow completely, or try to choose its form and/or content, in resistance to the will of A, in the case of coercion, or as a result of B's own will to integration, as a result of successful seduction.

A *integrates* B:
B *is integrated by* A:
A takes on signs of B's particularity. Generally, A is a relatively hegemonic identity, or group of identities, so that while it acknowledges or reproduces some signs of the Other as Self signs, these are only the

ones it *chooses* to acknowledge or reproduce. Again, B may attempt to stop the flow entirely, or try to choose its form and/or content, in resistance to the will of A, in the case of coercion, or as a result of B's own will to integration, as a result of successful seduction.

The line between coercion and seduction, and therefore between 'resistance' and 'freedom,' can only be drawn subjectively, in particular cases, and the drawing of such lines will give rise to statements of *value*; that is, a response to an attempt at assimilation or integration could appear as either 'self-determination' or 'rebellion,' depending upon the position of enunciation. In one formation that I will analyse – Canadian multiculturalism as state policy, which is discussed in chapter 8 – assimilation and integration have evolved specialized meanings, and a symbiotic relationship exists in which the terms have been richly 'confused' to achieve certain power-knowledge effects. When assimilation and/or integration are used within the discursive field being analysed, their particular resonances will be respected.

I should point out that by invoking the notion of 'relative power' above, I am speaking about the achievement of a hegemonic striation of spaces, bodies, and souls, an articulation of a nation-race-culture with a state form, to create a *society*. The *net* flow of signs enabled by a relatively successful striation tends to be from groups of greater structural power to those of lesser potential. I shall refer to this observation as the *power law of sign flow*. This is not to say that signs never flow in the opposite direction – they do – and when this occurs, I would cite an instance of relatively successful resistance. However, close attention to the net flow of signs over time is of great use in unravelling the complex relations that exist between self-identified groups of people who wish to perpetuate their own style of life at the expense of other styles, and I will make use of it throughout the analysis.

Herodotus, Father of Ethnography

In her study of the historical construction of ethnocultural diversity in the tradition of anthropology, Margaret Hodgen ascribes priority to the work of the ancient Greek historian Herodotus of Halicarnassus (Hodgen 1964: 20–1). Here, she argues, the rules and categories according to which Western philosophers, missionaries, and colonizers would describe and judge Others were first laid down. Hodgen notes that Herodotus shows great rigour in choosing a set of categories of differentiation and applying them systematically to the peoples described in his *Histories*. 'For each group,' she suggests, 'seven categories of cultural fact are given' (Hodgen 1964: 23). These include the place of residence and climate, language, dress, food and the means of acquiring it, dwellings, modes of making or avoiding war, and prestige as judges. The final category might be better reckoned as involving internal and external political relations, and Hodgen leaves out the important category of religious rites, especially those involving burial, but it does seem that even in his briefest descriptions, Herodotus adhered quite closely to this formula.

Take, for example, his estimation of the Indians, whom he held to be the most Easterly of all Asians:

> [T]hey will not take life in any form; they sow no seed, and have no houses and live on a vegetable diet ... All the Indian tribes I have mentioned copulate in the open like cattle; their skins are all of the same colour, much like the Ethiopians.' Their semen is not white like other peoples', but black like their own skins ... Their country is a long way from Persia towards the south, and they were never subject to Darius. (III.98)

In this, and in dozens of other descriptions, we can discern what Herodotus considered to be the essential pieces of information that were needed in order to know the Other. To some extent, we can make out a particularly Greek set of interests, in the concern to trace lines of descent and to document abilities in war and statesmanship. But what is perhaps more interesting about Herodotus's categories is that they treat of what can be seen from a distance – a distance not only optical but cultural, as well, the dis-stance of the one who observes but does not participate. And, even though his text is full of disclaimers, he often relied upon hearsay for observations that would have required great intimacy, as in his report of the outrageous hue of Indian semen. Yet, even when Herodotus appears to be recounting what he himself has experienced, we are left with the impression that his subjects are objects, that he has observed them in passing with a collector's eye.

This tendency is most pronounced as the reader is brought further from the Greek World, into distant reaches of the East, West, and North. The Androphagi, or maneaters, are given only a few lines, in which they are represented as 'the most savage of men, [with] no notion of either law or justice. They are herdsmen without fixed dwellings; their dress is Scythian, their language peculiar to themselves, and

they are the only people in this part of the world to eat human flesh'
(IV.105). The Neurians are reduced even further. All we hear of them is
that 'it appears that these people practice magic; for there is a story
current amongst the Scythians and the Greeks in Scythia that once a
year every Neurian turns into a wolf for a few days, and then turns
back into a man again' (IV.105). Herodotus quickly disclaims any belief
in this tale, but tells it nonetheless. The same goes for the headless
Blemmy, strap-foots, troglodytes, and the men who sleep for six
months of the year. All of these peoples, real or imagined, are reduced
to a single abhorrent characteristic, and thereby constitute a *de facto* category of their own: that of the monstrous semi-human being. At the
margins of the known world, we find monsters of all sorts, mythic
Amazons, amber, and gold. The terrible *and* the beautiful: indeed, anything but the everyday.

It is hard to argue that Herodotus was obsessed with tales of monsters, since the sections of the *Histories* devoted to them are quite few
and far between. But, even when he was dealing with the relatively
close and familiar, he was constantly operating in a mode of comparison between what he saw and heard and what he and his assumed
readership – Greek men – would have considered normal. We can see
this mode at work in the example cited above, where the members of
the Indian tribe are said to avoid taking life in any form (unlike a
Greek, who kills regularly for sport, riches, and glory); to sow no seed
(unlike the Greek agriculturist); and to have no houses (unlike the
Greek, who takes great pride in his *oikos*). In his attempts to spy the
Other through the scope of the Self, Herodotus earned his place as the
Father of Ethnography. But such comparisons cannot be achieved
without a prior assumption, still with us in even the most postmodern
of anthropological practices, which I will call the *law of individual-group
identification*. This law lets the one stand for the many, and vice versa,
and thereby allows the inquirer to know and describe that most useful
of abstractions, 'the people.' Such an effect always begins at home, of
course, for the first premise is that one's own people exists as a basis
for comparison, that there is a set of practices and appearances that
'we' all share. Certainly it is tautologically true that, within human
groups defined as such, some practices will be more common than others, more or less actively encouraged or discouraged, and it is this
observation that gives rise to the notions of culture, race, society, and
so on. Taken further, however, these premises are used to produce the
always doubtful, and sometimes dangerous, consequent that *all* who

appear to be 'part' of some people will share certain very particular characteristics: rather like dog's heads or goat's feet, but less marvelous – or even positively valued – and therefore more difficult to detect in passing.[1] Again, let us return to the Egyptians, 'much the most learned of any nation of which I have had experience' (II.77). *All* of them? What of the slaves, prisoners, street hawkers, women stuck at home tending an infinity of dependent children and men? The Royal Scythians, according to Herodotus, 'are the most warlike ... of their race' (IV.20), and the Issedonians, apart from eating their dead fathers, 'appear to have a sound enough sense of the difference between right and wrong' (IV.27). This is a far cry from what was to come, of course, when individuals would be torn to pieces by dogs because of qualities supposed to be inherent in their people, but the *modus operandi* is the same.

The use of stereotypical, reductionist formulas to describe peoples and all individuals considered to be 'of' those peoples was correlated in Herodotus, and in later formations of the European discourse on diversity, with a tendency to freeze these forms, to grant them a certain imperviousness to the ravages of time and change. Again, this is a regular feature of Herodotus's text that shows itself more clearly the further he ventures from home. The Egyptians at least *had* a history, though Herodotus didn't always agree with its claims. The more far-flung peoples, however, were granted their few attributes in perpetuity. Herodotus did not see cannibalism, for example, as a practice that might come and go, but as an essential characteristic.

While he tended to assume that each of the peoples he studied possessed an immutable nature, Herodotus was also very attentive, as I have noted above, to the existence of differences *between* these peoples. One 'explanation' for the observed variance in human practice was provided by the influences of climate and geography, two powerful and unchanging forces that shaped the nature of the peoples in a given region. Throughout the *Histories*, the land and its features figure prominently: 'Not only is the Egyptian climate peculiar to that country, and the Nile different in its behaviour from other rivers elsewhere, but the Egyptians themselves in their manners and customs seem to have reversed the ordinary practices of mankind' (II.36). The Scythians, with their nomadic relation to a hostile land, have managed to preserve themselves better than anyone else, since none who try to conquer them can cope with either the environment or the people (IV.46). A theory of human nature based on geography, climate, and group membership fits in with the general plan of the *Histories*, inasmuch as the counter assumption, that the nature of a people is variable, would mean that Greeks could suddenly begin eating one another and forget the difference between right and wrong. The possibility of such drift had to be excluded from Herodotus's text, lest it tear open the fabric of Greek life that his narrative so subtly weaves.

The terms the Greeks used to define the sorts of difference they found in the non-Greek world are important, to illuminate their usage in context, and to give, in anticipation, some sense of the connotations their derivatives carry today. *Ethnos* appears to have had a broad usage, covering groups of beings of many sorts:

> [W]e hear of *ethnos etairon*, a band of comrades, or *ethnos laon*, a host of men, in the Iliad; of *ethnos Achaion* or *Lukion*, the tribe of Achaeans or Lycians, also in Homer, along with *kluta ethnea nekron*, glorious hosts of corpses / the dead, in the Odyssey; of *ethnea melisson* or *ornithon*, a swarm of bees or flock of birds, again in the Iliad; *ethnos aneron* or *gunaikon*, the race of men or women, in Pindar; and to *Medikon ethnos*, the Median people or nation, in Herodotus. (Ostergard 1992: 31)

Ethnos was also used in contrast to *polis*. Greeks lived in a *polis*, a city-state with an obvious physical centre and a particular set of institutions. Non-Greeks lived in various sorts of regional or village affiliations, and lacked Greek political institutions (Humphreys 1978: 130–1). Those of an *ethnos* were commonly referred to by its name, or *ethnikon*, thus giving rise to the term *ethnikos*, often translated as 'heathen.' *Genos* was used by Herodotus to describe families or related groups within an *ethnos*, leading to the suggestion that '*ethnos* seems to be more suited to cultural than biological or kinship differences' (Ostergard 1992: 32). In the ancient usage of *ethnos* and its variants, we can see the basis for later transformations into the use of *ta ethne* to describe all groups except Christians and Jews (A. Smith 1986: 21); as well as for the current situation in which 'ethnic' is used in everyday language to refer to any person or group other than those whom the speaker considers normal or dominant, and, in Canadian multiculturalism policy discourse, to a people that does not, and should not, possess a *polis* (e.g., Kymlicka 1995: 15).

Herodotan ethnography was a practical attempt to answer the question How are the Barbarians different from the Greeks? Based on the way he tried to answer this question, Herodotus can be placed

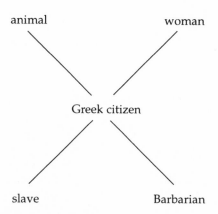

Fig. 3.1. The Herodotan wheel of difference

within the greater Greek scheme of things, as a precursor to the development of the notion of the Great Chain of Being. In her book *Centaurs and Amazons*, Page duBois argues that, prior to Plato, the Greek mode of reasoning about Self and Other was by way of polarity and analogy.[2] All Greeks were related in a network of likeness, set off in opposition to all Barbarians, who themselves were thought to share certain characteristics. To illustrate the analogy-polarity model, duBois uses the metaphor of a wheel. At its centre we find the network of Greek citizens – human, civilized, rational, autonomous males – alike in their possession of these highly valued qualities, bound by a 'logic of equivalence' (Laclau and Mouffe 1985). Radiating out from the Greek citizens were spokes of difference that defined an excluded periphery of animal, Barbarian, irrational, and female types, structured by a 'logic of difference' (see fig. 3.1). All of these were, of course, equivalent in their exclusion and presumed lack of possession of the central qualities.

Greeks were those who possessed the good, and lacked the evil. Non-Greeks were their complement, so that one could write an equation of identity in which Greek is the negation of all that it excludes: Greek = not animal + not Barbarian + not woman + not slave-like. Of course, a positive equation could be written as well, following the traditional line of thought on nations and ethnicities as 'shared' agglomerations of positive attributes.[3] But this approach tends to downplay very real and effective motivations and rationalizations for relations of

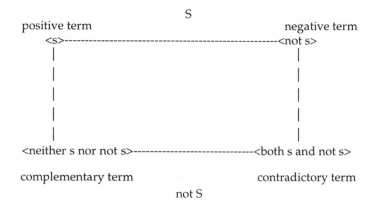

Fig. 3.2. The semiotic square

power between the Self group and its Others; 'not sharing,' that is, being 'different,' is a far less grievous sin than being a *negation* of all that 'we' stand for. The positive approach also makes it impossible to note how the excluded Other is in fact essential to the construction of a canonical identity, in the sense discussed in chapter 2.

While the wheel metaphor is interesting and enlightening, it models only binary oppositions, and therefore does not fully capture the subtlety of the semantics of identity in Greek myth, which, as duBois has noted, contains many 'fusions of oppositions' (105). What are we to make, for example, of the Centaur, who, as both man and animal, undermines the firm opposition between these two terms? Or the Amazon, who confounds the male/female dichotomy in possessing a woman's body but a man's warlike temperament? A.J. Greimas's method of the 'semiotic square' is a useful tool for analysing identification systems of this sort, especially in the diagrammatic form given in Ronald Schleifer's *A.J. Greimas and the Nature of Meaning* (1987: 25–33). Schleifer proposes a general representation of the square that can be rendered as in figure 3.2. Such a semiotic square is a formal method of exhausting the possibilities of signification inherent in a given concept or 'semantic axis.' S above is a semantic axis, which sets up a binary opposition between two terms. Given a unit of meaning <s>, the square provides a means of generating terms that are contrary <not s>, contradictory <both s and not s>, and complementary <neither s nor not s> to <s>. The complementary term is of greatest interest, in that it admits of many possible interpretations. This term is inherently 'synthetic,' since it points to that which cannot be contained within the axis inscribed in the terms of the square, and may lead, in practice, to an overcoming of the binary opposition in question.

To generate particular squares, I use a method adapted from a 'narratized' procedure that Schleifer attributes to Nancy Armstrong, which I present here along with an example that will help to clarify the process:

1. Choose a semantic axis <S>, and think of the name of the dominant or hegemonic entity within it (S = <gender in patriarchal societies>, s = <man>).
2. Think of the name of that which lacks the qualities of, must not 'be,' is the Other of s (not s = <woman>).
3. Think of the name of that which confuses the issue, which implies both the absence and presence of s (both s and not s = <drag queen>, <dyke>, which are not gendered identities).
4. Think of that which transcends the opposition between s and not s (neither s nor not s = <individual in a degendered society of the future>).

In this all-too-familiar example, the contradictory term tends to undermine the static binary opposition that forms the basis for the square (see Butler 1990). The complementary term is difficult to imagine, or even name, since discursive practice has not yet made known its positive content. Yet it is always there, promising relief from, or at least a change in the form of, the system of binary opposition in question:

> In actual practice ... it frequently turns out that we are able to articulate a given concept in only three of the four available positions; the final one [the complementary term] remains a cipher or an enigma to the mind ... the missing term ... we may now identify as none other than the 'negation of a negation' familiar from dialectical philosophy. It is, indeed, because the negation of a negation is such a decisive leap ... that we so frequently come upon a system in the incomplete state. (Fredric Jameson, cited in Schleifer 1987: 29)

Extra subtlety and completeness can be added to duBois's analysis of the Herodotan wheel of difference if each of the spokes of the wheel is considered to be the semantic axis of a semiotic square, providing

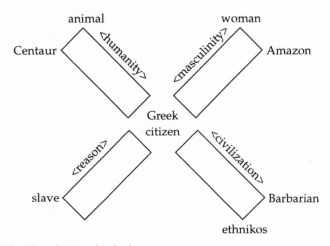

Fig. 3.3. The Herodotan wheel of squares

the full discursive resonance of each mode of opposition to the canonical Hellenistic identity (see fig. 3.3). With this model, we can see some of the complexity inherent in human language, which goes far beyond a mere diacritics of meaning. A 'picture' of language in use, or discourse, emerges, which Jacques Lacan has referred to as a 'chain' or 'network' of signifiers (Lacan 1981: 42–52). Any signifier, as a 'quilting point' (*point de capiton*), could be placed in the middle of a wheel such as that pictured above, although some signifiers have more connections than others. Most importantly, some also have stronger connections to the field of power (the Big Other), and thus are more likely to produce effects that striate thoughts, bodies, and geographic spaces. The signifier 'Greek' must be seen as a particularly powerful striative force, signifying for over two millennia as <Western civilization> itself.

Returning to Herodotus, his method, as far as it is relevant to the European discourse on diversity, can be summarized as follows. A set of categories is constructed and used as a basis of evaluation and comparison of various peoples. These categories rely upon what can be seen from a distance, and provide information about what is supposed to be the 'nature' of a people, which is also presumed to be influenced by the land they occupy. In all cases, the Self people provides a basis for comparison, with signs of similarity to the Self usually counting as possession of a good, and signs of difference indicative of a lack or deficiency. The nature of a people is assumed to be displayed in all individuals who are of that people, so that to know one is to know all and vice versa. Finally, the further one gets from one's own land, the stranger the peoples one encounters, until at the edges of the world there are only marvels and monsters to which the normal categories of evaluation scarcely apply.

Ancient Ionian Hellenism and the Destruction of the Inferior Other

While he used the binary mode, Herodotus also explicitly referred to certain peoples as 'the most barbarous,' 'the most knowledgeable' (outside of Greece), and so on, invoking a hierarchical comparison within the category of Barbarism. T.J. Haarhoff (1948: 6–19) notes that the strong split between the Barbarian and the Greek arose with what he calls the 'Ionian enlightenment' of the fifth and fourth centuries B.C. In this discourse of identity and difference – which I will from now on refer to as 'ancient Ionian Hellenism' – one can observe hierarchical differentiation *between* terms (e.g., in placing all Greeks above Barbarians), as well as *within* a given term, as in the division of Greeks into various classes of males, followed by females and slaves. The hierarchization of the category of 'Greek' can be observed in Plato's description of his ideal *polis*:

> While all of you in the city are brothers, we will say in our tale, yet God in fashioning those of you who are fitted to hold rule mingled gold in their generation, for which reason they are the most precious – but in the helpers silver, and iron and brass in the farmers and other craftsmen. (*Republic* 3.415a, cited in duBois 1991: 133)

Significant in their absence from this discussion are the slaves, whose place in Plato's republic is a matter of contention.[4] I find compelling the position put forward by Page duBois, who suggests that 'slavery's relationships of subordination and hierarchization' are archetypal to the differentiation of types at all levels in the Platonic scheme (1991: 139). Unlike Plato, Aristotle made his position on the 'nature' of the slave quite clear. In the *Politics*, the slave was not even given the status of a degenerate human subject, but was classed as an object, a 'tool,' a 'sort of living piece of property' (1253b23). Bracketing the question of whether certain philosophers thought their existence was 'justifiable' or not, the practice of slavery in Greek city-states, and the existence of slavery as a political-philosophical category of *inferior internal Other*, clearly show that slaves were simultaneously placed at the bottom of a hierarchical order of human types and at an excluded-included margin of the social world.

But these social categories were themselves part of a larger order. A.O. Lovejoy, in *The Great Chain of Being*, suggests that Plato bequeathed to Western thought a 'principle of plenitude,' which he defines as

> not only the thesis that the universe is a *plenum formarum* in which the range of conceivable diversity of *kinds* of living things is exhaustively exemplified, but also any other deductions from the assumption that no genuine potentiality of being can remain unfulfilled, that the extent and abundance of the creation must be as great as the possibility of existence and commensurate with the productive capacity of a 'perfect' and inexhaustible Source, and that the world is the better, the more things it contains. (Lovejoy 1936: 52)

To this notion Aristotle added a principle of 'continuity,' which is derivable from the principle of plenitude, and holds that there cannot be any 'gaps' between the beings of creation; if there were, then something possible would not have been realized, and the creator would have shown himself to be less than perfectly 'good' (Lovejoy 1936: 58). Thus evolved a conception of the universe as 'composed of ... an infinite number of links ranging in hierarchical order from the meagerest kind of existents ... through every possible grade up to the *ens perfectissum*' (59).[5]

Recalling the semiotic square of identity within ancient Ionian Hellenism, and continuing the quilt metaphor for semiosis, we can think of multi-levelled buttons, connected in a linear order by way of 'sewing them through,' the first sewn being highest, the last lowest, on the chain, and preserving the hierarchy that exists within each term. First the gods, in their order, followed by men, in theirs, and so on down the line. Thus, if the semantic axis is specified broadly enough, it is possible to collapse the spokes of the wheel into a single square, place the hierarchies inside their appropriate terms, and note that an implicit hierarchy exists, with the occupants of the positive term highest and those of the negative term lower down. In one sense, the occupants of the contradictory position are lowest on the hierarchy, as they lack

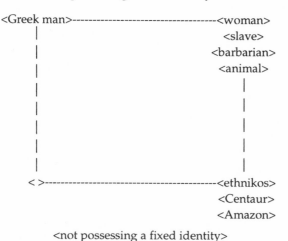

Fig. 3.4. The hierarchized square of ancient Ionian Hellenism

what is required for identity; but they can be seen as excluded from the hierarchy for the same reason. In practice, one finds both situations, with absorption of the contradictory term proceeding by way of a progressive inclusion within the hierarchy, accompanied by a shift in the semantic axis. This is the model I will use in examining the evolution of Canadian identity, as it is the most concise and compact way to signify all of the models that coexist; namely, the line (binary opposition), the square (contradiction and complementarity), the wheel (analogy within opposition), and the ladder (hierarchy).

Such is the problem of diversity in ancient Ionian Hellenism; but what of its solutions? One important response to the problem of diversity was to avoid trying to solve it at all. *Ignorance,* in the sense of an active, wilful desire not to know, was paramount, and helped to maintain its complement, *xenophobia.* This mode can be seen clearly in Herodotus, whose account of the Persians, while very detailed, contains enough spurious claims to make some commentators doubt whether he had any first-hand knowledge of his subjects at all (Georges 1994: 51–8). Greek ignorance can also be seen in poetry, drama, and comedy, where Barbarian stereotypes were used extensively to both define the Greek Self and keep the non-Greek Others at an absurd, mocking distance (E. Hall 1989; Georges 1994; Long 1986).

When non-Greek others absolutely had to be recognized, they were sometimes dealt with by way of tactics resembling present-day assimilation or integration (Dench 1995: 45–6). But the dominant active response was to attempt their *elimination* through destruction in battle or enslavement. In myth, the Centaurs and Amazons served as archetypal Others who were defeated and destroyed by Greek heroes (cf. duBois 1991: 49–77). In practice, the Greeks were constantly at war, both with each other and with non-Greeks. But there was an important distinction to be made between these two kinds of conflict. Plato has Socrates put it as follows: '[W]hen Greek fights barbarian or barbarian Greek we shall say they are at war, and are natural enemies ...; but when Greek fights Greek we shall say that they are naturally friends, but that Greece is torn by faction, and that the quarrel should be called "civil strife"' (*Republic* V.470). Socrates goes on to expect that 'brave and civilized' Greeks will 'love their fellow Greeks, and think of Greece as their own land, in whose common religion they share.' In victory, therefore, Greeks will not burn the land of Greeks, but only take a year's crop. Nor will they enslave the losers, the object of a fight being 'to correct a friend rather than to enslave and destroy an enemy' (V.471). Thus Aristotle: '[A]s the poets say, it is proper Greeks should rule non-Greeks, the implication being that non-Greek and slave are by nature identical' (*Politics* 1252a34). These statements indicate that, at the level of political discourse, there was a strong tendency to advocate the enslavement and destruction of problematic Others rather than their assimilation or integration.

Within ancient Ionian Hellenism, then, the methods of Herodotan ethnography were used to mark out the Greek Self from a range of Others. The notion of the Great Chain of Being placed these identities in a hierarchy, and political philosophy justified ignorance concerning, as well as destruction of, inferior beings by their superiors. As I will show, the idea of a ladder or chain of differentiated human types has persisted in Western thought up to the present day, and thus constitutes the most important contribution of ancient Ionian Hellenism to the Western discourse on diversity. The notion was passed down through the Middle Ages to the late eighteenth century, when 'most educated men were to accept without question ... the conception of the universe as a "Great Chain of Being"' (Lovejoy 1936: 59). The following sections will show how Roman, medieval, and Renaissance thought drew upon Ionian Hellenism, creatively reproducing its categories and contents and ensuring the continuity of the Great Chain.

Incorporation of the Other in Roman Imperialism

To the Greeks, the Romans were one among many Barbarian peoples; later, as they rose in influence, the Romans responded to this insult by adapting the Greek mode of Self / Other distinction, and setting themselves up as heirs to Ionian civilization. To the categories and contents of human diversity, the Romans brought little innovation. Pliny the Elder was one of the first miners of the ancient Greek vein, epitomizing and shuffling the words of Herodotus and his fellow Hellenes with a keen eye for tales of the monstrous and the wonderful. In all, he claimed to have consulted more than two thousand books and over one hundred authors in writing his *Natural History*, completed in approximately A.D. 77 (Preface, 17). The Great Chain of Being was taken over by neo-Platonism, and by this route passed from Greek to Roman to Christian thought (Lovejoy 1936: 61 ff). According to Plotinus, beneath God were the Celestials (*daimones*), and below them, human beings, all of these three still partaking of the good. By becoming 'evil and inferior,' the soul produced 'the animal nature' (*Enneads* VI.7.7), and proceeded on down to the vegetable and the mineral. Also important for later Western thought was the continuance of the idea that inequality and diversity were natural features of a divine order: 'The question is not whether a thing is inferior to something else but whether in its own Kind it suffices to its own part; universal equality there cannot be ... the inequality is inevitable by the nature of things' (*Enneads* III.3.3).

In the area of responses and solutions to the problem of diversity, Roman imperialism was much more creative. As a strategy of efficient management in the context of rapid expansion, violent invasion followed by toleration, assimilation, and integration was favoured:

> You, Roman, remember to govern
> The peoples with power (these arts shall be yours), to establish
> The practice of peace, spare the conquered, and beat down the haughty
> (Virgil, *Aeneid* [1962]: 6.860–3)

The case of the pacification of Britain, as related in Tacitus's *Agricola* (ca. A.D. 100), provides a detailed account of developed Roman thought and action in such matters. The model Conqueror, Agricola, when he comes on stage, alternates between the two methods of brute force and seduction. After several chapters of successful military exploits, he has succeeded in instilling fear into the many tribes, who have submitted to him. Now begins the real work of empire. Since the details are varied and interesting, and the conclusion so forceful, I quote this section at length:

> The following winter [after the campaigns] was spent on schemes of social betterment. Agricola had to deal with people living in isolation and ignorance, and therefore prone to fight; and his object was to accustom them to a life of peace and quiet by the provision of amenities. He therefore gave private encouragement and official assistance to the building of temples, public squares, and good houses ... And so the population was gradually led into the demoralizing temptations of arcades, baths, and sumptuous banquets. The unsuspecting Britons spoke of such novelties as 'civilization,' when in fact they were only a feature of their enslavement. (Tacitus, *Agricola* [1954]: 21)

Even local kings could be put to good use. Aulus Plautius, the first governor of Britain, knew what to do: 'Certain domains were presented to King Cogidmnus, who maintained his unswerving loyalty right down to our own times – an example of the long-established Roman custom of employing even kings to make others slaves' (14). Within the discourse of Roman imperialism, unlike that of ancient Hellenism, Others, especially the upper strata, were actively encouraged to take on signs of Romanness, and it was even thought that these Others could, in time, *become* Roman. The process of assimilation used to achieve the pacification and enslavement of Others was, by the time of the Conquest of Britain, quite well developed and codified, so that it could form a central theme in what is obviously an idealized 'great man' narrative.

While assimilation was a vital component of its practice, it must be remembered that imperial Rome was willing to take on at least *some* signs of the external Others it engulfed, as can be seen most obviously and famously in the polytheistic structure of Roman religion. As long as a sacrifice could be made to them, a Conquered people's gods could be set up alongside the ancient Roman deities:

> We do not conceive of the gods as different among different peoples, nor as barbarian and Greek, nor as southern and northern; but just as sun and moon and sky and earth and sea are common to all men, but have different names among different peoples, so for that one Reason ... different

honours and names have come into being among different peoples according to their customs. (Plutarch, *On Isis and Osiris* 67.377, cited in Whittaker 1984: 268)

Of course, not all gods were created equal, and there were fads and shifting hierarchies amongst those installed in the pantheon, with the Greek gods and those acquired in the early days of Roman expansion providing a sort of elite cadre (Wardman 1982: 3). But the Romans were quite willing to extend their hegemony, and swell their pride, by taking on gods with the same glee as they took on new territories. With the world composed of an endless diversity of peoples, one could count on an equally endless supply of gods. The system was inherently open and unfinished, since it was 'always possible for Rome to come into contact with the new gods of other societies who should be won over, or who may suit a Roman need' (3). Yet, through all of this change, the founding gods remained in place, rendering the system 'both conservative and acquisitive' (3).

Certain others, however, were not extended the gifts of Roman tolerance – the case of the Jews comes to mind here. Philostratus was disgusted by their 'unsocial existence,' and felt that they had 'nothing in common with other men, either food, or libations, or prayers, or sacrifices.' This 'failure' to assimilate to Roman practices left Philostratus feeling that the Jews were 'more remote in these respects from us than Susa or Bactria, and more alien than the Indians' (*Vita Apoll.* V.33, cited in L.A. Thompson 1989: 128–9). Continued Jewish resistance culminated in the revolt of A.D. 66–70 and the destruction of Jerusalem. Along with the Jews, the early Christians soon became official internal Others, and were blamed for any misfortune that befell the empire. Thus, when Rome burned in A.D. 64, 'Nero fastened the guilt and inflicted the most exquisite tortures on a class hated for their abominations, called Christians by the populace ... Covered with the skins of beasts, they were torn by dogs and perished, or were nailed to crosses, or were doomed to the flames' (Tacitus, cited in Green 1996: 16). Similar persecutions were carried out from time to time, until Valerian's edict of 258 that exposed all who were unwilling to accept Paganism to death (Green 1996: 17–20). Certain forms of difference inside the empire were neither tolerated nor adopted, but violently repressed by both physical and legal means.

Based on this cursory but, I hope, relatively uncontentious summary of the imperial Roman discourse on diversity, and again bracketing much particularity that can be constructed by way of historical and archaeological methods, the discourse of imperial Rome will be seen within my text as the epitome, within the Western tradition, of the strategy of *incorporation* of tamed Otherness. This could be done by way of both *assimilation* and *integration*, with limited tolerance granted as long as the Others being tolerated did not appear to be successfully resisting state striation by giving rise to, or perpetuating, local forms of organization. In cases where assimilation and/or integration did not seem to be proceeding as desired, violent repression by rational-legal methods and physical extermination was brought to bear upon the problematic population.

Early Christianity: The Missionary Urge

Through his prodigious effort at collecting facts, Pliny ensured that the lore of the Greeks was passed on, by way of Mela (*De situ orbis*) in the first century A.D. and Solinus (*De mirabilibus mundi*) in the third. According to Hodgen, Herodotus had described about fifty different peoples. 'Five to eight hundred years later, Pliny, Solinus, and Mela referred to thirty-four of the same peoples, and in terms that are either identical with or very similar to those used by the Greek historian. Though forgotten in name, the author of the *Histories* was honoured in imitation' (Hodgen 1964: 44). Along with Herodotus's monsters, late Roman and medieval Europe also inherited, and improved upon, Plato's and Aristotle's hierarchy of being. But now a powerful new interlocutor in the European discourse on diversity was emerging – Christianity. In *The City of God*, Saint Augustine devoted a very influential section to the question of whether the monstrous races spoken of by the Ancients were human or animal, in which he ambiguously concluded that 'accounts of some of these races may be completely worthless; but if such peoples exist, then either they are not human; or, if human, they are descended from Adam' (Augustine 1972: 16.8).

Of one thing, however, the early Catholic church was certain: that the Pagans and Aryan Christians constituted a serious threat to what remained of Graeco-Roman civilization after the withdrawal of Constantine to the East, and especially after the sack of Rome in 410. The emperor Theodosius, who took the Roman throne in A.D. 379, almost immediately enacted a 'Decree against Heretics' designed to ensure that all Roman citizens would also be Roman Catholics:

It is our will that all the peoples who are ruled by the administration of Our Clemency shall practice that religion which the divine Peter the Apostle transmitted to the Romans ... We command that those persons who follow this rule shall embrace the name of Catholic Christians. The rest, however, whom we adjudge demented and insane, shall sustain the infamy of heretical dogmas, their meeting places shall not receive the name of churches, and they shall be smitten first by divine vengeance and secondly by the retribution of Our own initiative, which We shall assume in accordance with the divine judgement. (Theodisian Code, XVI,1,2 [380], cited in Hillgarth 1986: 45–6)

Later on, all Pagan worship was prohibited, with detailed penalties such as the loss of one's home for burning incense in it; finally, by 435, Pagans became liable to the death penalty for the crime of observing their form of religious devotion (Hillgrath 1969: 47–8).

Such was the internal mission that was to be carried out against Paganism, which proceeded by way of the violent enforcement of legal prohibitions. But the Roman Catholic Church also saw itself as the bearer of civilization and 'proper' Christianity to the lost lands of the West. Bishop Daniel of Winchester, in his advice to Saint Boniface, suggested means by which he might 'overcome with the least possible trouble the resistance of this barbarous people.' The bishop gave details of theological arguments he thought would be successful in rooting out the 'absurd opinions' and 'disgusting rites and legends' that Boniface would encounter. Compared to the Christians, Herodotus appeared quite tolerant. But then Herodotus did not have the same kind of weighty task upon him. 'For what does the baptizing of children ... signify if not the purification of each one from the uncleanness of the guilt of heathenism in which the entire human race was involved?' (1 Dec. 722, cited in Hillgarth 1986: 135–6).

Prejudiced though they might be, the early Christian missionaries were not as credulous as their philosophers and cosmographers. Relying upon first-hand experience of the Barbarians who had taken over the western provinces of Rome, they were able to develop quite sophisticated and self-aware strategies for their conversion. The successful transformation of Constantine from a Roman Pagan to a zealous Christian was a move taken directly from the pages of the *Agricola*, and provided a model in imitation of which the monks sought to enlist the existing secular powers to use 'even kings to make others slaves.' This worked, around A.D. 500, with Clovis, King of the Franks, and in

589, with Recared, Visigoth ruler of Spain. Once converted themselves, these kings put the bureaucratic apparatus of their empires to work on the task of converting the (now internal) peoples subject to them.

This was a very effective method of assimilation in cases in which Aryan Christianity, and the means of mass coercion associated with it, already existed and could be used against both the remnants of Paganism and Aryan Christianity itself. A different game had to be played in England, however, where the Devil ruled supreme. When Pope Gregory sent monks there in 597, his instructions called for a strategy that was much more subtle and slow-moving:

> I have long been considering with myself about the case of the Angli; to wit, that the temples of idols in that nation should not be destroyed, but that the idols themselves that are in them should be. Let blessed water be prepared, and sprinkled in these temples, and altars constructed, and relics deposited, since, if these same temples are well built, it is needful that they should be transferred from the worship of idols to the service of the true God ... (Pope Gregory the Great, Epistle XI, 56, cited in Hillgarth 1986: 114)

After this were to come more priests, and bishops of the local 'race and tongue.' As we will see, a similar mode of nihilistic incorporation set the tone for the Jesuits, who, almost one thousand years later, would adapt these methods in their adventures in the New World. In the early Christian era, then, I wish to highlight and carry forward into later discussions several key themes: the creative reproduction of the ancient Hellenistic discourse on diversity via the appropriation of the Great Chain of Being; the imitative reproduction of the Roman imperial use of state forms to repress and eliminate internal Others; and the refinement of Roman imperial assimilation tactics through the strategy of self-conscious *conversion* of the Other into a form the Self can tolerate.

Renaissance Exploration and the New World 'Savage'

From Mela and Solinus, the torch of Herodotan ethnography was passed to Isidore's *Etymologies* in the seventh century, and thence to Bartholomew's *De proprietatabus rerum* in the thirteenth. Throughout this time, there seems to have been little change in the wide world at the expanding edges of Christendom; as far as one can tell from the European cosmographers, the same people and monsters lived in the same ways, in the same places, sporting the same odd characteristics, as they had always done. Undoubtedly this longevity should be attributed to the fact that many of these beings were living a life that was purely intertextual. Bartholomew, as soon as he felt the need to speak of lands beyond the European frontier, constantly fell back upon Isidore, Solinus, Pliny, and Herodotus. In India 'ther ben hilles of golde and it is impossible to come therto for dragouns and gryffouns and for many manere men wondirliche yshape, as Ysider saith ... Therefor Plinius telleth wondres of myth and multitude of the Indies ...' (Liber Quintus Decimus, Capitulum lxxv). Of Palestine: 'As Erodatus seith, thise men ben allweye fals and gyleful and wyly, greuvous enemys to the kyngedome of Israel' (Liber Quintus Decimus, Capitulum cxiii).

At the same time as the theologians and cosmographers were debating the meaning of ancient ethnographic data, Europeans began to travel and report in greater numbers, thus bringing new information to challenge and supplement what had been handed down. Marco Polo was one of the most famous of these medieval trader-Explorers who helped to keep the Herodotan tradition alive. In almost every section of his *Travels* (1968), we are introduced to a new people, told how they are governed, if they are subject to anyone else, and whether they have 'their own proper language.' Then comes religion – usually they are idolaters – a few comments on customs and diet, and, of course, commodities available for trade. Marco Polo was a competent amateur ethnographer, and was even so incredulous as to deny the existence of certain marvels and debunk a myth or two.

In these qualities, Marco Polo was not unlike another great Explorer who set himself the task of achieving his own visit to the court of the great Khan. Fully versed in European history, geography, and ethnography, Cristobal Colón (Columbus) set out for the East by heading west, and became convinced that he had achieved his goal. Las Casas says of Columbus's reading of Native reports of Cuba: 'he believed he understood that here put in ships of great tonnage belonging to the Grand Khan, and that the mainland was ten days sail distant' (cited in Todorov 1984: 31). As Todorov points out, what Columbus 'understood' was 'simply a summary of the books of Marco Polo and Pierre d'Ailly' (Todorov 1984: 31). For, although he never did meet the Khan, Columbus did encounter, or hear tell of, many of the other well-known marvels of the East. Cannibals abound in his narrative, and men with tails are to be found on at least one island ('First Voyage of Columbus,' 'Letter to Sanchez,' in Major 1961: 11). Amazons, women who 'employ themselves in no labour suitable to their own sex' but 'use bows and javelins' and wear 'brass armour,' are reported on another (15). As part of the proof of his theory of a pear-shaped world, he also reproduced the ancient connection between the south, black skins, and stupidity and laziness, and invoked the authority of Isidore, Pliny, Aristotle, and Saint Augustine ('Letter of the Third Voyage,' in Major 1961: 133–41). The voyages of Columbus clearly mark an important bifurcation in the European discourse on diversity, as ideas from the Old World were applied to the New, and later Explorers were told what to expect in their own travels.

Back in Europe, work continued apace on how to place the newly Discovered marvels. The old questions were asked, and the old answers given. Were the beings Columbus claimed to have met human? Dr Chanca, who accompanied Columbus on his second voyage, said of the people he encountered: 'they eat all the snakes and lizards, and spiders, and worms, that they find upon the ground; so that, to my fancy, their bestiality is greater than that of any beast upon the face of the earth' (Major 1961: 66). Generally, though, the 'Savages' of the New World were placed slightly higher, somewhere between beasts and men. The stories told of Barbarians far away to the east, over land, could quite easily be applied to those found to the west, over sea. Thus, in Muenster's *Cosmographia* (1544), Barbarians, Savages, and Monsters were lumped together as forms of the sub-human (Hodgen 1964: 127–8).

The question of the humanity of the New World peoples was not easy to settle, however, as demonstrated by the inconclusive results of the 1550 debate between Las Casas and Sepulveda.[6] The argument here might be seen as one between medieval theology and ancient philosophy. Sepulveda based his position upon Aristotle, claiming that hierarchy was natural, so that Savages, as inferior peoples, were born to serve the superior Europeans. 'In wisdom, skill, virtue and humanity, these people are as inferior to the Spaniards as children are to adults and women to men; there is as great a difference between them as there is between savagery and forbearance, between violence and moderation, almost – I am inclined to say – as between monkeys and men' (Sepulveda, cited in Todorov 1984: 153). Based on this reading, Sepulveda advocated a violent war of Conquest.

Unimpressed with the forbearance and moderation shown by the *Conquistadores*, Las Casas argued that the peaceful conversion of indigenous peoples was not only possible – that is, that they were human, and had souls – but also desirable, since God had commanded that all men be brought into his flock. 'Just as there is no natural difference in the creation of man, so there is no difference in the call to salvation of all men, Barbarous or wise, since God's grace can correct the minds of Barbarians, so that they have a reasonable understanding' (Las Casas, cited in Todorov 1984: 162). Of course, neither of the disputants brought into question the Conquest itself: rather, they debated how it was to be carried out, by physical elimination or assimilation to Christian civilization.

An epitome of these European notions about the Savage Other was given by Pierre D'Avity, who, quite in keeping with the principle of plenitude, worked out a scale of five degrees of Barbarism in 1614. Each level on the scale was predicated upon a lack of some European quality, the most important of which was the possession of reason, which implied knowledge of religion and abstinence from cannibalism. Descending the scale of 'brutality,' one encountered, in Herodotan style, those who 'sow not, nor have any tillage; those who go in nakedness; those without habitation, having no dwellings but caves and hollow trees; and those, the most brutish, deprived of government. For some being altogether barbarous, live without lawes or a commander, either in peace or warre' (D'Avity, cited in Hodgen 1964: 201; cf. Dickason 1984: 66–7). At this point, soon after the first voyages to the New World, the peoples of the New World were seen by some Europeans as beasts, by some as monsters, and by yet others as human; but, even when granted the gift of humanity, they were allocated an inferior status. This assumption was inherent in Las Casas's position, and shows up in the quote above: as they stood, Savages did not have reason, wisdom, and so on – but Europeans could teach them. And so they would, as European colonialism took hold throughout the New World, and fast-paced Discovery and looting gave way to more sedentary rhythms of domination.

From Prehistory to History: A Summary of European Contributions to the Problem of Canadian Diversity

Let us recall the question presented in the Introduction, and which has informed the analysis presented in this chapter: if it is true that there is a primordial tradition of diversity out of which Canadian multiculturalism has emerged, what are the relationships between the current system and that tradition? How are they the same and different, what rules and regularities do they share, and what are the lines of descent from the older forms to the new? I would suggest that ancient philosophers and statesmen, medieval theologians and missionaries, and renaissance travellers and Conquerors, all contributed to the construction and maintenance of a highly adaptable system, a sort of tool kit, ideally suited to the task of Self/Other differentiation and management. From Herodotus came the basic method of marking out visible differences between peoples, assigning to each people a set of timeless characteristics assumed to be representative of all who were 'part' of that people. Herodotus also supplied the rhetorical device of implicitly basing all comparisons on a silent but superior Self people, while covering this over with a gloss of detached interest and even occasional praise. Plato and Aristotle made explicit what was implicit in Herodotus, by providing the rudiments of a hierarchical gradation of all beings, placing the Self group at the top, just under the gods, and also providing justification for the particularly Greek responses of ignorance, xenophobia, and destruction. Roman civilization took on the fundamentals of the Barbarian typology and the hierarchy of beings, but tended towards strategies of assimilation, integration, and state repression in handling the problems it created for itself. Medieval Christianity expanded upon the ancient system of differentiation, providing justification for it in scripture, and also pioneered new methods in its successful conversion of all of Europe. Through the early Christian and medieval theologians there was a clear line of descent from Herodotus to the fifteenth- and sixteenth-century Explorers, who, steeped in the European discourse on diversity, quite 'naturally' applied the Old definitions and methods in the New World.

At one point in *Early Anthropology*, Hodgen marvels: 'One of the problems for the historian of European ideas is to account for the backwardness of ethnological thought despite sustained contact with non-Europeans' (80). Is this problem really so hard to solve? A 'backwardness' appears only if one gives priority to certain scientific narratives, which themselves reproduce many aspects of the tradition they are supposed to transcend. In backward times and places, as in more forward ones, the means by which the Other is separated from the Self allow her to be objectified, dehumanized, and thereby put to work. The European discourse on diversity, if it is indeed an 'error,' has been, and still is, a very useful and productive one. It is absolutely crucial to remember, though, that 'the Europeans' do not exist as a timeless entity with assignable group characteristics given by some 'nature,' any more than the Blemmy or the Acephales. In the Canadian case, this is true both in the sense that 'Europe' is a name for an idealization of an Old World, and because people, ideas, and practices associated with that World have been coming to Canada, with varying intentions and effects, more or less continuously over the past five hundred years. Whatever continuities there might be between a discourse on diversity that can be correlated with the signifier 'European' and one that might be designated 'Canadian,' the successive waves in which the former has broken on the shores of the New World have introduced discontinuities, as has the relatively separate development of the latter's local formations. At best, we can simply observe, at particular places and times, how a certain discourse (mis)informed by ideas and methods from the Old World reacted when it encountered (what appeared to be) Savages and Barbarians in the New.

Chapter Four

Two 'Canadian' Solutions to the Problem of Diversity

Spanish civilization crushed the Indian; English civilization scorned and neglected him; French civilization embraced and cherished him.

– Francis Parkman, *The Jesuits in North America*, 131

The greatest difficulty in constructing a history of *Canadian* diversity lies in the fact that 'Canada,' as a European outpost in the northeastern section of the continent now known as North America, has come to exist many times. Norse, Portuguese, Spanish, British, and French adventurers visited the coast, planted their crosses, and crushed, scorned, or embraced their Others at various places and times. Most of these attempts at colonization led to failure, though, with only the work done by the British and French remaining to create particularly Canadian problems and solutions. The purpose of this chapter is to show precisely how these two colonial discourses creatively reproduced their European antecedents in a new context, giving rise to the nascent forms of what would become known as the problem of Canadian diversity.

In this chapter, I also set out to achieve three more specific goals. The first is to produce a semiotic square of the system of identity that prevailed in each of the British and French colonial discourses, showing the positions created, how they were differentiated, and their placement in a hierarchical order. Recent work has clearly demonstrated that the European Explorers were steeped in the Herodotan tradition of geography and cosmography (see Dickason 1984: 5–25; Friedman

1981: 197–207). John Cabot, like Columbus, was seeking a sea route to the court of the Great Khan when he bumped into what he thought was northeast Asia in 1497. On his second voyage, he planned to hug the coastline to the south, sure that he would find the island of Cipangu, which Marco Polo had reported as the source of 'all the spices in the world, and all the precious stones' (letter of Raimondo de Soncino to the Duke of Milan, cited in Biggar 1911: 20). Jacques Cartier, in relating the story of his first voyage in 1534, claimed to have conclusively proven that the world was round by sailing westward to Asia (Cartier's account of his second voyage, cited in Cook 1993: 36). Unlike Cabot, Cartier spent a fair amount of time on rivers and dry land, and so was able to tell some tales when he returned home. He was not surprised to find the place populated by 'les sauvages,'[1] nor was he taken aback by reports of people with no anus, a single leg, and 'other marvels too long to relate' (Cook 1993: 82). These Explorers found, because they expected to find, monsters and Barbarians, gold and silver, spices and degenerate potentates; the Imaginary West, confused as it was with the Imaginary East, was in a sense fully mapped out before any European ever set foot upon it.

The second aim of this chapter is to provide an account of how European methods of managing problematic diversity were adapted and transformed by the French and British for use in the New World. In analysing this period, I will follow Canadian Native studies in dividing the history of European-Native interaction into three phases. First was the contact phase, during which 'the French explored, traded, and attempted to leave their permanent mark on the place. The Indians happily bartered but rejected the white men's presumption at erecting ... signpost[s]' (Miller 1989: 3–4). The next was the fur-trade era, in which the Natives were still possessed of their own economies and polities, and thus of a strong measure of self-sufficiency and power. In these two phases, the Natives and newcomers engaged one another, on relatively equal terms, in a Hegelian struggle to the death. This term should be taken figuratively, for the Europeans – or, more precisely, the French – were working hard to assimilate the Savage Other, that is, to have him carry out what Hegel would have seen as his own negation. At the same time, both the French and the British had recourse to a literal struggle to the death, which took the form of *extermination*. Here I am referring to attempts to totally eradicate signs of a problematic identity through killing *all* who are considered to partake of it. From extant documents, it is clear that the French were in horror of Native methods of individual torture; with time, Native peoples came to have the same fearful respect for the European ability to eradicate entire nations. The relative success of massacre over sacrifice tactics[2] led to a third phase, which has seen the creation of a system of 'tutelage' or 'unilaterally imposed administration of one party by the other' (Dyck 1991: 6), which would correspond to the Hegelian master/slave relationship. In addition to noting the use of some relatively well-known European methods during these three periods, I will also point out several more innovative and important contributions that are not so commonly discussed. From the French came what I will refer to as *strategic simulation of assimilation* to the Other; from the British, the discourse on Canadian diversity received the stance of *active ignorance,* as well as great refinements in methods of *distant microcontrol of everyday life* that anticipate the legislated environment being created for the postmodern Canadian citizen.

The third main theme in this chapter is the role played by 'hybrid' identities, that is, the *coureurs-de-bois,* 'Half-breeds,' and 'Métis,' which were deeply feared and repressed by both the British and the French state organizations, and continue to be marginalized today. Because of this marginalization, the terms 'Half-breed' and 'Métis' are highly charged. As with 'Savage,' 'Half-breed' will always be capitalized, to show that it is being used within a certain discourse and that I am aware of its use as a negative other-ascription. In the late 1800s, Half-breed was used within official and popular discourses in English to refer to both English- and French-speaking people assumed to be of 'mixed' European and Native parentage. Over the past few years, there has been an effort on the part of Métis organizations to replace Half-breed with Métis, but some of those who see themselves as English rather than French hybrids are currently trying to reclaim the term Half-breed as a positive self-identification. These identities, I will argue in chapter 9, can be seen as the semiotic ancestors of today's 'multiple origins,' and therefore provide clues as to how the much-lamented 'lack' of Canadian unity and identity might be understood and, to the greatest extent possible, overcome.

Before proceeding, I should point out that this section addresses material that has been widely discussed elsewhere, but has not, as I have suggested, been adequately situated in the broader context of the discourse on Canadian diversity. Thus, while those who are familiar with Canadian Native studies will find few surprises, it is nonetheless an essential part of my task to note certain features of the early colonial period. Where the relevant ground has been particularly well covered, I will provide minimal evidence for the claims made, so that more space can be allocated to relatively new or controversial aspects of the discussion. No text can please everyone in this respect, however, since a balance must always be struck between repeating common knowledge and making unsubstantiated claims; and, ultimately, the level of evidence required to be 'convincing' depends upon the values and beliefs each reader brings to the text.

The First Others of the New World

Although the British came first, the French stayed longest, and so they shall be given priority. And the first of the French, the Explorer Jacques Cartier, shall be seen as establishing the nascent forms that would be developed further by specialists devoted to the task of Conquest. Cartier's extensive journals make it clear that he had sufficient contact with 'Canadians' and 'Hochelagans' to comment on many aspects of what would now be called their 'culture.' Taking in order D'Avity's degrees of Barbarism – presented at the end of the previous chapter – we can see how Cartier's first impressions of the people of the New World were formed, and how they changed with further contact.

With regard to D'Avity's primary markers of civilization, reason and religion, Cartier's opinion appears ambivalent. Sometimes, it seems that he saw neither attribute, advising his king that the people of the New World lived 'without the knowledge of God and without the use of Reason' (Cartier's commission for his third voyage, cited in Cook 1993: 135). In the same passage, however, he is reported as describing them as 'well endowed in mind and understanding' (135). 'This people has no belief in God that amounts to anything,' he wrote after his second journey, but then continued the sentence: 'for they believe in a god they call *Cudouagny*' (Cook 1993: 68). Did they have a god or not? The apparent ambiguity can be reconciled if we remember that, for Cartier, there was only one religion that 'amounted to anything,' and that was Christianity.

Cartier also commented several times upon the Canadians' lax conduct regarding agriculture. He was impressed by the natural abundance of the New World, which included 'as good hemp as that of France, which comes up without sowing or tilling it' (51). Likewise the vines 'so loaded with grapes that it seemed they could only have been planted by husbandmen; but because they are never looked after nor pruned, the grapes are not so sweet nor so large as our own' (57). Later on, in Hochelaga, Cartier found 'that the land began to be cultivated. It was fine land, covered with large fields covered with the corn of the country' (61). But, even once he knew that the people of the New World were capable of agriculture, Cartier was not impressed with the effort they put into it. 'They are by no means a laborious people and work the soil with short bits of wood about half a sword in length' (69).

On the subject of clothing, there is also much to be learned from Cartier's narratives. During the first voyage, he used its lack as part of the justification for his conclusion that some people he met near the mouth of the Gaspé 'may well be called savage ... for they go quite naked, except for a small skin, with which they cover their privy parts and for a few old skins which they throw over their shoulders' (24). In his description of the Hochelagans, Cartier noted that 'the greater portion of them go almost stark naked' (62). The same went for the Canadians, who 'would come to our ships every day across the ice and snow, the majority of them almost stark naked' (70). That Cartier saw this form of clothing as a lack of something normal was made explicit later on, when he noted the various animals that inhabited the region. 'The people wear the skins of these animals for *want of* other apparel' (74, emphasis added).

Habitation also figured prominently in Cartier's records of his voyages. The people he met at Chaleur went 'from place to place maintaining themselves' (22), while those at the Gaspé had 'no other dwelling but their canoes, which they turn upside down and sleep on the ground underneath' (25). On the way to Hochelaga, Cartier noticed 'a large number of houses along the banks of the river' (57). In the village itself, the Europeans found fifty houses, the contents and use of which were described in such detail that it leads one to wonder if Cartier were not pining for his own beloved boards. Altogether, Cartier saw Hochelaga as the most civilized locale in the New World, and treated of it in unusual detail:

> This whole people gives itself to manual labour and to fishing merely to obtain the necessities of life; for they place no value upon the goods of this world, both because they are unacquainted with them and because they do not move from home and are not nomads like those of Canada and of the Saguenay, notwithstanding that the Canadians and some eight or nine other peoples along this river are subjects of theirs. (61–2)

Much can be made of this passage. First, it shows that Cartier was sufficiently familiar with, and open to, New World culture to begin to assign degrees of difference within it. It attributes to the Hochelagans several Christian virtues: a sedentary life, hard work, self-negation, other-worldliness, and, of course, the ability and right to dominate less civilized and hard-working peoples. The Hochelagans did not appear to Cartier to have a *polis*; but he thought they might be possessed of some sort of empire, the next best thing, and certainly an indication that they were not, like other peoples, altogether Barbarous and 'deprived of government.'

For Cartier, then, the peoples of the New World were of varying degrees of civilization, with most being quite Barbarous but some having achieved, if on a small scale, the level of empire-building. As to their humanity, Cartier seems to have been again ambivalent. The Canadians he found to be 'more indifferent to the cold than beasts' (70). His comments on the Beothuck of Newfoundland are similarly nuanced: 'there are people on this coast whose bodies are fairly well formed, but they are wild and savage folk' (10). Not monsters, he seemed to be saying, but certainly not Europeans either. The most compelling evidence of Cartier's opinion on this matter, however, can be seen in his immediate and ongoing conviction that he had found fertile ground for the cultivation of souls. During the first voyage, though he had shown no signs of knowing anything about their religious beliefs, Cartier twice stated his opinion that the people he had found would be easy to convert to Catholicism (22–3). It would seem that the Explorer followed his Church in believing that the inhabitants of the New World were convertible; that is, that they were human, and therefore had souls that could be saved.

The preceding observations suggest that in both the form and content of his narrative, Cartier worked within the genre of Herodotan ethnography and the categories of the European discourse on diversity. But he was also faced with the new task of reconciling the Monsters of the cosmographies and the Pagans of the Saints with the obviously human beings he encountered. Thus, during the phase of first contact, the New World Savage began quite quickly to be transformed from an unknown, semi-monstrous, external Other to an ambiguously human, potentially *Useful* Other on the margins of an advancing civilization. In this shift, the French colonial discourse on diversity began to diverge from the ancient European system, and thus began to develop its own particularity.

Conversion and Extermination: The Cases of the Huron and the Iroquois

The French claimed the right not only to Explore, but also to Colonize the New World according to the ancient Roman civil law of *vacuum domicilium*, which allowed one to take possession of 'empty' or 'vacant' land (Dickason 1984: 131; Jaenen 1991: 24). This interpretation, which came to be known as the doctrine of *terra nullius*, was commonly used in royal letters patent granting Explorers the right to take possession of lands 'uninhabited and not possessed or ruled by any other Christian princes' (e.g., Roberval's commission, in Cook 1993: 144). Of course, the 'emptiness' of a territory was judged according to European standards; that is, it was said to be 'inhabited' only where the Europeans saw signs of agriculture, government, reason and religion, and so on. The problems posed by the fact that the New World was not truly 'empty' were acknowledged early on, and quickly solved with the help of Christian theology:

> The earth pertaining then, by divine right to the children of God, there is here no question of applying the law and policy of nations, by which it would not be permissible to claim the territory of another. This being so, we must *possess it and preserve its natural inhabitants*, and plant therein with determination the name of Jesus Christ and of France ... (Lescarbot 1907: 1.17, emphasis added)

From their first attempts at Colonization, marked by the third voyage of Cartier and the first of Roberval, the French, at least in their official documents, eschewed the ruthless Spanish quest for riches in deference to higher goals:

> His majesty [Francis] ... is not afraid to engage in new expense, to establish the Christian Religion in a country of Savages at the other end of the world from France, and where he was well aware that there were no gold or silver mines nor any other gain to be hoped for, other than the winning over of an infinite number of souls to God ... ('List of Men and Effects for Canada,' in preparation for Cartier's third voyage; cited in Cook 1993: 126)

This course appears to have been followed with the Huron nation, which I will treat as an epitomal application of 'soft' methods of preservation, conversion, and civilization. But the French, beginning with Samuel de Champlain, also made use of the 'harder' strategies of physical elimination through displacement, containment, and extermination, and thus acted out their desire to be involved in a life and death struggle for recognition with the peoples of the New World. The Sieur de Roberval, who was in 1540 appointed as the first Governor of Canada, was instructed to 'go and return to said foreign countries ... to bring them into our possession, through friendly means or amicable arrangements, if possible, and [if not], through force of arms, violence, and all other hostile means, to attack towns, fortresses, and habitations' (Roberval's commission, in Cook 1993: 144). The French hoped for the existing inhabitants to submit without a fight; if, however, they did prove to be free and human, then there was nothing for it but to engage them in a struggle to the death. This mode of relationship was quickly established with the peoples of the Iroquois confederacy, some of whom are still at war with the Canadian state today.

But let us deal with the 'soft' methods first. As early as 1621, Champlain tried to lure some Montagnais onto what must count as the first Canadian Indian reserve, in the hope of procuring some trustworthy guides. 'With this object in view I had cultivated the friendship of a savage named Miristou, who had a very strong and a very special liking for the French, and who, I saw, was ambitious of commanding and being the head of a band' (Biggar 1925: 5.60). Champlain thought that he could get his friend elected, but required that certain conditions be met:

> The first thing I said to that savage was that he and his companions, who numbered thirty, should cultivate the lands near Quebec, taking up their fixed residence there ...; if they did so, we should regard them as brothers. I reflected further that we should thus be giving a hint for the future to the other savages, that, when they wished to elect a chief, it would have to be with the consent of the French, which would mean that we should begin to *assume a certain control over them,* and be able the better to instruct them in our faith. (5.61–2, emphasis added)

Champlain did succeed with his intervention into local politics, but we hear no more in his journals of the fate of his reserve. Marcel Trudel, citing Sagard's history, says that some land was in fact cleared, but never cultivated, thereby earning the name *désert des Sauvages* (Trudel 1973: 143). It is very interesting to note how this experiment showed all of the features of the form that would eventually develop, even in the mode of its failure.

The task of initiating a flow of signs of French civilization to the bodies and souls of the New World was taken up in earnest by the Jesuits, who arrived in 1625. In the *Relations*, narratives sent back to France from spiritual labourers in Canada, Jesuit views on the people they encountered, the tasks they set out to achieve, and the methods they used are quite self-consciously and explicitly put forward, making these texts very useful in discerning how the Jesuits constructed and managed the problem of human difference. As epitomes of their type, that is, as bearers of theories and methods developed over a thousand years of Christian missionary work, I have followed the canon and chosen Father Jean de Brébeuf, who arrived with the first party, and Father Paul le Jeune, who came soon after.

Le Jeune's relation of 1632 sets to rest any doubt that the Jesuits were self-consciously applying lessons learned in the past to their new task. After giving his views on the 'wholly barbarous' dress, intelligence, and social mores of the Savages, and describing some of the tortures to which the Iroquois subjected their prisoners, le Jeune explicitly linked the Savages of New France to those of Old Europe:

> Let no one be astonished at these acts of barbarism. Before the faith was received in Germany, Spain, or England, those nations were not more civilized. Mind is not lacking among the Savages of Canada, but education and instruction. They are already tired of their miseries and stretch out their hands to us for help. (*Relations*: 5.32–3)

While the Jesuits used the common term Savage (*Sauvage*) in their descriptions of the people of the New World, one also notices the presence of the new (old) terms Pagan (*Payenne*) and Barbarian (*Barbare*). This change marked an important shift in perception, in that it tied the problem of New World diversity directly to ancient Europe. There was nothing like an abrupt transition, of course; but, with the Jesuits, the unknown, beast-like Savage one might only *hope* to save began to be transformed into a type that European civilization had *already* successfully assimilated many times. 'If we go outside our cabin, Heaven is open to us ... so that we can say our prayers in full liberty before the noble Oratory that saint François Xavier loved better than any other' (10.107). For le Jeune, and the many Jesuits who came after him, Canadians were exactly what northwestern Europeans had been one thousand years before: Barbarians begging to be given the gifts of Christianity and civilization borne by selfless priests.

Just as the early Christians had allowed Pagans to maintain their altars, the Jesuits were compelled to accept from their flock behaviours that would never have gone over back home in Europe. Indeed, Brébeuf's 1637 'Instructions for the Fathers of Our Society Who Shall Be Sent to the Hurons' concerned itself mainly with the 'hardships, annoyances and perils' of the mission:

> Leaving a highly civilized community, you fall into the hands of barbarous people who care but little for your Philosophy or your Theology. All the fine qualities which might make you loved and respected in France are like pearls trampled under the feet of swine, or rather mules, which utterly despise you when they see that you are not as good pack animals as they are. (*Relations:* 12.123)

Annoyances aside, the 'Instructions for the Fathers' was deeply structured by the conviction that, before the Barbarian could be expected to take on European signs, the European must display signs of the Barbarian. 'To conciliate the Savages, you must be careful never to make them wait for you in embarking' (*Relations:* 12.117). 'You should try to eat their sagamité or salmagundi in the way they prepare it, although it may be dirty, half-cooked, and very tasteless. As to the numerous other things which may be unpleasant, they must be endured for the love of God, without saying anything or appearing to notice them' (12.117). In his mission to the Huron nation, which is often considered the epitomal case of 'peaceful' conversion, Brébeuf followed his own rules, stepping very carefully around the civilizational minefields he encountered, and even backing down, for the time being, on confrontations with the Devil. 'Generally speaking they praise and approve the Christian Religion, and blame their wicked customs; but when will they leave them off entirely?' (*Relations:* 10.25).

Brébeuf's fears were well founded. But other forces would come to his aid, altering the balance of power so that the Huron would be reduced to such conditions of extremity that they had no choice but to try to accept what the Jesuits offered. In 1648 the Iroquois, who were known for assimilating and enslaving those they Conquered, began a series of attacks on Huron villages that gave every appearance of a Spanish-style war of extermination. The Jesuits retreated with their flock to the island of St Joseph, where they were 'compelled to behold dying skeletons eking out a miserable life, feeding even on the excrements and refuse of nature' (*Relations*: 35.89). There was not much to sustain the life of the Huron, but the priests managed to survive, and counted themselves lucky to obtain, after so much effort, a bountiful harvest of souls: 'it was in the midst of these desolations that God was pleased to bring forth, from their deepest misfortunes, the well-being of this people. Their hearts had become so tractable to the faith that we effected in them, by a single word, more than we had ever been able to accomplish in entire years' (35.91).

While they were willing to wait for the 'peaceful' conversion of the Huron, Champlain and le Jeune were convinced of the necessity of forcefully subjugating the Iroquois confederacy, which operated in its own best interests, resisted the flow of French signs, and was possessed of sufficient military might to operate as an equal power. In the summer of 1609, Champlain had participated in a raid on an Iroquois camp, where he and his firearms met with much success; the year after that found him again at war. In these 'battles,' Champlain showed no mercy, apparently not bothered by the fact that he had guns, and his enemies didn't:

> The Iroquois were much astonished that two men should have been killed so quickly [by gunfire], although they were provided with shields made of cotton thread woven together with wood ... [S]eeing their chiefs dead, they lost courage and took to flight ... whither I pursued them, and laid low still more of them. (Biggar 1925: 2.99–100)

During another such encounter, Champlain halted the slaughter when he saw that some fellow Europeans were about to join in; he wanted them to 'have their share of this pleasure' (2.132). The simple joy of killing should not be seen, however, as Champlain's main motivation. Twenty years after the founding of Quebec, he continued to blame his problems on the Iroquois confederacy, and had come to the conclusion that it was time to 'engage in [a] legitimate war, in which, by destroying those peoples, we should make the land and the rivers free for our commerce' (6.314). The Iroquois had become bearers of intolerable difference, Absolute Others who could not be assimilated, with whom one could not stand to integrate, and who must therefore be physically eliminated.

Later French governors followed Champlain in blaming their problems on the Iroquois. Jean Talon, known in the history books as the

'Great Intendant,' was instructed by Jean-Baptiste Colbert to 'carry war even to their firesides *in order totally to exterminate them*' (instructions to M. Talon, 27 March 1665, *PD-NYCD*: 25, emphasis added). Although the subsequent campaign was unsuccessful in achieving its ultimate goal – the Iroquois soon learned to elude large contingents of armed Frenchmen – it did allow European striation of the land to proceed apace: 'It is fine to see new settlements on each side of the St. Lawrence for a distance of eighty leagues ... The fear of aggression no longer prevents our farmers from encroaching on the forest and harvesting all kinds of grain' (Le Mercier, relation of 1668, cited in Chapais 1964: 48). This successful 'encroachment on the forest' was also, of course, encroachment upon the traditional lands of various Native peoples, more and more of whom found themselves in the position of the Huron, namely, without the means of subsistence and – for the moment – reduced to dependence upon handouts from the French. Now that the haughty had been beaten down, the conquered could be spared[3] – and further managed by the use of 'softer' methods of conversion and civilization. By 1668 there were Jesuits amongst all of the five Iroquois nations, ministering to both Iroquois and French and Huron captives (Chapais 1964: 94–5; *Relations:* 49.103–17). In 1703, the Jesuit historian Joseph Jouvency was able to report that 'there are numbered in this formerly solitary and unexplored country more than thirty very prosperous and well-equipped missions of our society' (Mealing 1963: 115).

In this way, France began to become a net exporter of signs to the Native peoples, who might then be counted as part of the population of New France:

> In order to strengthen the colony ... nothing would contribute more ... than to endeavour to civilize the Algonquins, the Hurons, and other Indians who have embraced Christianity, and to induce them to come and settle in common with the French, to live with them and raise their children according to our manners and customs. (Colbert to Talon, 5 April 1666, *PD-NYCD*: 43)

Lest there be any question as to the extent of the assimilation proposed by Colbert, his letter of 6 April 1667 makes known his hope that 'through the course of time, having only but one law and one master, they might likewise constitute only one people and one race' (*PD-NYCD*: 59).

It is crucial to note that, while the French were able to expand their regime, they were not able, and *have never been able*, to entirely eliminate the more 'problematic' Native peoples, whose acts of resistance often take the form of violent engagement. While the historical evidence for it is easy to find, the use of physical elimination as means of managing Canadian diversity has been quite effectively covered over by mainstream Canadian history. I am referring here to the sentiment expressed in Parkman's famous quote cited at the beginning of this chapter, and echoed elsewhere. 'The aboriginal was never regarded as an alien in New France; he was looked upon as a subject. He was not to be liquidated; he was to be civilized' (Stanley 1949: 334). A comparison is also commonly made between an American preference for war and a 'kinder' Canadian approach of peaceful assimilation. In this vein, Thomas Berger has claimed that 'on the great plains the Indians ... would be sought and destroyed by the now far superior military power of the United States. In Canada there was no predisposition to eliminate the indigenous population except through assimilation' (Berger 1991: 64).[4] When not completely hidden from view, this inglorious aspect of the history of Canadian diversity has been glossed with a rhetoric of 'just cause,' from Champlain to Talon to the present day.[5] There is no doubt, however, that the French attempted to exterminate the Iroquois nations many times, and the only thing that stopped these peoples from being wiped out was their own ability to bend with and redirect the tide of death flowing their way. The coexistence of this struggle to the death alongside the master-slave relationship imposed upon the Huron makes it clear that *Geist* lost sight of its goal as it drifted over to the Americas, and allowed stages that should have been sublated to remain operative as forces of contradiction and antagonism. Indeed, the most striking feature of the early history of Canadian diversity is not its tendency to progress towards mutual recognition and unity, but rather its constant impediment by the complex knots into which the New World Spirit had wound itself.

The *coureurs de bois* as a Repressed Hybrid Identity

If the missionaries were having some success in initiating a net flow of signs to the Savage, there were other products of the meeting of French and Native peoples who did not fit in so well with the Royal plan. Despite constant state intervention to prevent inverse sign flow, some of the French assimilated to Native ways of life, as best seen in the example of the *coureurs de bois*. Good colonists were supposed to stay in one place, till the land, and quietly reproduce the *ancien régime* categories of peasant, petty bourgeois, and seigneur. Those who chose instead to live a semi-nomadic life and take on the ways of the Native peoples posed an ongoing problem to the Jesuits, proper French visitors, and above all to the colonial administration. Themes of wanton alcoholism, interracial sex, and idleness were central to the evidence produced by Father Etienne de Carheil, in his relation of 1702 regarding the state of the mission at Michillimackinack, a centre for the activities of the *coureurs de bois* (*Relations:* 65.190ff). Trading in furs at such remote outposts, he argued,

> serves but to depopulate the country of all its young men; to reduce the number of people in the houses; to deprive wives of their husbands, fathers and mothers of the aid of their children, and sisters of that of their brothers; ... it accustoms them [the young men] not to work, but to lose all taste for work, and to live in Continual idleness; it renders them incapable of learning any trade, and thereby makes them Useless to themselves, to their families, and to the entire country ... (*Relations:* 65.219)

Seeing the combined forces of the traders and the military commanders arrayed against him, the Jesuit argued that the fur trade should be limited to Montreal, and the young men kept at home, along the St Lawrence (65.220 ff).

The Baron de Lahontan was also unimpressed by what he saw of these young men, even when they were among the more civilized *habitants*:

> You would be amaz'd if you saw how lewd these Pedlers are when they return [from trading expeditions]; ... the Batchelors act just as our East-India-men, and Pirates are wont to do; for they lavish, eat, drink, and play all away as long as the Goods hold out; and when they are gone, they e'en sell their embroidery, their Lace, and their Cloaths. This done, they are forc'd to go upon a new Voyage for Subsistance. (Lahontan 1940: 20–1)

The comparison of the *coureurs de bois* to pirates seems to have been a common rhetorical trope of the late seventeenth century, as seen in Talon's complaints below, which also refer to some of the many attempts to legislate the 'illegitimate' traders out of existence:

[P]roclaiming the intention of the King, I caused orders to be issued that the volunteers (whom on my return, I found in very great numbers, living, in reality, like banditi) should be excluded from the [Indian] trade and hunting; they are excluded by the law also from the honours of the Church, and from the Communities if they do not marry fifteen days after the arrival of the ships from France. (Talon to the King, 10 Sept. 1670, *PD-NYCD*: 65)

Frontenac, who governed New France after Talon, shared his predecessor's fear and disdain of *the coureurs de bois*, and also tried, with the help of Colbert, to use state power against them. He thought it was crucial to the peace of the country to prevent 'the disorders of the *Coureurs de bois*, who will finally become, if care be not taken, like the banditti of Naples and the Buccaneers of Saint Domingo ... Their insolence ... extends even to the formation of leagues, and to the distribution of notices of rendezvous ...' (Frontenac to Colbert, 2 Nov. 1672, *PD-NYCD*: 91).

Of course, such attempts failed. French state power was never able to eradicate these hybrid identities, and so they formed an important, though mostly ignored, undercurrent within mainstream historical accounts. They are of particular interest with regard to the continuous efforts of the French colonial government – and every state seeking to control the shifting territory known as Canada since then – to suppress any spontaneously emergent forms that might have resulted from the European invasions. What the state absolutely forbids is that any group might begin to striate its own space according to its own rules, to make alliances and set up meetings. Like the Iroquois confederacy, the *coureurs de bois* were relatively successful *competitors* for organized control of geographical space, especially as they were seen to be taking on the socio-political forms of the Native peoples, which were fundamentally nomadic – in the sense discussed in chapter 2 – and therefore appeared as a challenge to sedentary society. Again, the Jesuit opinion is quite informative:

The Savages ... imagine that they ought by right of birth, to enjoy the liberty of Wild ass colts, rendering no homage to any one whomsoever, except when they like. They have reproached me a hundred times because we fear our Captains, while they laugh at and make sport of theirs. All the authority of their chief is in his tongue's end; for he is powerful in so far as he is eloquent; and, even if he kills himself talking and haranguing, he will not be obeyed unless he pleases the Savages. (*Relations:* 6.243)

As representative of a nomadic – that is, emergent, local, decentralized, and non-authoritarian – mode of organization, the *coureurs de bois* constituted the first repressed *semi-internal* Other in the history of Canadian diversity. Eventually driven out of the Great Lakes region by the decline of the fur trade and the incursions of American settlers (Peterson 1985), they form one line of descent to the Métis of the nineteenth and twentieth centuries, who have yet to be fully recognized as either Canadians or as a sovereign people in their own right, and therefore still occupy a liminal and contradictory position within the discourse on Canadian diversity (Adams 1995; 1989). More importantly, however, their treatment shows the extent to which Canadian state organizations have been deeply *fearful* of emergent forms, and have been on an endless quest for a single hegemonic striation of as much space as possible by the largest possible rational-bureaucratic apparatus.

The System of Difference in French Colonial Discourse

It is not so hard to penetrate the mists that hide Canada's primordial multiculturalism – the documents are there, at least from the French point of view, and they allow us to construct a semiotic square (see chapter 3) of those who could be considered <subjects of New France>. The positive term here was obviously <French>, the negative term – the name of the Other – was <*Sauvage*>, and the basis for the distinction was given by the possession or lack of <civilization> and <Christianity>. Within the negative term, there was a hierarchy, differentiated by degree of assimilation to the French, ranging from the Huron on down to the less assimilated Native nations. The contradictory position was taken up by the <*coureur de bois*>, who displayed the qualities of both <French> and <*Sauvage*>, and therefore threatened to undermine the system of binary opposition. In the sense that they were cast as roving bandits, these were not proper subjects of the French King; inasmuch as they were not seen as possessing a right to a group identity of their own, they were prevented from organizing as a distinct society. What was neither <French> nor <assimilated *Sauvage*> and had the potential to bring this system crashing down? The troublesome <Iroquois Confederation>, the external Enemy who had to be exterminated. As in the ancient Greek case, it should be noted that within this

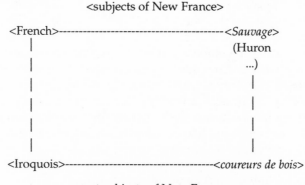

Fig. 4.1. Group identity in French colonial discourse (<Canada>)

square there was another implicit hierarchy, which had the Self group at its apex, descended through the primary Others, down to the complementary position, viz. French, *Sauvage* (Huron ...), *coureurs de bois*, Iroquois.

When we part the mists and look at the relations that existed under this system of primordial multiculturalism, what we see is not 'harmonious coexistence,' but a number of groups struggling to the death for hegemony. What we also see in this 'origin' is the Europeans pulling on their history to achieve as much as possible given their inferior position. The most important strategy they adopted was to *appear to give in the short term to win in the long term.* This form of *strategic simulation of assimilation* to the Other was perhaps the greatest innovation of the French in the New World, and would be put to good use as the history of Canadian diversity played itself out. For, despite ongoing resistance and mutual assimilation and integration, it is obvious that the net flow of signs has not been equal. Very few Québécois now live in open-roofed longhouses and speak Algonquin tongues, but many Algonquin live in bungalows under the eye of a paternal state and speak French, or, more likely, English. Mohawk warriors are dragged into Quebec courts, but do not have the right to subject Canadian and Québécois armed forces and police to their own forms of justice.

Thus we might summarize the French handling of the problem of Canadian diversity during the time of the establishment of New France as follows: for 'friends,' that is, those who did not fight to the death to maintain their style of life, there would be seduction, displacement, de-nomadification, and containment on 'reserves,' leading to a state of dependency conducive to civilization and conversion; for 'enemies,' a war of extermination would be carried out to strip the competing society of its demographic, social, and political power, and reduce it to the state accepted 'voluntarily' by the 'friends.' Of course, neither of these solutions could be implemented just as the French would like, so that they were also forced to assimilate and to integrate their Others to whatever extent was necessary to guarantee the survival of their project. Thus was one 'joining' of the 'Europeans' and the 'Aboriginal peoples' accomplished. But before we emerge from the mists of history, there is another tradition that must be unveiled, that inaugurated by the British with their many attempts at the still unfinished business of Conquering and colonizing not only the Natives, as first Other in the New World, but also the French, who were themselves soon to feel the sting of Conquest.

How Canada Became British

In the previous sections, I have presented the French colonial discourse as one of the 'two Canadian solutions to the problem of diversity' to which I refer in the title of this chapter. In the immediately preceding section, I have outlined how the French colonial discourse adapted an ancient European system of constructing and managing diversity to the conditions of a New World, and tried to point out some of its more interesting innovations. In the following sections, I will address the second 'Canadian solution,' as it is found in the early British colonial discourse. Again, I will discuss the means used by the British to distinguish themselves from the people they encountered, but as there is little difference here from the French system, I will treat this issue in only a cursory fashion. The use of the methods of displacement and extermination against the Beothuck of Newfoundland will be noted, but more attention will be paid to the strategy of *ignorance of the Other* that contributed to the demise of this group. The Hudson Bay fur trade will be presented as an example of British adoption of the French method of integrating the Other in a capitalist economy, but again the emphasis will be placed on an innovation – that of distant microcontrol of everyday life. As in the French case, even this concerted attempt to lock bodies into systems of state striation could not succeed in achieving the stage of 'apparatus.' British fur traders took Native women as wives, increasing their capital (in Bourdieu's sense) in the local branch of the colonial economy, giving rise once again to what was perceived by the British as a surplus, hybrid population of Half-breeds. I see this combination of ignorance and failed attempts at microcontrol as being eminently Canadian in its basic outlines, as I will show in the chapters on post-Confederation formations (6–8). This is what makes the early British colonial discourse important for the history of Canadian diversity, and this is one sense in which I hope the title to this section might be read.

When comparing the British and French systems, one finds that similar questions were asked, and similar answers were provided, regarding the humanity, civilization, and convertibility of the peoples of the New World. Sir George Peckham's 1583 *True Report of the Late Discoveries ... of the Newfound Landes* argued that the New World 'Savages,' lacking government and agriculture (Quinn 1979: 3.54) and going about naked (3.54), could only benefit from the 'relieving of the miserable and wretched estate' of their 'sillie soules' (3.41). If they would only follow his advice, Peckham asserted, the English would join the proud company of ancient biblical heroes – and contemporary Spaniards – in taking on a task 'as well pleasing to almightie God, as profitable to men ... as lawfull as it seemed honourable' (3.41).

Peckham was aware of the possibility that the 'Savages,' in their 'ignorance,' would not appreciate the kindness being shown them, and might resist being lifted to the level of European civilization. Drawing a page from Virgil's exhortation of the Romans to imperial glory, he advised that if persuasion proved to be necessary, peaceful means were to be preferred, such as letting it be known that the English had come to bestow gifts and to do no harm, offering beneficial trade and protection from their enemies (3.44). This was, however, only one method of 'planting' available to England as a Christian European power:

[I]f after these good and fair meanes used , the Savages nevertheles will not be heerewithall satisfied, but barbarously wyll goe about to practise violence either in repelling the Christians from theyr Portes and safe Landinges or in withstanding them afterwardes to enjoye the rights for which both painfully and lawfully they have adventured themselves thether. Then in such a case I holde it no breache of equitye for the Christians to defende themselves, to pursue revenge with force, and to doo whatsoever is necessary for the attayning of theyr safety: For it is allowable by all Lawes in such distresses, to resist violence with violence. (3.44–5)

This circle of retribution – which does not address the question of what one might call the 'first violent act' – was taken up and advocated by both the younger and elder Hakluyt (see Quinn 1979: 3.61ff), and soon became quite firmly established as the correct method of dealing with the problem of diversity in the New World.[6] Thus, at least in the official-intellectual discourse, the British took up a policy very similar to the French. They were to offer kindness to their inferiors, whom they would 'elevate' if possible; but, if the gift were declined, they felt compelled to engage in a life and death struggle. Such was the state of British 'theory' regarding the means of differentiation and methods of management appropriate to New World 'planting.' In the following sections, I will examine two characteristic instances of the application of this model.

Ignorance and Extermination in the New Founde Landes

The 'disappearance' of the Native people of Newfoundland has been much discussed, even elevated to the status of a myth: a 'vanished race' that 'passed out of existence as mysteriously as they entered thereupon,' still in a condition of 'primitive ignorance and barbarity' (Howley 1974: 62). Did the Beothuck just 'vanish'? Some claim that, with the silent complicity of various levels of government, they were displaced and exterminated to make way for British settlement and exploitation (Kelly 1974; Marshall 1996; Rowe 1977). Some deny that the Beothuck were exterminated at all or, if they were, that this was something the British set out consciously to achieve (Upton 1992). The records left by the early Explorers and Colonizers are of some help in examining this dispute, although the British never produced anything like the detailed 'ethnographic' studies of Cartier and Champlain.

Edward Hayes, who was on the second voyage of Sir Humphrey Gilbert in 1583, provided an account of the flora, fauna, and mineral wealth of the New World, which runs to more than ten thousand words. But there is scant mention of the human inhabitants, other than to hammer home that they are 'barbarous' (Quinn 1979: 4.24), 'pagans' (4.24), 'poore infidels captived by the devill, tyrannizing in most woonderfull and dreadfull maner over their bodies and soules' (4.24) – none of which seems to be based on actual encounters, or even observations, and hence gives the appearance of a simple restatement of established prejudice. Hayes admits that 'in the South parts we found no inhabitants, which by all likelihood have abandoned those coastes,' and gives no evidence of having met anyone in the North (4.33). The New World Savage was, for the British at this time, very much an imaginary apparition.

From 1610 on, various public and private efforts at colonization led to a slow growth in the British presence in Newfoundland, as well as that of the other European nations fishing off the coast. Among them, by the middle of the sixteenth century, the Europeans had taken over most of the shore of the island, where the means of subsistence were most plentiful, driving the Beothuck inland (Marshall 1996: 22). In the early seventeenth century, Lord Falkland recommended further displacement and containment in his instructions to 'the well affected planters in new fownde lande,' whom he advised to 'plante in the most extreme parte of the land northwestwarde ... to keepe the natives out from the maine land ...; which being Carefullie donne & observed, they will have the better parte of 2/3 parte of land of the bignes of Ireland to themselves ('Lord Falkland's Instructions to his Settlers,' in Cell 1982: 244). In this manner, the British slowly but surely progressed around, and then penetrated into, the whole of the island. Yet by 1760, when primary sources again began to appear, Sir Joseph Banks's report showed that a century and a half of coexistence had done little to bring the Beothuck out of the realm of fantasy: 'Of the Indians that inhabit the interior parts of Newfoundland, I have as yet been able to learn very little about them. They are supposed to be the original inhabitants of the country' (Banks's journal, cited in Howley 1974: 28).

While this lack of knowledge shows that there was little in the way of friendly intercourse between the two groups, they do appear to have interacted in other ways. Explicitly planned missions of extermination equivalent to the French forays into Iroquois territory were undertaken by the British settlers, usually justified by a claim of retribution for the loss of *matériel* to the Beothuck. The historical literature abounds with such tales, with various commentators taking positions regarding their veracity. Even the most doubtful of historians, however, tends to grant credence to the evidence collected by Captain G.C. Pulling, which appears in a transcription of his 1792 report on the state of Native-settler relations in Newfoundland (Marshall 1989).[7] Various governors of the colony issued proclamations apparently intended to stop the killing. The first and most succinct came out in 1769, and is worth citing at length as an epitome of the confluence and conflict between the official discourse at the centre of the British Empire and actual practice on the periphery:

> Whereas it has been represented to the King, that the subjects residing in the said Island of Newfoundland, instead of cultivating such a friendly intercourse with the savages inhabiting that island as might be for their mutual benefit and advantage, do treat the said savages with the greatest inhumanity, and frequently destroy them without the least provocation or remorse. In order, therefore, to put a stop to such inhuman barbarity, and that the perpetrators of such atrocious crimes may be brought to due punishment, it is His Majesty's royal will and pleasure, that I do express his abhorrence of such inhuman barbarity, and I do strictly enjoin and require all His Majesty's subjects to live in amity and brotherly kindness with the native savages of the said island of Newfoundland. (Proclamation issued by His Excellency Capt. the Hon. John Byron in 1769, cited in Howley 1974: 45)

This proclamation, which eerily foreshadows the Canadian Multiculturalism Act of 1988, was reissued in 1775 and 1776, and a similar edict was put forth by Governor John Holloway in 1807. Even with repetition, these words had no effect, as magistrates regularly turned a blind eye to the killing of Beothuck by settlers, and no one was ever brought to England for trial as required by the proclamations.

After two centuries of colonial coexistence, the British were *still* in a first-contact stage, struggling to the death with a Savage Other, while occasionally sending out Explorers to acquire information on his manners and customs. Were the Beothuck human? Did they deserve protection? Such questions had not yet been decided when they became moot in 1829, with the death of the last Beothuck known to Europeans. British ignorance of the plight of the people of Newfoundland has been much lamented, but its value as a tool in the management of problematic diversity should not be overlooked. A person who might not exist or, more precisely, is not *known* to exist, in the sense of having been assigned a set of typical characteristics, is equivalent to a nonperson, and therefore need not be granted what are now known as 'human' rights. This point was made forcefully to the 1837 Select Committee of the Parliament of the United Kingdom on Aborigines (British Settlements):

On our first visit to that country [Newfoundland] the natives were seen in every part of the coast. We occupied the stations where they used to hunt and fish, thus reducing them to want, while we took no trouble to indemnify them, so that doubtless many of them perished by famine; we also treated them with hostility and cruelty, and many were slain by our own people as well as by the Micmac Indians, who were allowed to harass them ... Under our treatment they continued rapidly to diminish ... In the colony of Newfoundland it may therefore be stated that *we have exterminated the natives*. (Cited in Bartlett 1990: 7, emphasis added)

Thus the Beothuck entered, passed through, and disappeared from European history as a 'mysterious' people who did not receive any of the gifts that Civilization had to offer, and themselves made no 'contributions' to an emerging Canadian diversity.

Microcontrol and Hybridity: The Hudson's Bay Company and the British Fur Trade

The Hudson's Bay Company was, it is true, a keen trader, as the motto 'Pro Pelle Cutem' – 'skin for skin' – clearly implies. With this no fault can be found, the more that its methods were nearly all honourable British methods. It never forgot the flag that floated over it.

> – George Bryce, *The Remarkable History of the Hudson's Bay Company*, 19.

The stance of fortuitous ignorance did not – and could not – exist where the British came with the express purpose of establishing themselves in the fur trade, and this shift in goals was accompanied by a shift in the terms of the discourse on diversity. The category of 'Savage,' drawn from the cosmographies and histories, was dominant during Exploration and first-contact stages, when extremely little was known about the peoples of the New World. 'Indian,' although derived from the widespread and long-lasting European conviction that the New World was in fact a piece of the Old, appeared as a post-contact term ascribing an increasing measure of particularity and humanity to these peoples. That this was not a purely chronological progression can be seen from the fact that while Governor Byron of Newfoundland was out to protect 'Savages' in the 1769 proclamation cited above, Zachariah Gillam had set off to trade with Hudson Bay 'Indians' one hundred years earlier (answer of Sir James Hayes to a letter from Labarre, 1683, *HBRSS*: 11.70). The change did not happen fully, quickly, or without contradiction, but, as we will see in the discussion of Hudson's Bay Company sources, the term 'Indian' was much more common than 'Savage,' and the increase in its usage was accompanied by a decline in the use of, or at least official ignorance of the unofficial use of, the method of physical extermination.

The British, of course, learned everything they needed to know about working with Indians from Radisson and Groseilliers, two notorious French *coureurs de bois* (instructions to Captain William Stannard, in Nute 1935: 419–20). It seems that the backers of the company 'knew,' at some level, that they would have been unable to gather a single fur if they had relied upon the 'honourable British methods' of ignorance, displacement, and extermination used by the quickly bankrupted Newfoundland Company. Without admitting it, indeed likely without any conscious awareness of having done so, the British fur traders *assimilated with* New World practices evolved by the French and Native peoples, and ultimately gained, at least for the stockholders of the Hudson's Bay Company, immense profits from doing so.

This is not to downplay the original contributions made by the Company to the methodological arsenal of the discourse on Canadian diversity. One of these was a 'legal,' 'contractual' means of taking land from Native peoples, as described in the 1680 instructions to Governor Nixon:

> In the severall places where you are or shall settle, you [should] contrive to make compact wth. the Capns. or chiefs of the resepective Rivers & places, whereby it might be understood by them that you had purchased both the lands & rivers of them, and that they had transferred the absolute propriety to you, or at least the only freedome of trade, And that you should cause them to do some act wch. by the Religion or Custome of their Country should be thought most sacred & obliging to them for the confirmation of such Agreements. (*HBRSS*: 11.9)

The Company was later to claim that these instructions, which are reminiscent of the infamous Spanish *requerimiento*, were consistent with the actions of Zachariah Gillam in 1668, when he 'Discovered a river in the botome of the sd. Bay ... where he met with the Native Indians & haveing made a league of Friendship wth. the Capt. of the said River & firmly purchased both the river it selfe & the Landes there aboute, he gave it the Name of Rupert River' (answer of Sir James Hayes to a letter from Labarre, 1683, *HBRSS*: 11.70). As in the case of the Newfoundland proclamations, the key to this process is the difficulty of making it 'understood' to people who did not share European notions about 'ownership' and 'title' that they had signed away the right to occupy 'their' land. Those whose values and interests lie with the British interpretation will see this as an attempt at 'fair play' that goes beyond the simple use of violent force. Those whose do not will see yet another creative use of the strategy of ignorance to achieve ends that would, if one were to apply the principles of British justice to Indians, be unconscionable. Whatever its moral status, this strategy has maintained its usefulness down to the present day. According to Thomas Berger, in the 'adjudication' of land claims, it has been 'difficult to convince lawyers and judges that the Native peoples of Canada possess rights based on the indisputable fact that they occupied vast areas ... before the Europeans colonized it. They had their own institutions, their own laws. But of this lawyers and judges *remained unaware*' (Berger 1991: 150, emphasis added).

Another, less discussed, contribution of the Hudson's Bay Company was its development of methods of bureaucratic microcontrol of the daily lives of its 'Servants' and 'Home Indians.' This approach was made easier by the Company's charter, which famously granted it possession of all the lands whose rivers emptied into the Bay, gave it sole right to trade therein, allowed it to make and enforce laws, and even to 'make peace or Warre with any Prince or People whatsoever that are not Christians' (Newman 1985: 1.329). As E.E. Rich has pointed out, 'the whole Charter was, in fact, a magnificent grant of rights and privileges, not a specification of duties' (Rich 1958: 1.56). From its inception, the members of the Company Council wanted to know every detail of every action of everyone who set foot in what amounted to its own kingdom (*HBRSS*: 5.7). Once the trade was up and running, they did not relent in their attention to detail, requiring from each factor 'Journalls of what has been done in the respective factories & of all occurrances that have happened to them in the yeare past that we may know how they & those under them have emploied their time' (*HBRSS*: 11.73). A 1738 letter from Prince of Wales Fort, written in response to queries and concerns from London, has the men in the field answering fifty-three different questions, many of which seem to have been absurd in their quibbling. For example:

10th The large quantity of copper rivets we principally find useful in mending of kettles.
11th We have examined the state of provisions in the account book 1737 and we find it must be an oversight for the pork stand charged thus ... the beef thus ... so likewise the butter thus ... (*HBRSS*: 25.243)

Item 11 goes on to give details of where each cut of beef and firkin of butter has gone, and ends by declaring the Company's employees blameless in any misallocation of food. The Company kept this up for several hundred years, thereby amassing an immense pile of incredibly detailed documentation of its activities – or, at least, an official representation thereof. It is often thought that the globalization of capital requires a certain electronic infrastructure to be in place; but the British showed, three hundred years ago, that exploitation for the profit of distant capitalists was possible using only the ship, the pen, and the musket.

The many rules and regulations regarding trade and contact with the Native peoples are of particular interest. It is obvious that, at least insofar as they could be caused to yield up land and bring down furs, the Native peoples of the Hudson Bay area, unlike the Beothuck of Newfoundland, were from the beginning seen by the British as potentially Useful Others. The Company's instructions to Thomas Draper, issued in 1680, insisted that he 'use the greatest circumspection' in his dealings with the 'Northern Indians,' and that he *deal justly with them, and let no body offer them any ill usage to* provoke their revenge' (*HBRSS*: 11.14, emphasis in original). While the Indians were seen as Useful Others by the British, they were Useful *external* Others, definitely to be kept outside, both literally and figuratively. During trading, one person at a time was allowed to come up to a window, there to strike his bargain and yield his place to the next. No Native people were to be allowed in the storehouse, nor were they welcome on the ships (*HBRSS*: 25.128, 268). Private trade was repeatedly forbidden, and to discourage 'debauchery,' the Council did 'absolutely prohibit ... women to be entertained or admitted into our Forts or houses under the penallty of the forfeiture of their wages' (*HBRSS*: 11.75). Finally, at the conclusion of their trade, those Indians not of the 'Home Guard' were encouraged to migrate back inland, so that 'the less opertuney will be given to our serveants for private Trade or debauchery with them' (*HBRSS*: 11.76).

But colonial capitalist rational-legal domination, as effective as it might be, can never be perfect or total. Despite the official regulations, there was constant unofficial contact between the Servants of the Company and the Native peoples, for the exchange of pelts and bodily pleasures. At both Moose Fort and Eastmain, the masters took Indian wives, and their children became important players in the fur trade (Francis and Morantz 1983: 90). Jennifer Brown claims that 'it is possible to document at least fifteen instances of Hudson's Bay men ... taking Indian women as mates before 1770' (Brown 1980: 52). By 1821, 'practically all officers of the Hudson's Bay and Northwest Companies, and many lower-ranked employees as well, were allied with women born in the Indian country' (Brown 1980: 51). These alliances gave rise to a considerable, but widely scattered, Half-breed population which, along with retired White traders, was not seen as assimilable by either Canada or Great Britain, and was therefore cast as a surplus, problematic group:

> It comes to be a serious consideration how these people are to be *disposed of*. It is both dangerous and expensive to support a numerous population of this description in an uneducated and savage condition, and it would be impolitic and inexpedient to encourage and allow them to collect together in different parts of the country, where they could not be under proper superintendence. The establishment of clergymen and schools at the Red River Settlement, where means of instruction will be afforded them, and where they will be under a regular police and government, by the establishment of Magistrates ... points out the proper mode of disposing of this numerous class of persons. (HBC committee to Governor Simpson, 8 March 1822, cited in McLean 1987: 49; emphasis added)

Once again, difference – now only partially non-European, but that was enough – was to be collected and contained within a demarcated space, where it could be subjected to the salutary effects of European law and religion. Rather than solving the problem, however, this method of 'disposition' of problematic hybrid bodies only set the stage for their later displacement as the lands controlled by the Hudson's Bay Company were bought – or invaded, or welcomed into Confederation, as one will have it – by the Canadians.

The Early Colonial History of Canadian Diversity

By way of their operations up to the end of the seventeenth century, the British and French ensured, between them, that the methods of both the Greeks and the Romans were preserved and brought to bear upon the construction and management of the problem of diversity in the New World. Fabulous, semi-human beings, often right out of the cosmographies and histories, were 'discovered,' and dealt with by means of the interlocking systems of xenophobia–ignorance–extermination, and exploitation–knowledge production–assimilation. The European discourse on diversity was thus transplanted and reproduced; but this was a *creative* reproduction in a new context, which gave rise to novel forms. The French colonial experience contributed the notion that the existing peoples were to be 'elevated' to a state of civilization, and developed methods to carry out this task. This practice of tutelage, which can be seen as compatible with the modern European idea of educating the masses, was something that did not occur to Greeks and Romans, nor to medieval Europeans. In those systems, it was quite fine, if not preferable, to leave the people in ignorance, so as to render them more easy to govern. The French brought modern ideas about individual development to the New World, and showed how they could be used as a tool of exploitation and domination.

In the early colonial era, the particularity of the British contribution does not yet show up, except in nascent form. But already, in futile proclamations regarding the Beothuck of Newfoundland, and the 'land purchases' around Hudson Bay, we can discern the outlines of what would become the most important and enduring British contribution to the Canadian discourse on diversity: the adoption of a mode of *legalized* domination and disenfranchisement that allowed an astonishing variety of dishonest and inhuman practices to be implemented in the guise of high civilization and due process. The strength, usefulness, and longevity of this contribution can be seen in the particularly Canadian propensity for state-sponsored sinning – for example, invoking the War Measures Act against certain fragments of the population – followed by an attempt at gaining absolution through public confession at a commission of inquiry. The British, through the offices of the Hudson's Bay Company, also showed that distant, centralized control of a vast tract of land could be implemented with a rather startling degree of success given the technologies at hand. When it came time for Canada to graduate from colony to country, the methods of distant micro-management pioneered by the London Committee were not forgotten by those who took it upon themselves to do the same thing from their base in Ottawa.

But the greatest gift given by Europe to the Canadian discourse on diversity came from both the English and the French, in the form of a binary system of Self-Other distinction that allowed the immediate work to be done, but has also proven to be amenable to infinite multiplication and permutation as the problem of Canadian diversity has evolved. The early British-colonial square of <Group Identity> was similar to the French, except that <British> occupied the position of

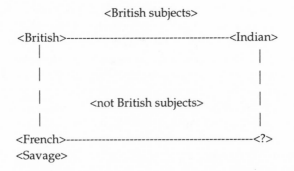

Fig. 4.2. Group identity in early British colonial discourse (<Canada>)

<French> as the dominant identity, and the distinction between Native peoples who would assimilate and those who would not was now marked through the use of different names: 'Savage' for the Useless external Other well beyond the pale of an advancing Civilization; and 'Indian' for the more Useful marginal individuals and groups who could not, or would not, choose either flight or extermination. Noting that the British and the French were locked in a battle to drive each other off the continent, we can see that they took on a mutually complementary relationship, in which each threatened the very possibility of existence of the other's system of identification. Thus 'French' belongs with 'Savage,' as neither 'British' nor 'Indian' and 'outside' the system. Since what would become known as the Half-breed identity did not yet possess any kind of official recognition, I will leave the contradictory term blank.

Through their mutual complementarity, the French and British came to be intimately connected as Imaginary Others, lurking just beyond the forest, one river or trading post away, or across the ocean in the Old World; never fully present, but never quite forgotten either (*Je me souviens* / What do they want from us?) However, this complementary system of British-French antagonism was far from stable. The crucial shift in relations between what are now known as the Two Founding Races came at the turn of the eighteenth century, when the ascending British Empire first glanced covetously, then stared unashamedly, at the prospect of taking as its own the whole of North America.

Chapter Five

Repetition and Failure in British North America

Open your eyes, Canadians, to your own interests ... We exhort you eagerly to have recourse to a people, free, honest, and generous ... For if you do not profit by this advice, you must expect the most rigorous treatment ...

– Proclamation by General Murray to the people of Quebec, 1759; cited in C. Nish, *The French Canadians 1759–1766*, 5

As I have shown in the previous chapter, it is not so difficult to dispel the mists, and the myth, surrounding the origins of Canadian multiculturalism. Contrary to what is still common wisdom, the British and French colonizers did attempt, like the much-vilified Spanish *Conquistadores*, to exterminate entire peoples, and in some cases they achieved their goals. What does this mean for the official history of Canadian diversity? Were these merely sad aberrations from what is otherwise a history of harmonious coexistence? If General Murray's warning to the French is any indication, the Roman imperial strategy of beating down the haughty and sparing the submissive was the norm rather than the exception, even when the colonial subjects to which it was applied occupied the highest position on the Great Chain of Being.

According to the ideology of European colonialism, though, the benefits of Colonization must not accrue only to the Conquerors; the Conquered must also be 'raised' by the destruction of their way of life and the removal of their autonomy. In his *Outline of a Project to Capture Quebec and Placentia* (ca. 1700), the Baron de Lahontan cunningly suggested that what the British had to offer to the French was exactly what the British and French had been offering to the Native peoples: the gift of a superior civilization: 'What makes me believe that the English will attain the end of this enterprise [the capture of Quebec] easily is the mildness of the English government ... There are not two hundred families in Canada who could not wish with all their hearts to be under English rule ...' (Lahontan 1940: 41). Thus the French in Canada were set apart as inferior and in desperate need of gifts that might improve their lot, the most important of these being a New World identity as Others within the British Empire. This, in its most concise form, is the source of the sting of Conquest; to be shifted from Self in one's own system to Other in an Other's, to go from providing solutions to problems to being managed as a problem oneself.

As is well known, the Conquest of New France was not quite as simple as Lahontan imagined. While the French army and bureaucratic infrastructure could be eliminated through brute force, the people were much more resilient. In Acadia they immediately showed their desire and ability to resist assimilation, to which the British responded with a disastrous and genocidal attempt at transportation. Later, in Quebec, the British allowed their new subjects to *preserve and maintain* signs of their problematic difference, making them the first group to be granted the gift of what is now known, within multiculturalism policy, as *integration*. A similar shift in management style was occurring in the British handling of 'the Indian problem.' Displacement – and the concomitant loss of the means of subsistence – now functioned as an indirect means of physical elimination, and the bodies that remained were collected together and put under a regime of *rational-bureaucratic tutelage*. In this chapter, I will outline the transition from methods of physical elimination to preservation and integration that occurred in the handling of the French and Indian 'problems,' and will suggest that this has become an archetype, providing a trajectory through identity-space that would be followed by each new group enveloped by the system of Canadian diversity. I will also show how a particularly 'British' North America was fashioned in the crucible of an advancing system of governmentality and rational-legal domination that sought – and failed – to contain a proliferating space of problematic diversity.

The Conquest of New France

Although much is made of the fall of Quebec, the Conquest of New

France began in 1710 with the capture of Port Royal. As I noted in chapter 2, the British effort to solve the 'Acadian problem' created by this 'victory' is often cast as one of those unfortunate exceptions to a history of emerging multiculturalism. As with the case of the Beothuck, historians dispute the details of cause, effect, and numbers dead. My main interest, though, is in how the British seemed to reach hastily for one solution after another, and ended by failing to 'solve' the problem of Acadian diversity in any definitive way. This, I would suggest, is the source of any historical embarrassment; not that ignoble methods were used, but that *all* methods, noble or otherwise, so obviously failed to achieve their goal in the face of Acadian resistance.

The guns hardly had time to cool before the first – and most radical – solution to the problem of Acadian diversity was proposed:

All French must be deported outside the country, save those who adopt Protestantism ... [I]t would be most advantageous for the Crown that this measure be effected with all possible speed and that they be replaced with Protestant families from England or Ireland. (Council of Victors, 14 Oct. 1710, cited in Arsenault 1966: 73)

Like the Beothuck and Iroquois before them, the Acadians were clearly 'in the way.' But their European connections meant that they could not be exterminated. Thus the Council of Victors quickly and intuitively found another way to justify treating the French as objects rather than subjects: a lack of Protestant religion. A method well suited to this sort of partial Otherness seemed to be *transportation*, which could appear as a 'soft' or 'humane' means of physical elimination. This strategy, especially when coupled with a subsequent importation of Desirable Selves – 'Protestant families from England or Ireland' – appeared admirably suited to the task of remaking the human landscape to suit the new regime of striation.

But, after some thought, it became apparent that even transportation might have ill effects on British interests, as the French of 'Nova Scotia,' once added to those already at Cape Breton, would be 'of the greatest danger and damage to all the British Colony's as well as the universal trade of Great Britain' (letter from Colonel Vetch to the Lords of Trade, 24 Nov. 1714, in Akins 1972: 18). The British then began to hope that *assimilation* would solve the Acadian problem: 'tho' we may not expect much benefit from them, yet their children in process of time may be brought to our constitution' (Lt. Gov. Caulfield to Board of

Trade and Plantations, Nov. 1715, in Akins 1972: 9). Indeed, a limited gift of *toleration* – the necessary counterbalance while waiting for assimilation to have its effects – had been bestowed upon the Acadians in article 14 of the Treaty of Utrecht of 1713. Those who wished to leave were given a year in which to do so, but 'those who are willing to remain here, and to be subjects to the Kingdom of Great Britain, are to enjoy the free exercise of their religion according to the usage of the Church of Rome as far as the laws of Great Britain do allow the same' (Akins 1972: 14–15).

Selves, of course, do not need to be tolerated: no special provisions need to be made for them; they are not even *noticed*. It is only when one is in the presence of what appears to be intolerable difference that tolerance becomes necessary and, in many cases, manifests itself as a gloss on hidden resentments. This the Acadians seem to have understood all too well, complaining often to the King about their treatment over the next several decades, as a battle of Oaths of Loyalty, trade in corn, and religious dogma played itself out. The British tried to hammer their recalcitrant subjects into submission rather than neutrality, claiming that 'they have remained upon their possessions in contempt of the Government, waiting the opportunity of a rupture between the two Crowns to re-establish their former Government, and in the mean time are daily in secret, inciting the Indians to robbery and murder, to the destruction of trade and hindrance of settling the country' (Gov. Phillips to Lord Carteret, ca. 1720, in Akins 1972: 19). For their part, the Acadians continued to complain that they had 'preserved the purest sentiments of fidelity to our invincible monarch' and had not been treated fairly in return (letter of the inhabitants of Acadie to Mr St Ovide, 6 May 1720, in Akins 1972: 25).

Royal tolerance proved to be short-lived, and more drastic measures were soon sought. But first the ground had to be prepared, by way of much hand-wringing over the intractability of the Undesirable bodies. Governor Lawrence was one of the most vocal in proclaiming the lack of efficacy of kind treatment, basing his opinion, in the anthropological style, upon first-hand experience and intimate contact with the Other:

> [The Acadians] have long been the object of my most serious attention, which, with the frequent experience I have had of them in the course of my duty, has enabled me to form an opinion of them and their circumstances that I shall now take the liberty to lay fully before your Lordships, together with such measures as appear to me to be the most practicable

and effectual for putting a stop to the many inconveniences we have long
laboured under from their obstinacy, treachery, partiality to their own
Countrymen, and their ingratitude for the favor, indulgence and protection they have at all times so undeservedly received from His Majesty's
government. (Lawrence to Lords of Trade, 1 Aug. 1754, in Akins 1972:
213)

The ethnographic style of intimate, first-hand knowledge displayed in
Lawrence's text is important, as it shows how the Acadians, who were
obviously 'human' and at least relatively 'civilized,' came to be
increasingly differentiated from the British as a separate 'people.' Later
historians, such as Francis Parkman, have clumsily painted this over,
by claiming that the problem with the Acadians was that they were of
a different *race* (e.g., Parkman in Griffiths 1969: 41; Brebner in Griffiths
1969: 92) – but there is no evidence that this innovation in human differentiation had infiltrated the official British discourse of the time.
Governor Hopson could not tolerate the Acadians because they were
'so ignorant and so bigoted a people' (Hopson to Lords of Trade, July
1753, in Akins 1972: 199); the Lords of Trade wrote of the lack of an
Oath as 'an Obstacle to the Industry and Quiet of these People,' and
did not object to 'sending proper Persons amongst these People, to
endeavour to quiet them' (Lords of Trade to Gov. Lawrence, 4 March
1754, in Akins 1972: 207); Cotterell, acting Provincial Secretary, felt that
it was 'both unsafe & unprecedented to trust our cause in the Hands of
people of their Persuasion' (Cotterell to Capt. Scott, 12 April 1754, in
Akins 1972: 208). The construction of the Acadians as an intractable
Other, a 'people' who could not be exterminated, assimilated, or tolerated, culminated in official acceptance of the strategy recommended by
Lawrence, which was the same as that of the Council of Victors in 1710:
'it would be much better, if they refuse the Oaths, that they were away'
(Akins 1972: 213).

The results of this forcible removal are now on record in English
Canada, thanks to books like the *History of the Acadians* (Arsenault
1966). The Acadians were rounded up by British soldiers, and in the
confusion 'women were loaded onto ships other than the ones which
carried their husbands, and children became orphans forever at the
very point of embarkation' (1966: 143). Many were taken by disease
during the journey or enslaved upon their arrival.[1] Not in the realm of
'common knowledge' – and certainly excluded from the multiculturalist history of Acadia – is the story of Lawrence's campaign of destruc-

tion of the countryside, whereby he hoped to burn, scalp, or starve out those who had escaped being loaded onto the ships.[2] What was supposed to have been a relatively 'soft' transportation led, once again, to enslavement and extermination, justified by the problematic Otherness of a people who professed the wrong religion, spoke the wrong language, and thereby forfeited what would otherwise have been a claim to full humanity. The handling of the problem of Acadian diversity starkly demonstrated the futility of rational-bureaucratic management of problematic human Others, as it cycled through military conquest, failed assimilation, and failed tolerance, to revert to physical elimination and extermination via transportation.

With the capitulation of Quebec, the British were once again faced with the same problem and, rather stunningly, attempted exactly the same solution. Under the terms of the 'Fourth Article of the Definitive Treaty of Peace' (1763), they allowed that 'the French inhabitants ... may retire with all safety and freedom wherever they shall think proper ... and bring away their effects ... the term limited for this emigration shall be fixed to the space of eighteen months' (Maseres 1772: 85). Always resourceful, the British had not relied entirely upon this one method of managing problematic diversity. A form of religious tolerance was granted, in both the 1760 'Articles of Capitulation' (nos. 27–35, in Maseres 1772: 77–8) and in the 'Fourth Article of the Definitive Treaty of Peace' (84–5). As a counterweight, British laws and political institutions were enforced upon the French population by the famous Royal Proclamation of 1763. The stated goal of this dual policy was to bring about 'the absorption of the French nation by the English, which in matters of language, patriotism, law and religion is evidently what is most desirable and could perhaps be realized in one or two generations' (Maseres, cited in Bergeron 1975: 49). Thus, as in Acadia, the gifts of religious tolerance and liberal political institutions were bestowed as stop-gap measures intended to encourage assimilation in the long run.

As is well known, this policy also failed to achieve its goal, and so the British soon found themselves forced to take on signs of Frenchness. By way of the Quebec Act of 1774, the British officially 'established' hated French Popery in Quebec, allowing that 'the Clergy of the said Church may hold, receive, and enjoy, their accustomed Dues and Rights' (*Revised Statutes of Canada* [1985], Appendix, No. 2, Article V). A new oath was designed for Roman Catholics, so that they could become civil servants (Art. VII). The British also conceded that their laws might not be universally applicable, by decreeing that 'in all matters of Controversy, relative to Property and Civil Rights, Resort shall be had to the Laws of Canada' (Art. VIII). Of course, the King reserved the right to provide support for the Protestant clergy and the 'Encouragement of the Protestant Religion' (Art. VI), and British criminal law would stay in place (Art. XI). Taken together, these measures constituted the first attempt at *officially integrating* a problematic 'Canadian' population that could not be eliminated or assimilated, and set a precedent that would be followed, over the next two centuries, by each new group in an expanding ethnocultural economy.

The Emergence of the Two Founding Races

The Quebec Act was quickly passed into law, but it was not long before the American Revolution brought several thousand British 'loyalists' to the Province, thus exacerbating the rather paradoxical problem of British diversity in a British colony. These new Canadians had just fled from thirteen colonies that were becoming far too un-British for their liking; what a surprise to find themselves surrounded by Frenchness in their place of refuge! Like the English merchants who arrived to exploit New France after its Conquest by arms, the American Immigrants had high expectations for their new home; precisely, *they expected to assimilate it, rather than have it assimilate them.* Certainly this sort of behaviour would not have been tolerated if it had been displayed by any other 'minority group.' But this group received a sympathetic hearing from the Lieutenant Governor of the time:

> A principal object for the consideration of the Legislature is the arrival in this Province of numbers of Englishmen or the descendants of Englishmen who must abhor their being subjected to an authority they have been unacquainted with, and to men whose language & customs they are as yet strangers to. Provision by Law should be made to conciliate these people, and if possible prevent complaint by anticipating their grievances. (Hamilton to Sydney, April 1785, in *DRCHC*: 1.527)

Conciliation of the British-American Immigrants came in the form of the Constitutional Act of 1791. Canada was split into two large pieces, with one (Upper) space for those who identified with Britishness, and one (Lower) for those who preferred Frenchness. In its Preamble, the Constitutional Act noted that the Quebec Act had been found 'in many

Respects inapplicable to the present Conditions and Circumstances' of the Province (DRCHC: 1.696), and was therefore to be repealed. Of course, the Quebec Act was itself supposed to have been a solution to the problems created by the Royal Proclamation of 1763, which was intended to solve the problems of military rule. In its first thirty years, Canada had already gone through four constitutions.

But separate development was no solution, as was clearly shown by the violent rebellions, in both Canadas, of 1837–9. The fact that physical force had been necessary to keep down supposedly loyal colonial subjects attracted the attention of the British Parliament, which sent out Lord Durham to report on the state of affairs. As a 'High Commissioner,' Durham took it upon himself to bring about a quick, yet final, solution to a *crisis* situation, using language that is all too familiar to Canadians who have seen dozens of such commissions come and go. 'Every day during which a final and stable settlement is delayed, the condition of the Colonies becomes worse, the minds of men more exasperated, and the success of any scheme of adjustment more precarious' (Durham's *Report*, in Lucas 1912: 2.10). To fulfil his mandate, Durham provided yet another definition, and proposal for the solution, of the problem of Canadian diversity. In the Introduction to his report, he noted that his opinions on the Canadas had changed upon crossing the Atlantic. The common wisdom in England, which held that the problems were caused by inappropriate design and implementation of political institutions, was off the mark:

> I expected to find a contest between a government and two nations warring in the bosom of a single state: I found a struggle not of principles, but of races; and I perceived that it would be idle to attempt any amelioration of laws or institutions until we could first succeed in terminating the deadly animosity that now separates the inhabitants of Lower Canada into the hostile divisions of French and English. (2.16)

Thus the notion of *racial* difference lodged itself in official Canadian political discourse, playing the explanatory and causal role that had previously been allocated to the concepts of nation and people. Because of its genesis in natural history,[3] Durham was able to use race as a means of assuring himself, and his audience, that there was a scientific-transcendental 'cause' for the problem of Canadian diversity in the 'fact' of racial divisions, and the possibility that the hatred of the French for the English had something to do with the former's violent incorporation into the Empire did not have to be considered. It was all in the bodies, the 'blood' – it was *natural*.

If Durham was original in giving the problem of Canadian diversity a basis in race, he was not so innovative regarding the political course needed to achieve racial harmony. He was afraid to allow further integration of the French, or even to reconvene the Assembly of Lower Canada, which had been once again 'prorogued': 'In the present state of feeling among the French population, I cannot doubt that any power which they might possess would be used against the policy and very existence of any form of British government' (Lucas 1912: 2.306–7). Thus he conceived the idea that 'tranquillity can only be restored by subjecting the Province to the vigorous rule of an English majority; and that the only efficacious government would be that formed by a legislative union' (2.307). What was 'efficacious' was, as always, determined by the power-law of sign flow, now adapted to parliamentary rather than physical warfare. Durham did the numbers:

> If the population of Upper Canada is rightly estimated at 400,000, the English inhabitants of Lower Canada at 150,000, and the French at 450,000, the union of the two Provinces would not only give a clear English majority, but one which would be increased every year by the influence of English immigration; and I have little doubt that the French, when once placed, by the legitimate course of events and the working of natural causes, in a minority, would abandon their vain hopes of nationality. (2.307)

Durham felt that re-unification under more pleasant demographic circumstances than those which obtained in 1791 would lead to French assimilation and would 'at once decisively settle the question of races' (2.309).

Despite objections from both Upper and Lower Canada, the British centre accepted Durham's recommendation of re-unification. With uncharacteristic dispatch, the Union Act was passed, creating the Province of Canada and, it was hoped once again, solving forever the problem of Canadian diversity. We now know this to have been rather optimistic; being placed in a minority and having their language rights revoked did not diminish the national aspirations of French Quebec by any means – rather than solving the problem, re-unification just shifted and intensified it. The British desire to take and hold 'Canada,' however 'Canada' might be defined, has proven to be a source of endless problems and solutions, countless states of crisis, along with an infinity of commissions, legislation, and constitutional reforms, which have each time been trumpeted as the End of the Problem, and have always failed at providing any sort of solution at all. Already, by 1841, the full gamut of Old and New World strategies for the management of problematic internal Others had been applied to the French and found lacking. No new ideas seemed to be forthcoming; history, as is its wont, was beginning to repeat itself, in the form of failed, repetitive gestures, twitches of the British muscle brought on by frustrated ethnogenetic desire.

Rational-Bureaucratic Tutelage: The Indian Problem under British Rule

Established in small communities under the Jesuits and Recollets, acting as allies in war and the fur trade, and having proven themselves, under Pontiac, to be capable of successfully resisting the expansion of European civilization into their traditional lands, the Native peoples of the St Lawrence region – unlike the Beothuck of Newfoundland – could not be ignored by the new British regime. However, while they were definitely *seen* by the British, they were not seen as *equals*. To the British mind, the Indians were even more incapable of appreciating the subtleties of parliamentary democracy and capitalist entrepreneurship than the French. Thus they were to be *protected* from European depredation, as prescribed in the Royal Proclamation of 1763. This document, which we have encountered in the discussion of the 'French problem,' set aside a large 'reserve' for the use of the Indians, who were to function as semi-Useful external Others, according to the Hudson Bay model, but now under the legislated care of the King (*Revised Statutes of Canada* [1985], Appendix, No. 1).

Unfortunately, the protections offered by the British King and his bureaucratic apparatus turned out to be as ineffective as the edicts against killing Beothuck in Newfoundland, since the Proclamation also provided a *legal* means by which Native people could continue to be exploited and displaced:

> [I]f at any Time any of the Said Indians should be inclined to dispose of the said Lands, the same shall be Purchased only for Us, in our Name, at some public Meeting or Assembly of the said Indians, to be held for that purpose by the Governor Or Commander in Chief of our Colony respectively within which they shall lie. (128)

That master of the interlocking colonial system of law, politics, and capital accumulation, the famous Governor Simcoe, was able to carry out an expansion of the boundaries of the Euro-Canadian *ecumene* that was 'orderly and fully consistent with the dictates of the Proclamation' (Henderson 1980: 8). Thus the Native nations were driven further into what at first seemed to be a hinterland of infinite expanse, 'as settlement of the country advanced, and the land was required for new occupants, or the predatory and revengeful habits of the Indians rendered their removal desirable' ('Report on the Affairs of the Indians in Canada ... 1845' [*Bagot Report*]: 5).

The results of this expansion are well known and documented (Berger 1991; Cardinal 1969; Cumming and Mickenburg 1972; Henderson 1980; Leslie and Maguire 1978; Waubageshig 1970). With the rise of European self-sufficiency, the declining importance of the fur trade, and relative peace with the United States, the Native peoples on the margins of an expanding Canada were no longer needed in their traditional roles, and thus were progressively transformed from relatively Useful semi-external Others into a large, Useless, and problematic, *internal* population:

> You came as wind blown across the great Lake. The wind wafted you to our shores. We received you – we planted you – we nursed you. We protected you till you became a mighty tree that spread through our Hunting Land. With its branches you now lash us. (Mississauga Chief to William Graves, ca. 1820, in D.B. Smith 1989: 43)

British colonial policy now shifted again, to allow for the conversion, civilization, and eventual assimilation of those Native nations that had been '(p)reserved' and thereby reduced to a state of relative submission. In 1775 a 'Plan for the Future Management of Indian Affairs' divided British North America into two districts, each with a Superintendent of Indian Affairs and a number of deputies. The Superintendents were granted sole power to purchase lands, apply British civil and criminal laws, and appoint Indian leaders (*DRCHC*: 1.428). To control the body, one must also control the soul, and, as the Society for the Propagation of the Gospel was chased out of the United States by the American Revolution, it began to do this sacred work in the Canadas. In 1782 a missionary was sent to Six Nations at Niagara, and in 1784 to the Mohawk at Kingston. From 1820 to 1830 the reports and recommendations came thick and fast, as French experiments from the 1600s were repeated by the British: houses were built; missionaries and agricultural tools were sent out; and six Indian boys were placed in a school in Lower Canada (*Bagot Report*: 7). However, none of this activity had the desired effect, so that in 1836 Sir Francis Head declared the 'attempt to make farmers of the Red men has been generally speaking a complete failure' (Parliamentary Papers [1839]: 125; cited in *Bagot Report*: 11).

But this did not stop the rational-bureaucratic machine – it only spurred it on to further action. A flurry of legislation followed the Bagot Report, beginning with the 'Act for the Better Protection of the Lands and Property of the Indians in Lower Canada' (*Statutes of the Province of Canada*: 13 & 14 Victoria Cap. 41–2, 1850), and the 'Act for the Protection of the Indians in Upper Canada' in the same year (*Statutes of the Province of Canada*: 13 and 14 Victoria, c. 74). The Protection legislation, designed to keep the Indians in their assigned places as problematic internal Others, was soon followed by a complementary Civilization Act, which was supposed to make them less problematic. The 1857 'Act to Encourage the Gradual Civilization of the Indian Tribes' sought to 'encourage the progress of civilization among the Indian tribes ... and the gradual removal of all legal distinctions between them and Her Majesty's Canadian Subjects' (*Statutes of the Province of Canada*: 20 Victoria, Cap. 26, Preamble). As the writers of the Bagot Report noted, this expansion of the social space of the Canadas left the Native peoples in 'a state of tutelage, which although devised for their protection and benefit, has in the event proved very detrimental to their interests' (6).

Thus was the first bureaucratic machine for microcontrol of 'Canadian' lives instituted; a hybrid of British rational-legal authoritarianism and French paternalism, it survives to this day as the model of interaction between European and Native societies, and arguably is being extended to cover *all* individual-state relations. In commenting upon this system, Noel Dyck has described it as 'coercive tutelage,' or 'a form of restraint or care exercised by one party over another as well as the condition of being subjected to such protection or guardianship' (Dyck 1991: 24). He has also noted how the history of 'the Indian problem' has seen 'both active and passive modes of resistance,' which have 'served to validate the assumptions that underpin institutionalized tutelage. Indians' refusal to respect the authority of their tutors has been interpreted as a further sign of their confusion and inability to know what is best for them' (27). This refusal, of course, is used to justify a further round of futile activity. I would see this system of tutelage as an instance of what I have described, in chapter 2, as a self-reproducing problem-solution set based on proliferating rational-bureaucratic action. Just as the possibilities of handling the French had already been exhausted by the middle of the nineteenth century, the Indian problem was similarly set in its groove and showing signs of desperate, imitative reproduction.

To summarize this section, as Canada became British the discursive position of the Savage – uncivilized, Useless, external, monstrous Other – gave way to that of the Indian under tutelage – the semi-wild, Useless, internal, inferior but definitely *human* Other. This period saw a shift from past methods of ignorance and physical elimination by extermination to softer forms of physical elimination, involving orderly, legal displacement. When the limits of displacement were reached, the Indian was then acknowledged to be 'inside,' placed on reservations and subjected to various forms of rational-bureaucratic management designed to eliminate *signs* of difference via assimilation. In this way, the British adopted methods pioneered by the French, and added a gloss of 'due process' to make them all seem quite proper and legal. The British also used Canada to further develop their early experience with the micro-management of distant lands and peoples via the Hudson's Bay Company. Out of this confluence of early French and British methods of managing human diversity, there emerged a particularly Canadian form of paternalistic rational-legal domination – through integration and administration – that has come to define, more than any other characteristic, the Canadian Way.

Group Identity in British Canada

In this chapter I have shown how, from the eighteenth century on, the British reorganized their systems of human differentiation and management to adjust to the problems of diversity created by their expanding empire. It was no longer a question, as in the early colonial era, of dealing with – or ignoring – semi-human, semi-civilized, semi-Useful external Others; the Others were now internal as well as external, Civilized as well as Savage, and very obviously existing and present. Thus, with the rise of British control over the territories that would become known as Canada, there was a compensating shift in the discourse of identity, to make way for the Second Others of the New World: the *Canadiens*. Just as the French in New France were shifted from the posi-

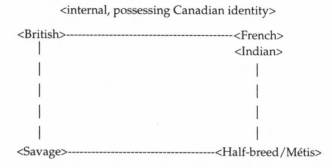

Fig. 5.1. Group identity in British Canada

tion of external Others to internal Selves, the contained Savage became the Indian and moved from the complementary position to the contrary. In the territories exploited by the Hudson's Bay Company, the emergence of British–Native Half-breeds added to the problem of contradiction attributed to the French hybrids. The particular shifts that occurred as Canada became British can be inscribed on the square of <group identity> in British Canada (fig. 5.1).

I have suggested that, despite these efforts, the British were unable to solve the problems they set for themselves, and fell into a stupor of imitative reproduction that lingers to the present day. But this 'failure' was, paradoxically, also a success, as it ensured that the problem of Canadian diversity would *multiply*, that those who declared the necessity of ever more intrusive methods of population management could justify their practice. The British failure to solve the problem of Canadian diversity ensured that the discourse itself would live on, as an adaptive, self-reproducing, public problem-solution set, to Conquer new regions of space, time, and individual-group identity. For, just as the French were brought inside and put under tutelage, so were the Indians, and so, with the passage of time, would be *all* who allowed themselves to be called Canadians.

Chapter Six

The Dominion of Canada and the Proliferation of Immigrant Otherness

The virgin soil, the primeval forest, and the teeming seas and lakes and rivers all possess undeveloped riches. Man alone is apparently the missing quantity, and his energy, industry and capital are the required elements in developing this young, but sturdy Dominion into the Greater Britain of the West – the worthy scion of the grand old Motherland across the seas, whose pride is in the colonial gems which adorn the imperial diadem, of which Canada is one of the brightest and most valued jewels.

> – Preface, *The New West* (Canadian Historical Publishing Co. 1888)

This chapter tracks the emergence of 'Canada' proper, that is, the state form which, from its base within the British colonies, extended its regime of striation until it claimed a right to govern half the continent. As I will show in the following sections, the Canadians self-consciously set out to create and maintain an 'empire,' drawing strategies from both the ancient European discourse on diversity and its New World adaptations. Their first adventure was the military invasion of the Red River region, which was followed by the deployment of a civilian force to shift the balance of the population towards a British-Canadian majority. But this plan, like all before it, came off miserably, and only succeeded in bringing on the greatest proliferation ever seen in the discourse on diversity, through the rise of dozens of categories of non-British, Immigrant Others.

This profusion of new identities quickly overwhelmed the system of classification the Canadians had inherited. The Great Chain of Being, based on humanity and civilization, could neither differentiate between various types of Immigrant, nor adequately separate the Immigrants from proper Canadians. In response, there emerged the Great Chain of Race, a creative confluence of Herodotan ethnography, European natural history, and North American social science, which I will present as it is found in the work of J.S. Woodsworth. Along with this new means of classifying human diversity, there arose new attempts at solving the problems it created. After toying with transportation and assimilation, the Canadians began to make use of the unique characteristics of the Immigrant – his qualities of having *come from afar* and of being *in transition* – to evolve the methods of deportation, disenfranchisement, and internment. For those who had not already found their way 'inside,' immigration laws were used to try to ensure the *exclusion* of individuals identified with groups considered 'Undesirable.' In this way, the English-Canadian state creatively responded to the proliferating problem of diversity created by its desire – perpetually unattained – for unity, identity, and the status of Great Nation.

Clearing the 'Empty' West

The origin myth of Canadian Confederation suggests that Canada was founded by an agreement between four provinces, which were 'joined' by other groups and individuals later on.[1] This myth has been challenged by writers such as Howard Adams (1995) and Himani Bannerji (1996), who argue, respectively, that 'Aboriginal' and 'Immigrant' are colonized identities within the purview of the Canadian state. It is interesting to note that certain contemporaries of the 'Fathers of Confederation' were in agreement with what has now become a 'radical' stance. Canadian Rev. A.M. Dawson, in a lecture delivered to the Mechanics' Institute of Ottawa in 1864, declared that 'every people, when they have reached a certain degree of power and renown, ought to aim at possessing colonial dependencies' (Dawson 1870: 45). William Norris echoed this sentiment and invoked both ancient and modern European antecedents as a guide for the future of Canada:

> Every known nation at present in being ... has at first been a colony ... In ancient history, the nation the most famous in war, in oratory and art ... was Greece. That this nation was once a colony, it is not necessary to

prove. The same may be said of Rome ... but the precedent which ... more particularly concerns the inhabitants of this country, is that of England – the motherland ... At first the attempt to colonize the Island was made from Rome, and it is more than probable that the Romans laid the foundations of those great institutions which have since been the means of England's greatness. (Norris 1875: 27–8)

Driven by visions of the glory of empire, those who identified with the new Dominion invoked the European dictum of *terra nullius* to construct the space they desired as empty, unstriated, and therefore fair game. Henry Hind, sent out on an 'Assiniboine and Saskatchewan Exploring Expedition' by the Province of Canada in 1858, reported on the 'vast unpeopled wastes – often beautiful and rich, often desolate and barren – of the great North-West' (Hind 1859: 1). *The New West*, a pro-colonization pamphlet published in Winnipeg in 1888, described the Northwest as containing 'countless thousands of leagues of territory on which the foot of man has never trod, lying tenantless and silent' (Canadian Historical Publishing Co. 1888: Preface).

Finding 'empty' land, however, was only half the battle. According to E.G. Wakefield's influential pronouncements on British colonial policy, 'the elements of colonization' were 'waste land' *and* 'the removal of people,' that is, an inward flow of Europeans to fill the empty land (Wakefield 1929: 30). In an 1876 report, the Commander of the Canadian Militia showed that he had read up on his colonial theory:

The appointment of magistrates, and encouragement of missionary labour are questions also becoming prominent in the dawning development of that noble territory, not long ago only known to the wild Indians of the mountain, the forest, and the prairie, to the dissipated, nomadic half-breed, and to the hardy trapper, but now silently and patiently awaiting the approach of the immense wave of human life which must shortly overrun the fair and productive soil of those remote and beautiful solitudes. (Report of Major Selby Smyth, cited in Canada 1876: 131)

While these dreams of striating an apparently empty space were quite in keeping with building an empire on the Roman-British model, there were some difficulties to be overcome. Here Smyth's and Dawson's vision of an empty land awaiting 'human' settlement are telling, for as Smyth's own text notes, this space was already the home of a number of Native nations, Métis settlements, Hudson's Bay Company forts, and, of course, the Red River colony. This was not an exceptional case, in Canada or elsewhere. It seems that everywhere the Europeans went, the 'waste' lands turned out to be occupied. There was, therefore, an element missing from Wakefield's formula for colonization: before the 'waste' lands could be populated, they had to be de-populated; that is, their emptiness had to be constructed in colonial practice so as to correspond to colonial theory. The proven way to do this was to remove from the existing bodies their possession of full human subjectivity by setting them up as Others to the colonizer's Self.

In the case of the Canadians and the Indians of the Northwest, the means of differentiation, and a method appropriate to it, were already at hand in the form of the myth of the doomed Savage:

> The policy of peace and protection towards the Indians has proved a wise one. It has *cost far less* than the aggressive policy of the United States towards the tribes within their boundaries ... For the sake of our own interests, if not from pity for a race destined apparently to extinction, we should deal with these Indian tribes kindly, and let them pass from the world unstained by the shedding of English blood. (Charles Marshall, *The Canadian Dominion*, cited in Canada 1876: 117, 130; emphasis added)

While there were proven methods in place for dealing with the Indians, the difficulties presented by the people of the Red River settlement posed a problem as yet unsolved by any colonial power. Emitting contradictory signs of all of the identities within the system of human difference the Canadians inherited from the British (see the previous chapter), the settlement was too Savage to be tolerated and too European to be destroyed. In the report of an 1857 expedition, the writers were overjoyed to Discover 'attractive and substantial' Christian churches, as well as a church and school where 'the congregation appeared to be exclusively Indian; in their behaviour they were most decorous and attentive' (Canada 1858: 332). But they also felt compelled to give their impressions of the 'darker' side:

> On two Sundays during my stay, at the time when Divine service was being celebrated in all the churches of the settlement, the heathen Indians held their dog feasts and medicine dances on the open plain. [T]he evil spirit was invoked, the conjurer's arts used to inspire his savage spectators with awe ... (333–4)

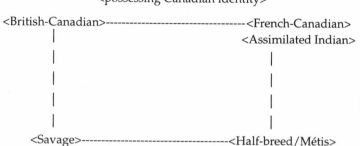

Fig. 6.1. Group identity in Canadian colonial discourse

How could the local Christians stand it? To the Canadians, this could only be the result of the impure blood that flowed through their veins:

> These hardy and fearless children of the prairie [the Half-breeds] constitute a race ... endowed with remarkable qualities ... It is, however, much to be regretted that ... many of them are fast subsiding into the primitive Indian state; naturally improvident, and perhaps indolent, they prefer the wild life of the prairies to the tamer duties of a settled home; this is the character of the majority, and belongs more to those of French descent than of Scotch or English origin. (353)

This passage shows the full scope and force of the Canadian adaptation of the British colonial discourse on diversity. Both the British Half-breeds and French Métis were set apart as separate races, and were simultaneously held to be inferior in humanity and civilization, with the French hybrid appearing as even more inhuman and uncivilized than the British. Lowest of all on the Great Chain of Race were the unassimilated Native nations who, being in the way of the Canadians, seemed to have 'regressed' from the days of the Hudson's Bay Company and, once again, were being named as Savages. Except for the addition of 'Canadian' to the tail end of 'British' and 'French,' the semiotic square and hierarchical ordering of Canadian group identity was taken over directly from the British colonial regime.

The 1857 Report made use of the hierarchy implicit in the separation of these groups in assuring its readers that the sorry state of the settlement was not the fault of the land. The few Full-breed Europeans who were there had managed to produce all the signs necessary for a Canadian to feel at home: 'Mr. Gowler, Mr. Gladieux, Mr. Flett, the McKays, and several others that might be named ... farm with industry and economy' (360). All that was needed, then, was to move out the Savages and hybrids so the pure stock could move in. There was, however, a problem. In the interval between the transfer of control over their lives from the Hudson's Bay Company to the Dominion of Canada, the people of the Red River settlement had set up their own government. As had the Iroquois confederacy and the *coureurs de bois* before them, they were striating their own space, and appeared to have at their disposal the means of defending that space against violent intrusion, as they had shown in preventing the Canadian-appointed Governor from entering the area. They were also able to express themselves in a style that showed fluency with the civilized humanist discourse that was being used to justify their displacement:

> Whereas, it is admitted by all men, as a fundamental principle, that the public authority commands the obedience and respect of its subjects. It is also admitted, that a people when it has no Government, is free to adopt one form of Government, in preference to another, to give or to refuse allegiance to that which is proposed ... [W]e refuse to recognize the authority of Canada, which pretends to have a right to coerce us ... ('Declaration of the People of Rupert's Land and the North-West,' 8 Dec. 1869, in Oliver 1914: 904–6)

Casting this resistance to invasion as a 'rebellion,' the Canadians sent in troops as soon as they could. They also incorporated many of the demands of the Red River Provisional Government into the Manitoba Act of 1870 (33 Vic. c. 3), which attached a hopefully tamed new province to the Dominion. Manitoba was presented to the Métis as a guarantee of their rights and lands and was supposed to 'extinguish' Half-breed title (Article 31). But, as in the case of the Indian reserves under the 1857 Civilization Act, the Half-breed Homeland was designed to self-destruct. This time the method was not enfranchisement, but the scrip system, through which Half-breed adults and children were issued certificates that could be redeemed in land or money. Individual and institutional capitalists from Canada were quick to grasp this opportunity to put their capital to work by buying up scrip certificates at discount prices. According to Donald McLean, a Métis historian, 'the chartered banks were the largest dealers in scrip throughout the Northwest territories, purchasing about 60% of all scrip sold' (McLean 1987: 108). Research done by the Métis and Non-Status Indians of Saskatchewan has shown that '90 per cent of scrip certificates ended up in the hands of bankers, lawyers and merchants, bought at prices ranging from 25 to 33 per cent of face value' (cited in Purich 1988: 116–17). Dispossessed of their land by the Canadians, many of the Métis of the Red River region moved further north and west, hoping to escape the strange machinations that the gifts of civilization and representative government had brought to them.

As the existing people of Manitoba were cleared out or contained, Canada was able to begin importing Anglo-Saxons, following the plan of 'a conquest and military rule, until a Canadian immigration can outvote the present inhabitants' (Taylor to Fish, 27 April 1870, in Stanley 1961: 132). John A. Macdonald felt that 'these impulsive Métis have got spoilt by the *émeute* [uprising] and must be kept down by a strong hand until they are swamped by the influx of settlers' (Macdonald to John Rose, 23 Feb. 1870, cited in McLean 1987: 105). And so they soon were. The 1870 census of Manitoba showed that the population of 11,963 was divided into 9,840 'Half-breeds' and 558 'Christian Indians,' as opposed to 1,565 'Whites' ('Abstract Statement of Census,' *SPHC* [1871], no. 20: 92). Fifteen years later, the situation looked quite different. The total population according to the 1885–6 census was 108,640, and the 'blood' ratios were radically altered (StatsCan 1887: 7). The province was bigger now, and Indians and Half-breeds were counted whenever they could be found, but even so there were only 7,985 people who claimed to be Half-breeds, and 5,575 Indians, for a total of 13,560 non-White bodies. The White population, however, had increased dramatically, to about 84,000, or 80 per cent of the population.

Ironically, the displacement of the people of the 'empty' Northwest, while it achieved a short-term goal, had the long-term effect of exacerbating the problem of Canadian diversity. The initial invasion of 1870, and subsequent attempts at legislating away the Half-breeds and Indians, caused a series of displacements that led to further violent confrontations in 1885, which in their turn have left a legacy of disputes to this day. There was, and continues to be, much debate over the means by which the displacement of the Métis and Indians was carried out. Was it moral? More importantly for Canadians who share the New World obsession with the bottom line, was it legal? Will the government have to dole out more blankets, pouches of tobacco, tractors, and, now, millions of dollars in cash? These questions linger, but are of greater importance at the end of the twentieth century than they were at the end of the nineteenth, when it appeared that colonial practice had finally caught up to colonial theory. Moving steadily outward from their base in Manitoba, the Canadians quickly cleared out or contained the Half-breeds and Indians, so that by the 1890s all of the Northwest was 'awaiting only the advent of the Anglo-Saxon race to be transformed into a prosperous and thriving country' (Canadian Historical Publishing Co. 1888: Preface).

An Explosion of Racial Subject-Positions

Unfortunately for the ambitious new nation, filling the Northwest with the Anglo-Saxon race proved to be much more difficult than clearing out the existing inhabitants. It was obvious from the beginning that this task would require many more Canadians than presently existed and were willing to leave Central Canada, and so the politicians and businessmen in Ottawa looked to immigration to help make up the difference. To this end, two pieces of legislation were put in place: the Immigration Act of 1869 (32–3 Vic. c. 10); and the Dominion Lands Act of 1872 (35 Vic. c. 23). The purpose of the Immigration Act, as gleaned from its explicit inclusions and exclusions, was to open Canada to healthy, wealthy, Anglo-Saxon bodies.[2] In order to provide places for these bodies, the Dominion Lands Act required that those parts of Manitoba and the Northwest Territories which were not currently being used by Anglo-Saxons be carved up into squares – agriculturally striated – and offered up to chosen Immigrants for free, provided they made certain 'improvements' to the land within three years (Section 33). Under the direction of the Department of the Interior, which replaced the Hudson's Bay Company as the apparatus of distant microcontrol in what was now the Canadian Northwest, these two acts set up the legal means by which colonization by proper British-Canadian types could proceed.

   In the 1870s, the ships' manifests used to record statistics on Immigrants had only four categories of 'Nationality': English, Scotch, Irish, and Foreigners (NAC, RG 76, series C.1, books 16–24). These forms reflected the British-Canadian hope for Immigrants from the Old Country, and the lack of any perceived need to differentiate among those few who might come from elsewhere. That hope was quickly dashed, however, as ships began arriving with 400 out of 500 passengers listed as Foreigners, mostly with names like Pedersen, Larsen, and

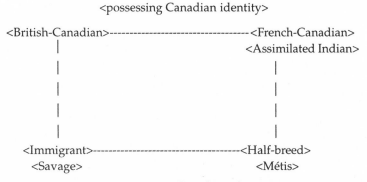

Fig. 6.2. Group identity in Canada, 1870s to early 1900s

Andersen. Immigration officers tried to make up for the lack of an officially supplied category by writing in 'Scandinavian' as a 'Nationality,'
but the system was soon expanded to include English, Irish, Scotch,
American citizens, Germans, Scandinavians, French and Belgians,
Mennonites, Icelanders, and Other Countries (NAC, RG 26, series C1,
vol. 25, book 2). These immigration numbers are notoriously 'unreli-
able,'[3] but whatever their value as an objective measure of diversity,
they clearly contributed to the creation of an entirely new subject-posi-
tion – that of the Immigrant, the non-British, non-French, non-Indian
internal Other.

In 1896, Clifford Sifton took over the Department of the Interior,
after having promised in his election campaign to overhaul the system
and solve the Immigrant problem. But his regime also failed to secure a
sufficient supply of Desirable bodies, claiming that while 'the British
immigrant is by far the more desirable ... the difficulty is, that in Great
Britain ... there is only about one million people all told, who are
engaged in agricultural pursuits ... It is therefore necessary to look to
other countries' (JHC [1900], v. 35, App. 1: 308). From this point on, the
official line was that anyone who could till the land could be a Canadian: 'Our desire is to promote the immigration of farmers and farm
labourers. We have not been disposed to exclude foreigners of any
nationality who seemed likely to become successful agriculturalists'
(Sifton to Laurier, 1901, cited in Knowles 1997: 62). While it is true that
the Anglo-only policy was largely abandoned, Canada was not really
accepting 'any nationality.' Sifton's policy was clearly oriented to find-

ing agriculturalists who were, if not Anglo-Saxon, at least European, and therefore second best.[4] Another innovation of Sifton's regime was the easing of regulations regarding block settlement of Immigrants. There were, in 1896, thirty-six such settlements, comprising over 37,000 people, mostly German and Russian Mennonites, along with some Eastern Europeans (*SPHC* [1897], no. 13: 124–5). Sifton's department altered the established policy by allowing more and larger settlements of Doukhobors attempting to escape Old World religious persecution in the New, and by admitting 'Galicians' – a catch-all category for anyone appearing to be from eastern Europe – attempting a similar improvement in their material well-being.

While the Department of the Interior tried to present these policy changes as improvements, the people of Canada were quick to notice that although the new Immigrants might be 'European,' they were clearly not 'Canadian.' Yet another attempt to solve the problem of diversity had only served to exacerbate it, as was immediately apparent in the House of Commons. As soon as Sifton's Deputy Minister, James Smart, had revealed that his ministry was 'looking to other countries' than Great Britain, the Select Committee on Immigration turned to a discussion of the 'comparative value' of immigration from these 'other countries.' From this discussion, a clear picture of the hierarchical arrangement of Immigrant identities emerges. American settlers were classified 'next to the British settlers – if not equal or in some instances superior' (*JHC* [1900], v. 35, App. 1: 309); Germans were seen as quite Desirable, although difficult to acquire. Belgium was considered to be too small, and the Swedes seemed to prefer the United States. Russia was possessed of a great stock of 'desirable classes' but, like Germans, they were hard to come by.

The discussion then turned to the Doukhobors, who were the only people – besides nihilists and anarchists – with whom the Russian government was willing to part. Whereas the Committee had been content to listen quietly to the Deputy Minister's exposition concerning the previous groups, now the questions began to fly. Five hundred Doukhobors had come to Canada. Where were they now? Was it true that they were leaving for the United States? Next, and even more problematic, came the Galicians, lumped in with the Doukhobors as fast-breeding Undesirables:

Q. Do the Doukhobors and Galicians have large families?
A. I think so, yes ...

Q. I have a statement from a party in the locality where the Doukhobors are that where they have settled the land has gone down in value, as Canadians do not like to settle there but sell out and leave. Do you know anything of that?
A. ... It may be so, I won't say. (*JHC* [1900], v. 35, App. 1: 319–20)

Both in and out of Parliament, the dawning understanding that they had failed to realize the fantasy of Anglo-Saxon purity incited fear, rage, and civil disobedience in British-Canadians, which was acted out upon those whom they saw as the source of the problem. In the Prairies, it was the Doukhobors and Galicians who took most of the blows. Under the title 'Misfit Immigration,' the *Calgary Herald* took on Sifton and Smart directly, calling the recent report of the Select Standing Committee 'one of the most amusing books of the season, as funny as Three Men in a Boat and as pathetic as Dodo':

What is this country coming to? Doukhobors pouring in by thousands on the eastern slope, Galicians swarming over the central portions, and rats taking possession of Dawson City, one would imagine that Canada has become a veritable dumping ground for the refuse of civilization. (*Calgary Herald*, 1 Feb. 1899)[5]

In British Columbia, which Canada acquired in 1871, nativism took the form of a particularly virulent anti-Asian sentiment. All of the rhetorical stops were pulled out in the attack on the Chinese, as seen in an address to the 1902 Royal Commission on Chinese and Japanese Immigration, which invoked a litany of all the modes of differentiation available to construct a stupid, inhuman, uncivilized Other:

The foundation of all social order is based upon a vigorous and intelligent people and the state cannot long endure whose foundation rests not upon those of its own race and kind, but upon a race not only alien in so far as their birth is concerned, but of a different type of humanity and civilization ... who do not assimilate with us, who would not if they could, and who could not if they would ... (Evidence of C. Wilson, *SPHC* [1902], no. 54: 282)

Several thousand petitioners for Oriental exclusion announced their devotion to the high principles of British-Canadian nationalism, declaring that 'it is in the interests of the Empire that the Pacific province of the Dominion should be occupied by a large and thoroughly British population rather than by one in which the number of aliens would form a large proportion' (279). To show that they were serious, the Canadians of British Columbia took it upon themselves to solve the problem of Asian Otherness by a series of attacks on people and property, culminating in the infamous riot of 1907.[6]

Canadian nativism was not, however, a purely English-Canadian phenomenon. French nationalism was as strong as ever, and its adherents also had their concerns about the racial content of the Northwest. Henri Bourassa, for example, accepted the empty land thesis, and the basic tenets of Canadian expansionism. But his imaginary Northwest differed in one very important respect from that of British Canada:

> [W]hen they [the fathers of Confederation] considered ... those virgin lands, when they threw open to civilization those immense territories which had theretofore been only the domain of the Indian and the buffalo, what was the idea which dominated their minds? It was to introduce there an idea that would include both nationalities, to introduce an idea that would bring together the French and the English; it was to create there a British colony, but also an Anglo-French alliance that would endure for all time. (*DHC*, 28 March 1905: 8588)

While the British might not have been winning the demographic battle in the Northwest, they were not losing it as badly as the French. Already, Bourassa had noted that the pattern of immigration was again making it possible to use 'democracy' to further marginalize the French in Canada:

> The Solicitor General, I was sorry to hear, made an argument this afternoon that because the French Canadians are less numerous in the Northwest than the Germans, or the Scandinavians, or the Doukhobors, there is no reason to grant us the official use of the French language. (*DHC*, 28 March 1905: 8588)

Despite having different ideas about what they had founded, there was a rather unusual level of agreement between the Two Founding Races that incoming Otherness was a threat to their existence. Each race felt its hold on its Homeland declining, and the Northwest, rather than becoming British and/or French, was once again refusing to follow design parameters and giving rise to all manner of emergent forms. To French-Canadian nationalism, this meant an intensification of the minority status of French language and culture outside Quebec, and another reason to fear the loss of an existing, but always threatened, identity. For English Canada, the situation was a little different; rather than worrying about *protecting* an identity, there was a fear of *never achieving* one. Through its failure to acquire pre-striated Self bodies through immigration, and its 'success' in escalating the number of types of Immigrant Other to seventy-nine by 1903 (NAC, RG 26, series C1, vol. 26, book 3), English Canada dealt itself a wound that continues to fester to this day.

Restoring Order: J.S. Woodsworth and the Great Chain of Race

What was to be done? A 'flood' of lectures, articles, and books poured out into the Symbolic, in the hope of countering the Imaginary flow of incoming Otherness – the problem of Canadian diversity had come into its own. 'Canada is today the Mecca of the world's emigration,' R.G. MacBeth declared, 'and those who are coming are by no means immigrants like ... the early settlers in the Province of Ontario, or the Maritime Provinces or the Red River country, who took no rest till they had erected churches and schools and colleges ... For the most part those who have been coming in recent years are of inferior races and lower civilizations' (MacBeth 1912: 20–1). R.G. Macpherson, Liberal MP for Vancouver, agreed with MacBeth, and pushed the proud lineage of Canada's Foundational Stock back to ancient Rome:

> The men who built up this country, who hewed homes out of the forest, were men of first class, A1 stock, and the responsibility they left us is great. The sentiment expressed in the proud phrase, *Civis Romanus sum*, becomes the citizen of Canada as well as it became the citizen of Rome. A race of men who cannot appreciate our mode of life, our mode of education, all that goes to make up Canadian citizenship, are not fit immigrants of this country. (Cited in Ward 1978: 84)

'These indeed are perilous times,' intoned Arthur Hawkes in *The Birthright* (1919). 'Those who suppose that dangers can be overcome by prophesying smooth things concerning them will find no lullabies here. If we daren't be frank we had better be dead' (xvii).

One of the first, and most famous, to sound the alarm was J.S. Woodsworth, in his very popular *Strangers within Our Gates* (1972a

[1909]). I have chosen to treat this text in detail as it displays a fascinating – and influential – confluence of discursive forms: Herodotan ethnography is revived and applied to the study of Immigrants as *internal* Others; European racialism, with its hierarchy of White, Yellow, Black, and Red, finds a permanent home in Canada;[7] North American social science, with its charts, graphs, tables, and diagrams, is deployed to highlight the objective-natural quality of the problem of Canadian diversity; and the discourses of socialism and the social gospel provide a bias towards the use of the institutions of the state and civil society to solve the problem of Immigrant diversity. *Strangers within Our Gates* is also a valuable compendium of the work of a number of writers, brought in to give their opinions on various issues and immigrant groups, and thus represents a cross-section of 'informed opinion' at the time.[8]

Woodsworth's goal, as stated in the Preface, was to 'introduce the motley crowd of immigrants to our Canadian people and to bring before our young people some of the problems of population with which we must deal in the very near future' (9). Much of the book is devoted to a discussion of the relevant characteristics of this amorphous heap of problematic Others, taking on both the method of Herodotan ethnography and its obsession with the seven categories of cultural fact: place of residence and climate, language, dress, food, dwellings, religion, and political organization. The categories were updated where necessary, but there can be little doubt that, as the problem of Canadian diversity expanded in size and scope, the ancient methods of cataloguing diversity were revived and put to productive use.

'Country of Origin' – with the usual confusion of races and places – provides the main structure for the presentation of subjects in *Strangers within Our Gates*, standing in quite easily for place of residence when the Others are inside rather than out. In its presumed influence upon character, climate also plays its ancient role: 'taken all in all there is no class of immigrants that are as certain of making their way in the Canadian West as the people of the peninsula of Scandinavia,' Woodsworth proclaims. 'Accustomed to the rigours of a northern climate ... they will be certain of success in this pioneer country' (77). Language is also invoked as a means of discrimination, with four pages (92–6) devoted to a table giving the 'linguistic differences and affinities' of the European races. J.C. Speer, Woodsworth's correspondent in 'Chinatown,' found it 'pleasing to hear words of our own tongue' from the 'little strangers' – children – he met there. 'One is reminded that some of them are as much Canadian as are we of Anglo-Saxon speech' (145). Speer found further evidence of strangeness in the Chinese mode of dress: 'the Chinese ladies wear no head covering, but seem to find their chief pleasure in the most elaborate toilet' (146). Finally, eating habits come under his scrutiny and, as in the ancient and medieval cosmographies, the descriptions sometimes veer into the fantastic: '[The Chinese] are by no means vegetarians, as so many people believe, but they can live on rice exclusively when it is necessary to do so' (147). This is surely a feat worthy of the Apple-Sniffers and Lotus-Eaters of yore!

The religious and political propensities of Woodsworth's Others also merit frequent comment. The arrangements adapted by the Mormon communities are given a great deal of attention, since Woodsworth feared that the 'octopus of Mormonism' was reaching out from Salt Lake City to grasp hold of Canada (66). After enumerating the many heresies of the Mormons, Woodsworth declares that 'these doctrines are obviously inconsistent with the teaching of Christianity,' and can only lead to 'the end of all free government' (71). In the allusion to ignorance of the value of a hat, in the assumption that English words are the only Canadian words, that rice is not a Canadian food, that the principles of British liberalism and European self-determination are the only valid form of political organization, we see at work the Herodotan trope of implicit comparison with a standard assumed to be shared with the reader, but not with the object, of the text. Neither Woodsworth nor Speer was expecting his words to be read by a Chinese woman or a Mormon bishop, but intended them only for a hidden, Invisible Self group which he identified as 'normal.'

Without doubt, Woodsworth was reproducing ancient prejudices. But his reproduction was creative, as it introduced certain metaphors, theories, and methods that have had a profound influence on the twentieth-century discourse on Canadian diversity. For example, he and his colleagues helped adapt the ancient system to a modern world motivated increasingly by, or shall we say obsessed with, the achievements of *science*. Following the lead of government bureaucrats, and preparing the ground for the later contributions of professional ethnic demographers, *Strangers within Our Gates* makes copious use of tables showing the numbers of people arriving in Canada, arranged according to 'birthplace,' 'race,' and 'nationality,' thereby providing 'concrete' evidence of the existence of the problem of Canadian diversity. To help convince the reader that the problem is getting worse, the tables are placed in chronological order, so that even the most doubtful can see the distressing trends. No Bulgarians at all arrived in 1900, but each year after, with the exception of only 1904, the numbers steadily increase: 1, 7, 14, 2, 71, 896, 1802 (23). 'Figures talk' (17), Woodsworth declares, then abruptly backs off from his own empiricism: 'if only we could read into these figures their real meaning!' (22).

While it might have been hard to read the 'real' meaning of social-scientific tabulations, it was relatively easy to use them to magnify the Immigrant problem until it took on the proportions of a crisis. For this purpose, the text makes use of the Flood metaphor for incoming diversity, which I have discussed in chapter 2. The Flood is invoked incessantly by Woodsworth and the other contributors, providing a sort of *basso continuo* that underlies and sustains the rhetoric of the text. It first appears in Sparling's introduction, as quoted above, with a reference to 'the incoming tides of immigrants.' Then, in the introductory section, 'Immigration – a World Problem' (attributed to WHELPLEY [sic]), the Flood metaphor is applied to immigration from 'the remote and little known regions of northern, eastern, and southern Europe: Like a mighty stream, it finds its source in a hundred rivulets. The huts of the mountains and hovels of the plains are the springs which feed; the fecundity of the races of the Old World the inexhaustible source' (13).[9] At the end of the second chapter, the Flood metaphor is again invoked, to put to an end any doubt that 'we' are facing a problem of great importance: 'We have entered a new era in our history. The immigrants are upon us! For good or ill, the great tide is turning our way, and is destined to continue to pour in upon us' (29).

The utility of charts and tables is not exhausted in providing objective 'proof' that a mass of problematic Others is threatening the Nation; they can also be used to *organize* this mass according to a system of categories. These categories can act as a series of dykes, keeping the Flood at bay; or perhaps, better yet, as *channels*, directing the flow into productive tasks, such as the construction of known and manageable identities. For, once the identities and differences have been worked out, the 'tide' does not seem so amorphous and frightening: it can be seen to contain 439 Chinese, 1,200 Ruthenians, 4 Quakers, and so on, ad infinitum, until every last shred of difference has been accounted for.

We have, of course, encountered this will to exhaustive naming before – in the principle of plenitude that accompanies the Great Chain of Being. It, like Herodotan ethnography, reappeared in Canada at the start of the twentieth century, taking a form I refer to as the Great Chain of Race, which structured thought, action, and even the table of contents of Woodsworth's book. Reading its chapters, one descends the Chain from pinnacle to base, following the contours given by Linnaeus's *Systema Naturae* (1740). In the final version of his taxonomy, Linnaeus included humanity, under the classifications *Europaeus albus*, *Americanus rubescens*, *Asiaticus fuscus*, and *Africanus niger*. These categories were put into an explicit hierarchy of human-ity and civilization by LeBon, viz. White, Yellow, Black, and Red (Todorov 1993: 107 ff). Again, Woodsworth was not doing something entirely unheard of in Canada. The order he presented followed that given in the reports of the Department of the Interior from 1896 on. But he was innovative in his ability to lay out the entire structure and justify its arrangement, with the sort of meticulous attention to com-pleteness and detail that one would expect from a modern social sci-entist following in the footsteps of medieval natural historians and ancient Greek philosophers.

The discussion begins with 'Immigrants from Great Britain,' who are the most Desirable type for Woodsworth's vision – which he assumes is shared with his reader – of a White Anglo-Saxon Protestant Canada. The British are 'among our best citizens' since they bring with them 'more of our own blood,' and can 'assist us to maintain in Canada our British traditions and to mould the incoming armies of foreigners into loyal British subjects' (46). Next on Woodsworth's scale, and in keep-ing with the official government line, are Immigrants from the United States. 'Desirable settlers? Yes' (65). These are followed closely by the Scandinavians – 'they easily assimilate with the Anglo-Saxon peoples and readily intermarry' (76). Next come the Germans, who are 'among our best immigrants' (84). 'Even those who detest foreigners make an exception of Germans, whom they classify as "white people like our-selves"' (84). Woodsworth places 'The French' fifth on his scale of White Desirability, and even then allocates only a single page to his discussion. 'Up to the present time the French immigrants have formed no large colonies,' he declares, seeming to forget the entire history and even the simple existence of Quebec (90).

The descent down the Great Chain of Race takes the reader to South-eastern Europe, where 'we enter what is to most of us a *terra incognita*' (92). Again, one can note the assumption that the reader – one of 'us' – is not a Southern European. Here Woodsworth stumbles, and almost falls off the structure he is working so hard to complete: 'We plunge into an apparently inextricable tangle of nations, races, languages, and religions. On what principle are we to adopt a working classification – geographical situation, political allegiances, national ties, racial characteristics, linguistic affinities, religious beliefs, social distinctions, or some group of these?' (92).

If it encounters difficulties outside of northwestern Europe, social science fails utterly when it reaches the Orient. At this point, a long description of 'Chinatown,' attributed to the Rev. J.C. Speer, is inserted into the text, in which the many strange differences of 'The Chinese' are enumerated. They are 'clumsy men' who play 'outlandish fiddles' (148), make use of 'ill-smelling punk-sticks' (150), and have 'peculiar' funeral customs (151). Turning to the 'Hindu,' Woodsworth declares that 'they are very slow, and do not seem capable of hard, continuous exertion. Their diet is light, and physically, they are not adapted to the rigorous climate of Canada' (154). This litany of tragic differences leads to an inevitable conclusion: unlike even the most southerly or easterly of Europeans, 'the Orientals cannot be assimilated' (155).

Proceeding down the Chain, Woodsworth arrives at the Black and Red in a chapter entitled 'The Negro and the Indian.' Short though it is, this chapter is quite interesting for both its explicit statements and inadvertent admissions. 'Neither the Negro nor the Indian are immigrants,' Woodsworth notes, 'and yet they are so entirely different from the *ordinary white population* that some mention of them is necessary if we would understand the complexity of our problems. We group them merely because both stand out entirely by themselves' (158, emphasis added). The Invisible Selves – the 'ordinary white population' – are named explicitly, in terms of their Invisible Colour, against which the Blacks and the Indians 'stand out' for the writer and assumed readers of the text. For his description of the 'unmanly' and 'undemocratic' traits of the Negro, Woodsworth cites an American 'expert,'[10] and then finishes his discussion by saying that 'we may be thankful that we have no "Negro problem" in Canada' (158). Quite true. While the semi-Whites and Yellows in Canada were despised as Useless internal Others, the Blacks fared even worse – so low on the scale of Desirability that, despite the fact that there were Black slaves in Champlain's Quebec and a continuous, but tenuous presence ever since, this 'type' had been so successfully prevented from obtaining a place in the history of Canadian diversity that it could not even become part of the problem.[11]

With regard to the Indians, whom he describes as 'grossly pagan ... half civilized ... debauched,' Woodsworth has little to say, other than to cite the necessity of providing them with the gifts of Christianity and civilization (160). Woodsworth's attempt to consider the problems of the Indian and the Immigrant *together* was important, though, in that he was forced into it by his desire for a complete description of the Great Chain of Race. The Indian was not an Immigrant, but still he was part of the problem of Canadian diversity, and thus had to be included in any enumeration of its content.

In codifying, clarifying, and completing the Great Chain of Race, in recovering useful ancient, medieval, and early Canadian colonial forms, and in providing these with a sound basis in New World social-scientific observation and commentary, J.S. Woodsworth made an outstanding contribution to the problem of Canadian diversity. But this was not all. Woodsworth also turned his attention to the need for solutions, bringing to bear the same literary flair and social-scientific attention to detail. The Flood metaphor was crucial here, as it reinforced the idea that the incoming Others were not human subjects but natural objects, and made it possible to consider state policy intervention as providing a 'tap' to control their 'flow.' Yet, as the experience of the previous decades had shown, even the Canadian state was being overwhelmed: 'Government policy may to a small extent quicken or direct the flow, but great economic laws rather than Government policy are responsible for the rise of the tide' (29). With the help of the Flood metaphor, the diversity that threatened Canada was simultaneously objectified, problematized, publicized, and rendered insoluble. For what could be done in the face of a natural disaster arising from intractable economic laws?

Despite his lack of faith in government policy, Woodsworth had no intention of being swept away in the Stream. He had a plan, but first he had to dismiss a competing paradigm that will be familiar to late twentieth-century readers as a form of 'melting-pot' ideology: 'There is an unfounded optimism that confidently asserts that all this mingling of the races is in the highest interest of our country. We get the strength of the North, the beauty of the South, and the wisdom of the East; such is the line of thought often presented in after-dinner speeches' (182). Anticipating the theory of complex systems, Woodsworth perceived that 'the newer nations are in a state of unstable equilibrium' (182), poised on the edge of order and chaos, ready to give rise to new forms. Fearing these *emergent* forms because they were unpredictable, he presented his own *design* plan for enabling a 'higher type' to be developed:

English and Russians, French and Germans, Austrians and Italians, Japanese and Hindus – a mixed multitude, they are being dumped into Canada by a kind of endless chain. They sort themselves out after a fashion, and each seeks to find a corner somewhere. But how shall we weld this heterogeneous mass into one people? That is our problem. (167)

Here Woodsworth provided the first concise formulation of the problem of Canadian diversity as it would develop during the twentieth century, as a *perpetual lack of unity caused by the presence of a disordered chaos of non-canonical Others.*

To help Canada achieve its destiny, Woodsworth advocated a two-pronged attack: assimilation to an Anglo-Canadian model for those Others already within – the mass that needed welding – and exclusion for those who could not be expected to 'assist us to maintain in Canada our British traditions' (46) – the flow that required direction *away* from Canada:

We, in Canada, have certain more or less clearly defined ideals of national well-being. These ideals must never be lost sight of. Non-ideal elements there must be, but they should be capable of assimilation. Essentially non-assimilable elements are clearly detrimental to our highest national development, and hence should be vigorously excluded. (202)

In the following two sections, I will discuss each of these solutions, and others adopted by the Canadian state, in order to see how Woodsworth's social-scientific theories and methods influenced the realms of state policy and popular culture.

Managing the Strangers within Our Gates: Assimilation, Transportation, Deportation, and Internment

Dealing with the Immigrant problem was, in a sense, nothing new to those who wished to construct a British Canada, as they had been struggling for centuries to displace, contain, exterminate, and assimilate a growing field of problematic Others. In each of these cases, a period of violent struggle had subsided into a master-slave relationship – without, of course, leaving behind the possibility of further eruptions of violence. While the Immigrant Other was never engaged in a literal struggle to the death, other forms of physical and semiotic elimination were most certainly deployed. Assimilation was for some time the dominant paradigm, in what I will describe below as both its *passive* and *active* modes. But, try as they might, early twentieth-century Canadians could not assimilate their Others as fully or completely as they (the Canadians) might desire. So, while the federal government continued to leave most of the work to the provinces, via their compulsory education systems, and the churches, via their missions and settlement houses, it also began to take seriously its responsibility for 'directing the flow' of Undesirable Immigrants. Because these identities occupied a low position on the Great Chain of Race, bodies associated with them could be treated like objects and moved about with relative impunity. This, combined with their lack of full British-Canadian subjectivity ('naturalization'), provided some new possibilities for physical elimination. Two of these were *deportation* of individuals, and mass deportation, or *transportation*, of groups. The Immigrants' 'lack' of full citizen status also facilitated their *disenfranchisement* and *internment*. With these methods, the Canadian government was able to remove certain Undesirable bodies from the sight of proper citizens, thereby achieving an effect similar to earlier, more literal, forms of physical elimination. Each of these methods will now be discussed, beginning with assimilation.

It was not uncommon for British Canadians of the early twentieth century to expect that Southeastern Europeans, as members of the White race, would simply 'be assimilated,' in the passive tense. This assumption can be seen in the response of Deputy Minister James Smart, when questioned by a member of the Select Standing Committee on Immigration and Colonization:

Q. Are the habits of the Doukhobors like those of the Mennonites, who want to make everything themselves?
A. Yes, largely the Doukhobors are the same. They make their own shovels, spades, boots, clothing and all that; many of them are blacksmiths ...
Q. They will get over that in time?
A. I have no doubt that after rubbing against Canadians, they will change their habits. (*JHC* [1900], v. 35, App. 1: 314).

The Canadian government had always been against 'assisting' immigrants too much, so that, when questioned by the same committee, a later Superintendent of Immigration was forced to admit that he knew very little about the bodies that his department attracted, processed, and deposited 'on the land':

Q. I understand you follow the immigrant on his arrival in Canada by one of your agents all the way through to his destination in the Northwest?

A. No.

Q. You know nothing about them after they arrive?

A. After they land in Canada, we know they are ticketed to a certain point by the railway.

Q. Do you find out where they are going, whether they are going to friends in the Northwest, or simply going without any connection?

A. No. (*JHC*: [1906], v. 41, App. 2: 476)

Being dumped into the Prairies to rub up against Canadians did not seem to be enough to transform Immigrants into British Canadians, and so there was a growing feeling that more active measures had to be adopted. Again, Woodsworth was a leader. As a follower of the social gospel, linking the salvation of the individual to the salvation of society,[12] he was of the opinion that 'special attention should be drawn to the necessity of mission work in our cities' (Woodsworth 1972a: 256). He himself had put in his time 'where the white harvest stan-deth,' at the All Peoples' Mission in Winnipeg, as Chair and Superin-tendent of its operations. In his more methods-oriented volume, *My Neighbour*, published in 1911, he spelled out in detail how the task of assimilation was to be carried out. As indicated by its name, his mis-sion really did attempt to be all things to all people, including among its twenty-one 'Departments' Kindergarten, boys' and girls' social and educational classes, clubs, gymnasiums and baths, libraries, night schools, concerts and lectures, Sunday meetings, monetary relief, religious services, and hospital and home visits (Woodsworth 1972b: 210–16). Reminiscent of the colonial fort, the mission was an outpost of civilization in a wilderness of Barbarism which, in a telling metaphor, acted like a 'focusing glass' to direct rays of assimilative energy onto the homes of Immigrant families (183).

In *The Education of the New Canadian: A Treatise on Canada's Greatest Educational Problem*, J.T.M. Anderson also came out against the theory of passive assimilation: 'There seems to be a too prevalent idea,' he argued, 'that each and every male and female new-comer may, irrespective of age, and after being subjected to some more or less in-definable process, which we call "assimilation," enter the ranks of full-fledged Canadian citizenship (Anderson 1918: 7). Citing Woods-worth, whom he presented as 'one of the best Canadian authorities on the subject of racial assimilation' (29), Anderson was concerned that

THE ASSOCIATED CHARITIES.

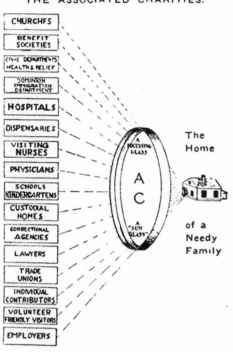

A FOCUSSING GLASS—A SUN GLASS.

Fig. 6.3. The mission as agent of rational-bureaucratic discipline

the new Immigrants would never become 'true Canadian citizens, imbued with the highest Anglo-Saxon ideals' (8). As an Inspector of Schools in Saskatchewan, he tended to favour compulsory education in British language and culture as the means of avoiding this unpleasant prospect, and operated on the assumption that 'the cry of the foreign child for better schooling must be heard and answered' (121). Like the Savage before him, the Foreign child was to be taken from the care of his parents for his own good, and any local attempts at his education were to be forcibly defeated. Anderson had high praise for how 'sensibly and fearlessly' the Alberta authorities dealt with difficulties arising in 'foreign' districts, by swooping in and appointing school boards where they were not happy with the policies adopted by those who had been democratically and legally elected (99–100). Certainly, if anyone had chosen to fight harder, there would have been yet another rebellion in the Northwest, as distant microcontrol was once again imposed in an attempt to force people's lives to conform with a distant ideal of British-Canadian identity.

Such was the treatment of the Strangers within the gates of a frightened and insecure British Canada. But what about those who threatened from without? Frank Oliver, who took over control of the immigration 'tap' from Clifford Sifton in 1906, began what was to become a century-long attempt to classify, manage, and solve the problem of Canadian diversity through state control of immigration. His first action was to present a bill to give the government new discursive and legislative powers over Foreign bodies, both incoming and existing: 'This Act is designed to enable the Department of Immigration to deal with undesirable immigrants – that is the sole purpose, as I understand it. We provide certain definitions, which will give us necessary authority over the people it is desired to reach' (*DHC*, 13 June 1906: 5201). Oliver referred to the 1906 Immigration Act as a 'weapon of defense,' which included sections allowing the Minister, or the Governor in Council, to deport, exclude, and prohibit from landing various 'classes' without consulting the legislative or executive branches of the Canadian government (The Immigration Act of 1906, 6 Ed. VII, c. 19).[13] From 67 in 1903, the number of deported Immigrants increased to 137 in 1906, after which it doubled every year until it reached a high of 1,748 in 1909 (Urquhart 1965: A342–7). During this time, total immigration decreased, from 211,000 to 173,000, so that it seems Oliver had provided a weapon that was quickly put to good use.

The Canadian tradition also included a more radical, *en masse* form of deportation, which had been used to shuffle various Native peoples about within the Dominion as it expanded, and had also informed the less successful British handling of the problem of the Acadians. Despite its mixed results, the government again tried *transportation* as a method of dealing with some of those Immigrants who apparently could not be welded into the Canadian mass. In 1908, shortly after the anti-Asian riot in Vancouver, there was an attempt to send 'some hundreds of unemployed Hindoos now in B.C. to West Indies as indentured immigrants' (NAC, RG 7, file 507, reel C220: 84). Observers were sent out, but when they reported back that the Honduras was swampy and infested with mosquitoes, the idea was rejected at a meeting organized by the Khalsa Diwan society (Singh 1994: 42–3), and the scheme was abandoned. Again, transportation had proven itself to be a less than adequate means of solving the problem of human diversity.

With the beginning of the First World War, Canadian fear and anger also came out under the cover of protecting the Homeland from 'enemy aliens.' In what looked like a single stroke, 'immigrants of German or Austro-Hungarian nationality' – who had previously occupied a high position on the scale of Desirability – became Others to be tracked and managed. Any individual who was associated with these now dreaded nationalities became a potential Enemy, and was required to take an oath 'in consideration of ... exemption from detention,' and 'to report to such official and upon such terms as the Canadian authorities may from time to time prescribe' (Proclamation of 15 Aug. 1914, section 4, *Canada Gazette* 48: 617). Anyone who refused to submit to Canadian racial discipline could be 'arrested and detained' (section 1) and, if 'the officer or authority making the arrest was not satisfied' with their pledges of allegiance, they could be interned (section 5). These provisions were expanded to cover Canadian citizens by the Wartime Elections Act, which revoked the franchise for 'naturalized enemy aliens,' except those who were serving in the Canadian armed forces (7–8 Geo. V. c. 39 s. 154). Regardless of one's citizenship, beliefs, or personal history, having as one's 'mother tongue ... the language of an enemy country' was enough to make one an official Enemy.

On 6 November 1914, an 'Internment Operations' branch – rather ironically attached to the Department of Justice – was created by Order in Council, to be headed by W.D. Otter (PC 301). Over the six years of its mandate, the Internment Operations Branch processed 8,579 people, identified in Otter's 1921 report as consisting of 6,954 'Austro-Hungarians, covering Croats, Ruthenians, Slovaks, and Chzecks,' 2,009 'Germans,' 205 'Turks,' 99 'Bulgarians,' and 312 'Miscellaneous' (*Report on Internment Operations, 1921*; reprinted in Gregorovich 1983: 79). Of these, Otter states that 'not more than 3,138 could be correctly classed as prisoners of war' (79). He suspected that 'the tendency of municipalities to "unload" their indigent was the cause of the confinement of not a few' (80). Not only their indigent, perhaps, but their Others, defined as indigent, then redefined as Enemy Aliens? Thus did deportation, transportation, and internment function as methods of physical elimination of problematic bodies: methods that provided modern equivalents to colonial extermination, displacement, and containment. Just as the extermination of Savages was justified on the basis of their lack of humanity and civilization, the treatment of Immigrants as inhuman objects was predicated upon their lack of 'suitability' for a Canadian life. Once again, it would seem that such treatment was not the exception, but the norm, giving us further cause to doubt both the received history of Canadian diversity, and the policy of multiculturalism that claims to emerge out of it.

Excluding the Strangers Without

While deportation and internment were repeatedly and widely deployed, these methods were of minor importance compared to the Canadian state's efforts to regulate the flow of incoming Otherness through immigration restrictions. Section 30 of the Immigration Act of 1906 provided, for the first time, a broad legal basis for these exclusionary practices: 'The Governor in Council may, by proclamation or order, whenever he considers it necessary or expedient, prohibit the landing in Canada of any specified class of immigrants, of which due notice shall be given to the transportation companies' (6 Ed. VII, c. 19). As with the new rules regarding deportation, the courts and elected representatives could be bypassed, enabling decisions to be made by a small group behind closed doors. The use of the term 'class' is also important, as it was empty of specific content and therefore provided a wide-open category under which any group of people could be excluded for any reason. That Frank Oliver was aware of this potential is apparent in his answer when questioned on the relevant section in the House of Commons: '[T]here has been an immigration of gypsies lately and it is thought that such people are not desirable under any circumstances although they are physically and mentally fit, and that it would be quite proper to take power to say: You cannot come in' (DHC, 13 June 1906: 5253). Applicable without explanation or reason, without public knowledge or the potential for criticism, exclusion by 'class' was a perfect weapon of defence in the war on incoming Otherness.

Like deportation, exclusion was in fact practised prior to 1906. It had been possible since 1869 to prohibit the entrance of those seen as medically or psychologically unfit, and the Chinese had long had the 'honour' of being the first race to be excluded from Canada via a separate piece of legislation (Chinese Immigration Act of 1885, 48–9 Vic. c. 71). But formal, explicit racial exclusion was not commonly practised, either before the 1906 Act or after, as the Canadian government chose to do its work in roundabout ways. The 'continuous journey' legislation, which led to the *Komogata Maru* incident,[14] is one famous example of the preference for implicit rather than explicit discrimination. This tradition of claiming to be open and tolerant while actually being closed and afraid can also be seen in Frank Oliver's presentation of the 1910 Immigration Act as a triumph of egalitarianism: 'The intention of the Bill, and the policy of the government, is that all immigration shall be treated on exactly the same footing, on the same basis, according to their merits, irrespective of their race or religion' (*DHC*, 21 March 1910: 5505). This was an odd claim, since section 38 of the Act restated the continuous journey restriction, and also allowed the Governor in Council to 'prohibit for a stated period, or permanently, the landing in Canada ... of immigrants belonging to *any race deemed unsuited* to the climate or requirements of Canada, or of immigrants of any specified class, occupation, or character' (section 38c, emphasis added). Perhaps what the Minister meant was that everyone would be classed as Desirable or not based on the same set of racial principles?

Canadian exclusionism reached its mature form with the 1919 Act to Amend the Immigration Act. Section 3, which dealt with the 'prohibited classes,' was revised and extended from nine to twenty categories (9–10 Geo. V. c. 25). Of greater importance, though, was the broader latitude given to the Governor in Council for prohibiting the landing of

> immigrants of any specified class or occupation, by reason of any economic, industrial or other condition temporarily existing in Canada or because such immigrants are deemed unsuitable having regard to the climatic, industrial, social, educational, labour, or other conditions or requirements of Canada or because such immigrants are deemed undesirable owing to their peculiar customs, habits, modes of life and methods of holding property, and because of their probable inability to become readily assimilated or to assume the duties and responsibilities of Canadian citizenship within a reasonable time after their entry. (Section 13)

During the second reading of this bill, J.A. Calder, the Minister for Immigration and Colonization, spelled out its aim quite clearly. Although he held it to be 'self-evident' that Canada had to increase its population – to increase the tax base and size of markets, and for other reasons of capitalist exploitation summed up in the catch phrase 'people and production' (*DHC*, 29 April 1919: 1868) – he was concerned that the population thus acquired be of the correct type: '[F]or some years to come ... our policy should be directed along two lines, first, towards increasing our agricultural population; second, towards providing, under the existing law ... for the exclusion of certain classes of people who cannot be readily absorbed into our population at the present time' (*DHC*, 29 April 1919: 1876).

Eager to make use of his new powers, Calder allowed himself an orgy of expiatory exclusion, which began only three days after the Act to Amend the Immigration Act received royal assent. Order in Council 1202, issued on 9 June 1919, allowed Asians to be barred from British Columbia – and thereby from Canada – by prohibiting the landing of 'any immigrant of the following classes or occupations, viz., skilled and unskilled labour' at its ports (*Statutes of Canada* [1919], v. 1, Prefix to Statutes: ix).[15] Order in Council 1203, issued on the same day, prohibited 'immigrants who are alien enemies or who have been alien enemies during the war.' Next to go down were the Doukhobors, Mennonites, and Hutterites, for whom it seemed that the final lines of section 13 had been explicitly written. Order in Council 1204 of 9 June 1919 excluded them for their 'peculiar customs, habits, modes of life and methods of holding property, and because of their probable inability to become readily assimilated or to assume the duties and responsibilities of Canadian citizenship within a reasonable time after their entry' (x). At the same time as he was ridding the nation of its Others, Calder also achieved the goal of increasing the flow of incoming Selfhood. In 1918, 5,396 of 41,845 immigrants, or 13 per cent of immigration to Canada, was from Great Britain. The next year, the total had almost tripled, to 107,698, with 54 per cent from the Mother Country and 39 per cent from the United States, leaving only 7 per cent in the Other class (*B & B Report*: 4.238ff). In this way, Calder finally achieved what the Canadian government had been striving for since 1867.

Restrictions and prohibitions were added at a great rate, until the number of Undesirable categories vastly exceeded the Desirables, rendering it easier to specify which classes were *admissible* rather than those that were prohibited. This technique was used in an Order in Council of 1923, which limited entry to only a few classes: agriculturists with the means to begin farming; farm labourers with reasonable assurance of employment; female domestic servants with reasonable assurance of employment; wives and children of residents able to support them; U.S. citizens with means to maintain themselves until they could find employment; British subjects with means except, of course, those who were Asian; persons who could satisfy the Minister that their labour was required; and, finally, other relatives, not under eighteen, and not Asian (PC 183, 1923). The Chinese Immigration Act of

1923 took this same approach, and showed how the specification of Desirables could be used to totally exclude Undesirables without giving the appearance of having done so. For, while the title of the Act seemed to indicate that its purpose was to allow Chinese immigration, its effect was to shut it down entirely, by limiting entry to diplomats, returning children of Chinese descent, and merchants and students coming to Canada on a temporary basis (13–14 Geo. V. c. 38 s. 5). By denying entry to persons 'of Chinese origin or descent other than the classes mentioned' (s. 7), the Act was spectacularly effective; over the next twenty years, a total of eight Chinese are recorded as having emigrated to Canada (B & B Report: 4.238ff). In their close attention to economic conditions, their focus on classes of employment as a means of implementing an exclusionary policy, and in their specification of Desirables rather than Undesirables, these proclamations and Acts established the forms still followed by current Canadian immigration legislation.

The strategy of exclusion reached its zenith with the Great Depression, which provided the justification for a total prohibition of all Undesirable Others. In 1931 the landing in Canada of all classes and occupations was prohibited, with five exceptions: British subjects with means to maintain themselves; U.S. citizens with means; wives and children of citizens; agriculturalists with means; and fiancées who could be supported (PC 695, 21 March 1931). The sections allowing Americans and unspecified agriculturalists were further qualified by a proviso that these could not settle in a province 'which signified its disapproval of these sections.' Thus, the only way to get into Canada in 1931 was to be a non-Asian, relatively well-off British subject or American, or to marry your way past the border guards. And if you were already in, it was a good idea to stay off the dole. In 1929, 444 people were expelled from Canada for showing a likelihood of becoming a public charge – that is, for being suddenly Useless to Canadian capitalists. In 1930 this number increased to 2,106, doubled again in 1931 to 4,084, and rose to a high of 5,217 in 1932, a year when total immigration was only 20,591. By the 1930's, the immigration 'tap' had been shut off, and to a great extent the 'flow' of Otherness had been reversed. Canadian nativism – especially in its English variant, which hoped for the French to be excluded as well as everyone else – had found its expression in a restrictive immigration policy which made it very clear that Canada was, and would remain, British.

Identity by Design in Early Twentieth-Century Canada

Two central themes emerge from this chapter. First, we have seen that the early twentieth century was dominated by a *design theory of identity* that required strict conformity to an Anglo-Canadian model. The methods used to implement this model were primarily coercive, relying upon *removal and exclusion* of bodies that were not seen as conforming to the design parameters. Thus, over the first half of the century, physical force was systematically deployed in excluding, containing, and deporting, at one time or another, virtually every 'class' of person other than healthy, wealthy, British Canadians. Those whose bodies could not be eliminated were politically disempowered, through the removal of the franchise. It is crucial to note that these actions were always provided with a covering rhetoric of justification: they were intended only to protect the national economy, polity, or society; or were in the best interest of the particular Class of Immigrant involved; or, most commonly, some 'crisis' or 'emergency' – a war, depression, or strike – made it sadly necessary to deviate from the regular practice of an otherwise peaceful and democratic country. In this stage of the history of Canadian diversity there thus appeared a vital aspect of late twentieth-century multiculturalism – a desire for unity and identity achieved through rational-bureaucratic action said to be in harmony with liberal ideals.

Whatever justifications might be produced, it seems clear that the Immigrant was being blamed for the failures of the Two Founding Races to realize their respective National Dreams and, like the Jew and Christian in ancient Rome, served as a scapegoat whenever a plague fell upon the nation. The formulation of the problem of Canadian diversity in the early twentieth century, with its focus on the difficulties of racial assimilation, gives some clues as to precisely why and how the Immigrant was at fault. His greatest sin, it would appear, was first to behave like the British and French and attempt to striate his own bodies and spaces according to his own models; but worse than this, the unassimilable Other appeared to be *succeeding where the British and French were failing*, in being possessed of distinctive characteristics, in being part of an ongoing and lively culture which could give rise to strange churches, evil-smelling punk sticks, and outlandish clothing. Obsessively marked out as distinct from canonical Canadian society, the Immigrants of the early twentieth century, like the Savages and Indians before them, appeared to have precisely what those who would administer and assimilate them lacked – an identity. This was, I suggest, simply too much to bear. The British Canadians, as the occupants of the highest rung in the Canadian Great Chain of Race, knew all about 'swamping out' existing peoples by overcoming them numerically. They had done this across what was now the whole of Canada, with the glaring exception of Quebec, where it seemed that the French could never be outnumbered. Something had to be done if the nation were not to be broken into ten or a hundred Quebecs, a sea of Red Rivers, a cosmopolitan chaos in which Britishness itself might be at risk from the wild forces of unconstrained emergence.

Chapter Seven

The Rise of the Mosaic Metaphor

In the previous chapter, I showed how early twentieth-century Canada was dominated by a *design theory* of Canadian identity, which called for the assimilation or exclusion of Immigrant bodies. In this chapter, I will discuss two other lines of thought that were extant at the time. One, which I will describe as a *free emergence theory*, assumed that a 'proper' and 'desirable' Canadian identity would evolve on its own, out of an unconstrained mixing of 'racial qualities.' The third variant, which I call the *constrained emergence theory*, combined elements of both design and free emergence and, as we will see, was the ancestor of multiculturalism as state policy after 1971. In the remainder of the chapter, I show how the Canadian state began to *apply* this theory, through its attempts to produce integrated subjects who would perform according to a simulation model of an ideal 'Canadian citizen.' In summary, this chapter shows how, over the course of the twentieth century, state-sponsored seductive integration of cultural signs slowly replaced coercive assimilation of racialized bodies by civil society as the preferred solution to the problem of Canadian diversity .

Canadian Identity as an Emergent Phenomenon

As J.S. Woodsworth had noted in 1909, some concerned citizens around him were suggesting in 'after-dinner speeches' that assimilation to the British-Canadian model would not be the way of the future, but that 'the mingling of the races' was 'in the highest interest of our country' (Woodsworth 1972a: 182). Perhaps Woodsworth was referring to Professor Maurice Hutton, who, in a speech to the Empire Club in 1904, had argued that 'all great civilizations are created by a blend ... when one people of one type meets another people of quite a different type and by force of circumstances are compelled to ... add their joint civilizations together' ('The Canadian National Character,' in Clark 1904: 68). As a model for this process, Hutton invoked the ancient Greek experience, and spoke in the first person to one of its pre-eminent philosophers: 'Your own civilization of Greece, Plato ... was produced by a sturdy northern people coming down like a wolf upon the southern fold of a very ancient and rich civilization ... and these produced the many-sided, susceptible, marvelous genius of the Ionian Greek' (68–9). Hutton had big plans for the Canadian hybrid, which he expected would possess the qualities of the philosopher-king, the occupant of the highest rung on the Platonic Great Chain of Being:

> Plato, in his picture of an ideal state, asks himself this question – How am I going to combine the manly qualities which build up an empire, enterprise and self-reliance and high spirit and aggression, with the other qualities more gentle but more efficient in maintaining an empire, perhaps, when built? ... We are going to say to him, Plato, it is possible that in the Island of Atlantis you will find a people known as Canadians ... fitted ... for realizing this ideal character. (68)

In *The Foreigner*, a popular novel published in 1909, Ralph Connor presented a similarly stirring and hopeful vision of the future Canadian:

> In Western Canada there is to be seen to-day that most fascinating of all human phenomena, the making of a nation. Out of breeds diverse in traditions, in ideals, in speech, and in manner of life, Saxon and Slav, Teuton and Celt and Gaul, one people is being made. The blood strains of great races will mingle in the blood of a race greater than the greatest of them all. (1909: Preface)

Unlike Woodsworth, who argued for the use of agents of socialization to convert Foreign Others into Anglo-Saxon Selves, Connor and Hutton imagined that the Canadian type would eventually *emerge on its own*. They understood that the characteristics of this identity, as the result of a process of fusion and mixing, were essentially unknowable, but they were certain that it would be of the highest type. In that they (apparently) placed no limits on the mingling of races, and entrusted their future to superior 'blood stocks,' I refer to their vision as a *free emergence theory* of Canadian identity.

This vision did not catch on with early twentieth-century British Canadians, perhaps because it sounded too much like the all-American ideology of the 'melting pot.' However, an even more marginal – but homegrown – alternative, to both designed assimilation and free emergence, was also being advocated in Canadian public life:

> The day will come in Canada when each nationality, while preserving its own peculiar characteristics, brought up in the broad, strong, national life of Canada ... will combine to form the grandest race that the continent of North America or the world has yet produced. (Lieut.-Col. Sam Hughes, *DHC* [1902]: 3026-7)

The key innovation here is the suggestion that 'each nationality' will 'preserve its own characteristics,' but only within 'the broad, strong, national life of Canada.' The possibility that a total eradication of difference might not be attainable was already implicit in Woodsworth's metaphor of 'welding' together a series of 'elements,' or fundamental, indivisible units, but this implication was suppressed in his text. Hughes was willing to follow it through, however, to arrive at what might appear to be a logical contradiction. How could a singular form – 'the grandest race ... yet produced' – emerge out of a 'combination' of a diversity of preserved characteristics?[1] Like Hutton and Connor, Hughes hoped for the emergence of a single race, and he also expected that an essentially unknowable result would, by some necessity, be the best possible. But, in allowing for the contradictory existence of a diversity within this unity, and in setting limits to the realm of particularity, Hughes prefigured, without using the name, the integrationist approach that Canada would eventually adopt.

Charles McCullough, a founder of the Canadian Club, also weighed in on this theme. 'Let us be broad Canadians,' he argued, 'as broad as from sea to sea ... and from the south to the north; but in all our breadth let us endeavour to conserve the national spirit, but build up Canada in every possible way' ('Canadian Clubs and Canadian Problems,' address to the Empire Club, in Hopkins 1911: 220). McCullough pursued the theme of unity within diversity by noting that the Canadian Clubs had as their mandate the 'promoting of unity among ourselves' and the development of an ideal of 'toleration and respect' between the

French and English (222). This could be extended, he thought, to the other races, as well:

> In building up the walls of Jerusalem every one of the children of Israel enclosed their city with unusual strength of wall – the duty devolved upon them to build, and every man did his part. So, in Canada, it is by every one doing his part, men of diverse views, men of different races, men who have no knowledge of the liberty we enjoy in this Canada of ours, but who have come here to share in our privileges. (222)

Thus he added the idea that if problematic diversity were to be preserved rather than eradicated, it would be necessary for canonical Canadians to *tolerate* the resulting signs of Otherness.

These 'theorists' of Canadian identity did not yet have a name for their approach, nor did they share a common metaphor. But there were observable regularities in an emerging discourse that held to what I will call the *constrained emergence theory of Canadian identity*. An (incomplete) characterization of this approach as I have described it so far would note its assumption that *a unity of higher types will emerge through the preservation and tolerance of limited forms of difference*. As I have noted, this was a marginal view in early twentieth-century Canada. But greater hegemony for the idea of seeking unity within diversity would come in time, as the Mosaic metaphor for Canadian society made its first tentative appearance on the scene, and constrained emergence theory was further refined.

The Canadian Mosaic as a Constrained Emergence Theory of Identity

The story of the Mosaic began, not with a self-conscious attempt to provide a name for a particularly Canadian form of nation-building, but with a passing reference in a traveller's journal. The following passage, which is perhaps the first published invocation of the Mosaic metaphor for Canadian society,[2] is taken from Victoria Hayward's *Romantic Canada* (1922). It was prompted by her encounter with the Canadian Prairies, and occurred in the context of a discussion of the many 'New Canadians' who were to be found there:

> The New Canadians, representing many lands and widely separated sections of Old Europe, have contributed to the Prairie Provinces a variety in

the way of Church architecture. Cupolas and domes distinctly Eastern, almost Turkish, startle one above the tops of Manitoba maples or the bush of the river banks. These architectural figures of the landscape, apart altogether from their religious significance, are centres where, crossing the threshold on Sundays, one has an opportunity of hearing Swedish music or the rich, deep chanting of the Russian responses; and of viewing at close hand the artistry that goes to make up the interior appointments of these churches transplanted from the East to the West ... It is indeed a mosaic of vast dimensions and great breadth, essayed of the Prairie. (187)

Here one can discern again the operation of the tradition of Herodotan ethnography, in producing signs of Otherness from architecture, musical taste, mode of worship, and, of course, language and country of origin. The encounter with these Alien signs in a familiar pastoral setting among the Manitoba maples 'startles' the visitor whose senses are not accustomed to the assault. The diversity is there; it is multifaceted and real – and yet, it is a foreign figure set against a local ground.

A daunting profusion of differences, both natural and human, to be sure. But, for Victoria Hayward, Canadian diversity was not a problem – rather, it represented a positive and precious opportunity for a roving spirit with a collector's gleam in her eye. In the Introduction to the text, E.J. O'Brien applauded Hayward and her photographer companion, Edith Watson, for their loving attention to what made Canada particularly, and proudly, Canadian:

Those who know and love the by-ways of Canada have frequently encountered Miss Watson and Miss Hayward in the pursuit of a self-imposed task. Hardly a task we should call it, but a delight, to record with the camera and the pen those unique and beautiful racial traditions which have survived in Canada and flourished, which the passion for conformity to a provincial process of standardization has crushed in the United States ... That wise tolerance and appreciative catholicity which is not always found in a new land has preserved old loveliness here. (iv)

O'Brien's Introduction reinforced the articulation of Mosaic and race found in the form and content of the main text, with its reference to the 'beautiful racial traditions' that 'flourish' in Canada. It also noted the necessity of 'tolerance' in the presence of problematic difference.

It seems fitting that this celebration of Romantic Canada, like so much else that is Canadian, was a gift from two Americans. No matter:

the Canadians were quick to make use of a good thing, as can be seen from Kate Foster's publication, in 1926, of *Our Canadian Mosaic*. Foster followed Woodsworth's lead with her Section I, 'Immigration and Statistics,' which contains the requisite tables, and with Section II, 'At Our Gates,' which establishes the Tide of Immigrants as a *bona fide* national problem. She deviates from his line, however, in trying to make a distinction between 'assimilation' and 'amalgamation':

> In many minds the term 'assimilation' is confused with amalgamation. Does the former necessarily imply inter-marriage – the fusion of races? Is not assimilation rather the incorporating into our national life of all peoples within our borders for their common well being? Is it not the working together side by side for the common advancement, each race contributing something of value and so slowly but surely evolving a new people enriched by the diversity of its origin? (135, emphasis added)

What Foster calls 'amalgamation,' as a 'fusion of races,' is quite clearly a free emergence theory of identity. However, the status of 'assimilation' in her text is a little more difficult to discern. It is a process of 'incorporating ... peoples' that she expects will leave room for the 'evolving' of 'a new people.' The characteristics of this new people will be unknown, to the extent that they will be left to 'evolve'; but, to the extent that they will result from a process of incorporation 'into *our* national life,' they will not be *entirely* unknown. Thus, once the terms are sorted out, what Foster advocates appears as a version of constrained emergence theory.

In an attempt to give a concrete form to her idea, Foster became the first writer to invoke the Mosaic metaphor in the context of a discussion of Canadian immigration policy and nation-building. In justifying this choice, she wrote of the Mosaic's 'capacity to endure,' a quality 'essential in nation-building' (141). Equally important was the ability of the Mosaic to order and unify the Flood of chaotic diversity: 'In nation-building all manner of materials are required,' for the task involves the 'fitting together of many generally small pieces ... to form a pattern' (141). Even 'the humblest cube' was to be incorporated into the Mosaic, for it had a part to play in the overall design (142). Thus, *every* person was to be assigned a set of typical characteristics, and *every* set of characteristics was to be included in the Mosaic. But, while Foster advised that the variety of types should be brought together into a single (Canadian) pattern, it was equally important that they be kept separate, 'no one tesserae encroaching in the very smallest degree upon another' (142). Thus did the Mosaic display in its form the abstract notions of equality, diversity, and unity in diversity.

Foster went on to note that in Mosaic-building, 'as in other art, design is of paramount importance' (141). 'A principle of order must prevail in every ornamental composition – otherwise the pattern is spoiled and there will be disturbing patches' (142). A design, of course, implies a designer, and, in the spirit of Woodsworth's dedication to racial taxonomy, Foster was quick to point out that the designer 'must know his material or fail':

> The most glaring mistakes that have been made in the course of erecting our national structure have been due to ignorance in regard to its constituent parts ... Just as the use of pictorial and figure subjects demands comprehensive historical knowledge ... so the use of human 'tiles' demands that we native-born Canadians make it our business to know something of the background of our fellow workers. (143)

Foster expected that there would be great difficulties facing anyone 'who attempts to classify the human elements that must be fitted into our intricate Canadian pattern' (141). But, like Woodsworth, this did not prevent her from making an effort. Section III of *Our Canadian Mosaic* provided 'A Near View of Our New Canadians,' where, following the conventions of Herodotan ethnography, the various types and their characters were brought into relief. But mere knowledge was not enough. Well aware of the tendency of internal Others to create difficulties for the realization of the Canadian National Dream, Foster insisted that the designer must 'render the object which he produces *useful* ... It matters not how beautiful the object is to be, it must first be formed as though it were a mere work of utility; and after it has been carefully created with this end in view it may then be rendered as beautiful as you please' (141–2, emphasis in original). For the designer of the Canadian Mosaic, the program was clear: first, know the Other; then render him useful; later, use him to put a layer of attractive ornamentation on your creation.

Foster also spoke about the 'cement' used to hold together the pieces of the Mosaic, which for her could be nothing other than 'good will and friendliness born of natural respect and confidence between all peoples within our borders' (143) – that is, tolerance of the differences displayed in the preserved human tiles. Here, however, the limits to the realm of emergence in early twentieth-century Canada became clear: the only way to 'natural respect' was to ensure that everyone had more or less the same nature:

> We can surely learn a lesson from our great neighbour to the South for there is such a thing as a country being swamped by unemployable and undesirable immigrants. Thus Limited Selective Immigration is Canada's great need today. Prospective immigrants should be selected preferably from British stock or from among the more readily assimilable peoples of Europe. (11)

For all of her talk about Mosaics and 'evolving a new people,' Foster was, in the end, unable to take a step beyond an exclusionary and Eurocentric immigration policy.

As a further aid in the 'evolution' of a British Canada, and following her previous suggestions about knowledge and utility, she suggested increased intervention in the daily lives of 'the foreign born,' in the form of a 'Dominion-wide system of educating the aliens in Canada for citizenship' (128). As in the policy suggestions of the Canadian design theorists, the Immigrant Others were to be subjected to a system of tutelage and surveillance oriented to correcting their problematic difference. 'Isolation is the greatest wrong to the Foreign-Born. They should not be left to themselves' (128). Thus early twentieth-century constrained emergence theory shared with its ancient and colonial antecedents the characteristic orientation to *improvement of the lot of a sorry, inferior Other* who was seen to be begging for the gift of recognition from those in possession of a superior civilization. The Immigrant was to be lifted out of the muck, polished up, and cemented into a place of honour on the magnificent Canadian Mosaic.

Design, Designers, and the Social Sciences

After Woodsworth's and Foster's first steps, the theory and practice of Canadianization through rational-bureaucratic intervention would be refined and professionalized, with the help of the emerging disciplines of anthropology, sociology, and psychology. An important figure in this transformation was Robert England, whose *Central European Immigrant in Canada* (1929) presented a general theory of Immigrant assimilation. As the 'voice' of 'fifty experienced nation-builders' who had served in the educational wilderness of rural Saskatchewan (Preface:

x), England continued the social gospel tradition that had taken firm root in the Canadian psyche. But he had also attended the Collège Libre des Sciences Sociales in Paris, and was able to bring a profusion of social scientific insights to bear upon the problem of Canadian diversity. Thus did two new categories of human differentiation, *culture* and *ethnicity*, come onto the scene. England also *defined* the realms of constraint and emergence in the constrained emergence theory of Canadian identity, and *refined* the method of assimilation, by arguing that it must be seductive rather than coercive in nature.

In his first chapter, entitled 'The Problem,' England made the customary display of tables and invoked the Flood metaphor, ritualistically creating a difficulty of 'national concern' (3–4). He was worried that 'our British ideals' would 'go into a melting pot rather different from that which we have perhaps too superficially imagined' (8). For, competing with these ideals were others equally desirous of perpetuating themselves. Freezing his subjects in a Herodotan frame, England claimed that he encountered in Saskatchewan 'districts where the customs, habits, social and economic background of the people belong not only to another land but to another century. There has been the question of the education of a medieval people' (9). In his descriptions, England implicitly put to work many of the classic, medieval, and modern means of differentiating the Other: ability to function in a democratic *polis* and to use the language of the observer; intelligence; mode of dwelling; literacy; and, of course, the ubiquitous climate theory: 'The severe winter conditions which are a tonic to more Northern races must have confined in many a sod cabin in Northern Saskatchewan much home-sickness and regretful longing' (77).

But England, as a social scientist, also helped to push the frontier of the Canadian discourse on diversity into a new realm: that of *culture*. In one of its first appearances in a semi-official Canadian setting, culture leaned on the established authority of history, language, and race as axes of problematic difference: 'The linguistic problem ... emerges ... as the most urgent. Closely linked with it is the culture problem, which to some extent rests on historical development and racial differentiation as well as language distinctions' (60). Culture also had a certain scientific *cachet* borrowed from the discipline of anthropology: 'Anthropologists are beginning to discover how cultural influences reach down to our most deep-seated emotional tendencies. The whole machinery of logical thought may be affected by the type of culture' (161). Culture, it seemed, was so important that if one were to be abruptly deprived of its support, 'serious psychological' problems could result, and, as in the South Sea Islands, 'races' could 'die out' (162) from the effects of coercive assimilation.

Under pressure from exponents of the new science, the Canadian government had added several anthropologists to the staff of the Geological Survey of Canada, whose job it was to conduct research on the 'aborigines of Canada' and thus bring the equivalent to the tools of sociology to bear upon 'those members of the human species as have been supposed, rightly or wrongly, to come nearest the state in which we may imagine primitive man to have lived' (Sapir 1912: 62). Although still of dubious civilization and modernity, the Native peoples of Canada were finally being granted cultures of their own. As both Foster and Woodsworth had pointed out, one must know the Other in order to create and constrain her, and anthropologists were the specialists at this sort of knowledge production.

The new discourse of Mendelian genetics was also invoked in England's text, as a means to 'prove' the impossibility, or at the least the improbability, of the notion that a superior type could emerge out of a chaos of races:

> When the question of the amalgamation of racial stocks comes to be studied in the light of biology and anthropology, it is probable the results will not justify facile optimism as to the merging of characteristics. In accordance with Mendelian law dominant racial characteristics will be found to persist, Mediterranean will not become Nordic, nor Nordic Alpine. (England 1929: 65)

If the free emergence thesis was scientifically insupportable, and if coercive assimilation could cause mental illness and death, then what was Canada to do? Following Hughes and the 'evolutionary' undercurrent in Foster, and making use of yet another new category of differentiation – ethnicity – England proposed a strategy that involved the preservation and tolerance of difference, plus evolution/training to find 'common denominators' between the various 'elements' of Canadian society: 'The modern world is more sympathetic to the idea of ethnic individuality. We are beginning to realize that a primitive people has a right to preserve its own cultural background whether aesthetic or not' (163). The category of ethnicity will be discussed further, in the context of its rise to dominance in the 1960s. For now, it should suffice to note that England's usage contained a common 'confusion' or 'richness,' in that while Other groups – in this case, 'primitive people' – were seen as possessing ethnicity, anthropologists of the Self group were not. This tendency was in keeping with ancient Greek and early Christian usage (see chapter 3) and was perpetuated, as we will see, in the latter part of the century, as well.

At any rate, in anthropology's paternal relation to the cultures of Primitive peoples, England had invoked and expanded upon another key idea of constrained emergence theories of identity: not only must problematic Others be allowed to preserve signs of difference, but non-problematic Selves must be *trained* to tolerate these signs. It was not enjoyable – it offended the 'aesthetic' sense – but it was necessary. And, perhaps not too difficult, given the history of Canadian diversity:

> The British Empire has been fortunate in having administrators in colonial and mandated territories imbued with sufficient sympathy to realize that the type of social life to which a race has accustomed itself must be touched with care ... Ideas, customs, 'taboos,' which seem to us totally illogical and incomprehensible, are logically sound and completely comprehensible given the background, the mentality, and all the premises upon which the whole social structure is based. (163)

What forms of difference were to be tolerated by Canadians, according to England? First of all, he thought it unwise to 'expect or require' Immigrants 'to surrender anything that might be helpful to unity and progress' (184–5). The Immigrants would also be permitted to hang on to certain aspects of their particularity which, while they might not directly contribute to the greatness of the Dominion, would not pose a challenge to the canon of British-Canadian liberal-democratic capitalism. '[W]e need not care whether the peasant woman, for example, keeps or discards her head dress, unless it indicates adherence to a general scheme of custom and institution alien to the spirit of Canadian progress' (185).

While variation in customs was seen to be acceptable – as long as they were of no social or political consequence – no tolerance was possible with regard to the crucial issue of language: 'To understand and sympathize we must speak a common language, share a common opportunity fitted to our capacity, and thrill to common memories of mutual service rendered, of pain endured, of story, legend, tradition, and song' (185). England suggested that 'out of these [commonalities] will come inevitably similarities of custom and habit, a certain standardization of logical processes in thought, and even, perhaps a similar response to emotional appeal' (185). The common language, of course, would be English. Anyone who was not 'English-speaking' was an Other, including the French, whom England unceremoniously lumped in with types generally considered to be far lower on the Great Chain of Race in his enumeration of thirty-one 'non-English' rural districts in Saskatchewan: 'Table II shows that District No. 8 was Hungarian; No. 16 Mennonite; No. 5 German, Norwegian, and Anglo-Saxon; No. 6 Ukrainian-German; No. 30 Doukhobor; No. 2 French' (69). For England, language was the great assimilator.[3] If the Immigrants could be seduced into *speaking English*, they would eventually *become British*, and the problem of Canadian diversity would be solved.

Here, in the realm of intolerance, England was cautious to avoid the mistakes made by other Colonizers. Citing W.H. Rivers, he noted that 'the only way in which the culture of an immigrant people can be carried about the world is in a psychological form, in the form of sentiments, beliefs and ideas' (161). If cultures had an immaterial basis, then those who sought to manage them would have to take this into account: 'Fundamentally, the problem must be regarded to some extent as a psychological one and this, in turn, means that the institution which deals with the moulding of minds and wills must be operated efficiently, and the newer citizens must be shown especially how worth-while it is to make the institution ... theirs' (185). Thus, instead of a policy of coercive total assimilation, England argued for a subtler form that was partial and seductive:

> We cannot compel people to accept our standards, our customs or our ways. The work of assimilation must not be a work of putting into bondage. It must be a task of emancipation. It must be a challenge and a call to wider perspectives, saner ideals, better habits and customs ... (165–6)

In this way, he hoped that a 'bond of national unity' could be forged (168), warning that 'we must incorporate the races who have come to us into *one* people: otherwise our Dominion from sea to sea will perish in strife and anarchy' (173, emphasis in original).

Again, we see the fear of conflict and disorder that permeates the Canadian discourse on diversity, along with the equally ubiquitous dream of a perfectly striated space of social order that closes the Canadian ecumene, stretching between two 'smooth' seas. In his plan to achieve this ideal, England adhered to the constrained emergence theory of Canadian identity, placing in the realm of preservation-toleration-emergence what he calls 'custom,' and in the realm of constraint any social, political, or economic forms that he felt would threaten British-Canadian liberal-democratic capitalism. To convert these preserved Others into free Selves, England relied upon linguistic assimilation, which he assumed to be a powerful seductive force that could be harnessed to the task of producing an English-Canadian unity and identity. This continuation of the English-Canadian dream of Dominion, coupled with the assumption of the assimilative power of language, shows that the willingness to leave some differences in place and tolerate them was a self-conscious move in a long-term game. Even though it had failed miserably in both Acadia and Quebec, *strategic simulation of toleration of the Other* was being offered up once again as the solution to the problem of Canadian diversity. Blithely unaware of its own history, the English-Canadian tradition marched on, professing sympathy and liberal views and offering up the gifts of freedom and civilization, all in the name of gaining a much-coveted, but ever-elusive, national unity and identity. As yet, however, the Canadian state had not committed itself to this task, and continued to remain aloof. This would change with the Second World War, when relatively tolerable, somewhat Canadian Selves were once again transformed into monstrous Enemy Others whose mere presence constituted a national crisis.

WWII and the 'First Bureaucracy for Multiculturalism'

In this section, I set out to show how the constrained emergence theory of Canadian identity was taken up by the Canadian state as a solution to the wartime problem of European Immigrant diversity. The transfer of social-scientific knowledge to official policy came by way of two key figures: Tracy Philipps, whose intense lobbying helped to create the Nationalities Branch of the Department of National War Services; and Watson Kirkconnell, whose writing established the generic characteristics of the state-sponsored, academically produced pamphlets which are now ubiquitous. Through the efforts of Philipps, Kirkconnell, and other academic experts, the Canadian state began to take upon itself the role of 'policing culture' (Bauman 1992: 8), and it is in this sense that the Nationalities Branch, the form of which was maintained after the end of the war, can be considered as the 'first bureaucracy for multiculturalism' (Dreisziger 1988).

The Canadian government began its assault on the new Enemy

Aliens with the tried and true methods of bodily discipline. The War Measures Act, left over from 1914, was again invoked, and used to issue the *Defence of Canada Regulations* (Canada, Privy Council 1939). As in the First World War, one did not need to actually *do* anything to become an Enemy Alien; it was enough that one had lived in an occupied country, or that the Minister of Justice 'satisfied' himself that one might, in the future, act 'in any manner prejudicial to the public safety or the safety of the state' (Canada, Privy Council 1939: 29, s. 21). Such persons could be registered, detained, arrested, and interned, with no requirement for what is known as 'due process' within the tradition of Western liberalism.[4] While some people were disciplined for their former place of residence or supposed political beliefs,[5] others were deprived of their rights because of what appeared to the Canadian government as their 'racial origin.' Many whose origin the government identified as German or Italian were arrested and interned for having been so identified, and a large proportion of the interned Communists were classified/self-identified as Ukrainian or Jewish (J.H. Thompson 1991: 11–14). Perhaps the most famous internment of the Second World War was that of the Japanese, which also involved an effort in displacement and transportation the likes of which had not been seen in Canada since 1713.[6]

Although it depended heavily upon modern methods of discipline during the war, the Canadian government also took its first, tentative steps towards the adoption of a new, postmodern form. Following England, J.F. MacNeill of the Department of Justice wanted to abandon the use of 'repressive police measures' in dealing with the Immigrant problem, and advocated a shift to 'well written articles published in their own language ... printed and distributed free of charge' (cited in Dreisziger 1988: 5). Tracy Philipps, a widely travelled, multilingual diplomat and spy, was thinking along similar lines. Early in 1941, Philipps wrote a report on a tour he had made of the Immigrant heartland of the Western provinces, and addressed the means of attaining two goals:

A. *Immediate Aim.* To win the war.
B. *Ultimate aim.* Unity of the Canadian nation. (NAC, RG 26, vol. 1, file 22–2, vol. 1, 'Short Extract, Report Submitted on 16th January to the Associate Minister': 1)

Arguing against the strategy of 'attack' on the 'foreign element'[7] that had been used so far (section VI-1), Philipps proposed a method of seduction much more 'convenient to Nature':

> One gives the subject access to the sun. It illuminates, it enlightens and heals. One unearths their misapprehensions and their grievances. One treats these simultaneously and sympathetically ... This second process calls for far more patience. It is slower but surer ... The subjects spontaneously begin to detach themselves from their ancient backgrounds ... They are caught up into Canadianism of which at last they can be helped to feel themselves the co-creators. (VI-2)

To 'catch up' the problematic Continental Europeans, Philipps advocated a focused propaganda effort, arguing, after Woodsworth and Foster, that 'each national group has to be treated on its own peculiarities' (VI-3): 'The first hook-up has ... to be not between the divergent un-Canadianized groups themselves. Each community needs to feel itself separately and directly linked to the country's permanent government' (VI-4). On the level of tactics, Philipps advocated the Roman-Jesuit technique of 'employing even kings to make others slaves,' and seducing the Others into assimilation without their conscious awareness of what was taking place: '[O]ur first task is to work through the willing and already assimilated elements within each national group and of the same vocational class. Through them we can close up to other and older-Canadian contacts, until the new Canadians are *insensibly merged* into the main life-current of the nation' (VI-4, emphasis added).

As a complement to this effort, Philipps also suggested that the government seek to 'diminish Canadian disunity by interpreting sympathetically the less understood European Canadians to audiences of older Canadian stock' (VI-1). Like England, Philipps was assuming that the problem of European diversity must be officially addressed not only by removing signs of Otherness from bodies, but also by *trying to render these signs less offensive to those whom they offended*. Thus, for the first time, the Canadian government was to subject solid British-Canadian Selves to racial-cultural discipline, just as though they were Savage, Indian, French, or Immigrant Others. As an end-goal, Philipps visualized a constrained emergent Mosaic-like object, created through 'a process of building-in of a richly diversified human material into a very distinctive British-American edifice, identical with neither but drawing the best from both' (IX-2).

Throughout 1941, Philipps continued to argue for the establishment of a bureaucracy that would carry out this work, until finally, in December, he was hired as European Advisor to the Director of the Bureau of Public Information of the Department of National War Services, along with Professor George Simpson, who was to act as Senior Advisor (PC 103, 104, 3 Dec. 1941). This was an informal arrangement that seems to have served a mainly propagandistic function, the style of which can be seen in the pamphlet *Canadians All: A Primer of Canadian National Unity*. According to the Foreword, 'in this booklet, the authoritative pen of Prof. Watson Kirkconnell tells the story of the peoples of Canada, and points to a road for us to follow towards permanent unification of all our groups into one strong, resolute nation' (Kirkconnell 1941). Here, for the first time, academic authority and state power were brought together to produce seductive literature for mass consumption, with the goal – once again – of 'permanently' solving the problem of Canadian diversity.

In the first few pages, Kirkconnell follows Woodsworth's lead in laying out immigration and population statistics to prove the existence of 'the varied ingredients that history has poured into the huge mixing-bowl of Canada's national life' (7). Stealing a phrase from Foster, he declares that within this melange, 'no one element predominates' (7). The 'mixing-bowl' metaphor suggests that Kirkconnell adhered to a free emergence theory of Canadian identity. This tendency can also be observed in his claim that 'we are all minorities, but all Canadians, entering, each with his own capacities, into the richness of the national amalgam' (7). To justify this egalitarian rhetoric, and to counteract possible 'Nazi underground warfare,' Kirkconnell tried to discard the notion of race, calling it 'one of the most dangerous errors that can delude the human brain' (8), and declaring that 'there is no such thing as a French race, an Italian race, an Anglo-Saxon race, or a German race ... We are all mixtures' (11). Mixtures of what, one might ask? It turns out that 'to the scientist' – the Linnean natural scientist – there were in Europe 'three main subspecies of the human race, namely (i) the tall, fair-haired, long-skulled Nordic, (ii) the short, dark, long-skulled Mediterranean, and (iii) the stocky, broad-headed Alpine type' (8). Kirkconnell claims that 'every nation in Europe has been a mixture of these types,' and thus concludes that 'none of our national groups from Europe is really alien to the rest of us' (11).[8]

This equality effect can also be seen in the form and content of the mini-catalogue of human types that takes up the last half of the pamphlet. Here the focus is on the 'contributions to Canada' made by various groups. Equality is apparent in the fact that this section is arranged alphabetically, rather than in order of the Great Chain of Race as it was in Woodsworth's text. It is also worth noting that Kirkconnell's tone is decidedly more generous than Woodsworth's. The Indians and Eskimos are credited with having 'built up an extensive and typical American civilization' and with 'teaching the French and the Anglo-Saxons the arts of travel and survival in a vast new land' (37). Indeed, if he mentioned a group at all, Kirkconnell had nothing unpleasant to say about it, as he notes in his memoirs: 'I gave Oscar Cohen and the Canadian Jewish Congress a chance to vet my section on the contribution of the Jewish-Canadians. My one plea was that he should not try to inflate my text, since, in my effort to be generous to the Jews, I had given them more inches than any other group in Canada, including the French, the English, or the Scots' (Kirkconnell 1967: 273). These are signs that his pamphlet, of which 300,000 copies were distributed, was produced, not to aid bureaucratic action or edify academic colleagues, but for *mass consumption* by Canadians both problematic and canonical.

While he tried to set up a rhetoric of equality, a close reading of his text shows that Kirkconnell was not a free emergence theorist, but an advocate of a Canadian identity that would emerge only out of the White section of the Great Chain of Race, with these races renamed as nations. He writes, for example, that we 'should be careful never to assume that our fellow-Canadians, *of any origin*, are by nature unworthy of our sympathy, respect, and good will' (11, emphasis added). But this occurs in a paragraph which has as its topic 'our national groups from Europe.' In the discussion of races as 'mixtures,' he clearly states that 'none of our national groups *from Europe* is really alien to the rest of us' (11, emphasis added). Later, he suggests that 'all of us, of every origin, must resolutely repudiate' hatreds brought to Canada from abroad. Again, however, the only hatreds mentioned are those brought by 'our citizens from Europe' (12). Non-Europeans are never *explicitly* excluded from Kirkconnell's 'multi-national state' (12), but throughout the text the 'us' and 'we' that will contribute to the emergence of a Canadian identity are exclusively European. With its high rhetoric of equality masking a racialist limitation on the allowable parameters of emergence for a Canadian identity, *Canadians All* established the generic characteristics of the mass distribution pamphlets that would be produced by the Canadian state for the next fifty years, and which are still being pumped out by the hundreds of thousands.

This propaganda effort was given a more formal footing in 1942, with the creation, under ministerial authority, of the Nationalities Branch of the Department of National War Services. Also at this time, the Advisory Committee on Co-operation in Canadian Citizenship (ACCCC) was formed, to bring academic and other expert advice to bear upon the problem of the European Other. Its work, in the face of administrative and personal difficulties, is presented in glowing terms in Robert England's memoirs:

> Despite [some] handicaps, the committee and the branch continued to function, issuing a weekly release as to the use made of the Canadian topics in the foreign-language press, keeping liaison with the Red Cross, auxiliary services, the National War Finance Committee, and various friendship councils and community councils throughout the country, initiating helpful newspaper stories, and working actively with the various ethnic groups throughout the country. (England 1980: 137)

A similar résumé can be found in the pamphlets and speeches of Watson Kirkconnell, one of which was quoted at length in the House of Commons (*DHC*, 27 April 1944: 2417).

The records of the Nationalities Branch and the papers of Tracy Philipps in the National Archives corroborate these claims, but also add a little more to the story. The Editorial Section of the Nationalities Branch, under Vladimir Kaye, did indeed contribute to the foreign-language presses; but it spent much more time *monitoring* them, with the help of Kaye, whose multilingual skills were put to good use (NAC, RG 26, series B1, vols. 3–4, files 33-C-1 to 33-C-Z). Not only were Foreign presses watched, Foreign groups and individuals were tracked as well, and information exchanged with the police. In May 1942, Tracy Philipps sent a report on 'Communist Activity, Organization, and Plans' to Mervyn Black of the RCMP, and requested information on certain Slavic organizations and individuals. Black responded by naming several people as members of the Communist party, and also provided his opinion on the links between communism and Elements of Canada's Foreign population:

> An amalgamation of Slavic organizations took place in Hamilton during April and while there were included in this so-called United Slavic Organizations of Hamilton some church organizations, the Communist controlled language groups were overwhelmingly predominant. The

ostensible object of the conference held in Hamilton was, of course, for aid
to the Red Cross. (M. Black to T. Philipps, 22 June 1942, NAC, RG 30 E350,
vol. 1, file 8)

A similar exchange of correspondence, marked 'Secret,' took place in
November 1942, in which all of the directors of the United Slavic Organizations of Hamilton were provided with a communist or ethnic
nationalist connection. 'It seems quite obvious,' the Assistant Director
of Criminal Investigation for the RCMP concluded, 'that the Communists exercise considerable influence, if not control, in the Organization' (K. Duncan to T. Philipps, 23 Nov. 1942, NAC, RG 30 E350, vol. 1,
file 8). This was how the Nationalities Branch 'liased' and 'worked
actively' with 'various ethnic groups throughout the country' – it
subjected those Enemy Aliens who were not in internment camps to
surveillance and secret manipulation, in an attempt to assuage the
Canadian government's fear of the Red Menace.

Yet, despite its many activities – and perhaps because most of them
were kept secret – this early bureaucracy for the management of problematic Otherness atrophied and was faced with dissolution at the end
of the war, which had provided its *raison d'être*. Following what was
quickly becoming a great Canadian tradition of using academic exper-
tise to construct and justify the existence of the problem of Canadian
diversity, Robert England was brought in as a hired gun to help reorga-
nize the Nationalities Branch. His report made no new contributions or
innovations to the discourse on Canadian diversity, but was important
in that it recommended that the efforts of the Nationalities Branch be
continued during the peace:

> It was probable that we had before us at that time two or three more years
> of war succeeded by years of political adjustment in Europe, which
> would disturb many of our peoples of European origin. It was a measure
> of national wisdom to attach them closely to Canadian ideals and aspira-
> tions in the interest of their own peace of mind and the future welfare of
> their children. In view of this situation, I recommended the permanent
> establishment of a Citizenship Division ... (England 1980: 141)

A difficult debate ensued in the House of Commons (*DHC*, 27 April
1944: 2396 ff), with various members citing pamphlets, invoking the
Mosaic, and telling their personal stories of immigration. A Mr Pouliot
desperately pleaded for the Minister to 'get back to normalcy by

removing this item from the estimates' (2405), but there was a new normalcy on the horizon, and the item was passed. Not only was the Nationalities Branch – renamed as the Citizenship Division – saved, but its budget was more than doubled, so that it could carry on its dual mission of public friendship and secret surveillance, even though the National Emergency that had justified its creation would soon pass into history. Recalling this period in his memoirs, Robert England remembers that he had been asked 'facetiously' how he was getting on in the 'twilight zone' of the National War Services department. 'I was not quick enough to reply,' England writes, 'to the slightly pejorative term, by saying that I was midwife in the twilight sleep to the birth of a federal agency that would outlast the World War II defense agencies, and that the concept of citizenship was as vital to the survival of Canada as the Polymer Corporation or research into the splitting of the atom' (England 1980: 143). Plastics, atomic fission, and multicultural citizenship: harbingers of the coming postmodern age.

The Citizenship Machine

Having arrived at the safe resting place of the end of the Second World War, we might pause and consider the state of the problem of Canadian diversity at this crucial juncture. Coercive, total assimilation of European Immigrants was giving way to a more subtle form, in which the preservation of certain signs of Otherness was seen as permissible, perhaps even Desirable. The Canadian government was taking upon itself the task of not only training Others to be Selves, but of training Selves to accept the signs of Otherness that were being preserved. This strategy was adopted with the goal of helping European Others feel as though their nation was becoming an official state nation, and thus constituted a simulation of Self assimilation to the Other. This was a *strategic* simulation, however, because the long-term goal was still assimilation of these Others, the moment of preservation playing the role of 'ancient soil' brought along with the 'plant' to the 'new world,' where it would eventually be knocked off (England 1929: 187).

With the rise of the first bureaucracy for multiculturalism, the Canadian state began to expand its purview outside of the internment centres set up in times of 'national emergencies,' to attempt increasing everyday microcontrol of the lives of both canonical Selves and problematic Others. While I would not want to downplay the sufferings of those who have been held in concentration camps, both in Canada and elsewhere, there is a sense in which this form was being extended to cover those who, because of semiotic, financial, and physical limitations, could not be constructed as Enemy Aliens and interned. Rather than constraining the *bodies of some* of those who inhabited its territories, the Canadian government began to try to *constrain the minds of all.* This was the task allocated to the post-war Citizenship Branch, which, as I will show in this section, progressively extended its domain from the management of European Immigrants to include Indians and then canonical Canadians, until it became what I will refer to as a *citizenship machine.* In this way, the state emerged as the entity that would solve the problem of Canadian diversity once and for all, by providing a basis for unity that had otherwise been lacking.

A crucial event in the formation of the post-war discourse on diversity occurred in 1947, when the Canadian government announced that its new immigration policy would be 'based on the conviction that Canada needs population,' and would involve 'productive immigration measures.' In putting forth this 'new' policy, W.L Mackenzie King relied on some old arguments:

> [I]n a world of shrinking distances and international insecurity, we cannot ignore the danger that lies in a small population attempting to hold so great a heritage as ours ... A larger population will help to develop our resources. By providing a larger number of consumers ... it will reduce the present dependence of Canada on the export of primary products. (W.L. Mackenzie King, *DHC*, 1 May 1947: 2645)[9]

Past experience had shown that the procurement of Foreign producers and consumers usually led to trouble. But the Prime Minister hoped to avoid such problems by way of proper rational planning: 'The fear has been expressed that immigration would lead to a reduction in the standard of living. This need not be the case. If immigration is properly planned, the result will be the reverse ... The essential thing is that immigrants be selected with care, and that their numbers be adjusted to the absorptive capacity of the country' (2645). This planning and adjustment had as its goal the expansion of the size of the managed population available to the Canadian state and its capitalist economy, while preserving the state's articulation with that population through excluding Immigrants – for example, the 'oriental' – who would 'change' its 'fundamental composition' (2846).

This new immigration policy required, of course, a new bureaucracy.

King gave the Department of the Secretary of State, which had long been responsible for the *registration* of Canadian citizens, control of the Citizenship Branch, which was supposed to *create* them. The role of the Branch, as proposed by the Advisory Committee on Co-operation in Canadian Citizenship (ACCCC), was essentially propagandistic: to 'create among Canadians of French and British origin a better understanding of Canadians of recent European origin, and to foster among the latter a wider knowledge and appreciation of the best traditions of Canadian life' (Dept. of the Sec. of State 1949: 78). In carrying out its mission of peacetime propaganda, the Branch encouraged the provinces, which were responsible for education, to set up citizenship training classes. Seven of the ten provinces had done so by 1949, producing seventeen thousand new Canadians (Dept. of the Sec. of State 1949: 78). The task that had been formerly entrusted to the rubbing of shoulders and to Christians on internal missions was now being taken up by the Canadian state at both the federal and provincial levels.

To complement its new official policy for the production of citizens, Canada also required a new official history. This was provided by a booklet entitled *Our History*, ten thousand copies of which were printed in 1948 for use in citizenship classes. Here the Canadian government presented what was supposed to be 'a factual account of Canadian history under the general headings of Discovery and Exploration, Settlement, and Political Development' (Canada. Dept. of Citizenship and Immigration, Canadian Citizenship Branch 1961: 79). It is worth examining what was included in and excluded from *Our History*, as this pamphlet was periodically revised and reprinted up until its last edition in 1967, and the sanitized narrative it presented is still being recited as 'fact' to anyone who can be forced or seduced into listening to it.[10]

The English colony at Newfoundland is discussed in *Our History*, but the Beothuck are not (26). The Acadian transportation is given a few lines, and some attention is paid to the 'hardships' that were endured. But the events are treated as a sad necessity, the fault for which is laid at the door of its victims: 'Their refusal to swear allegiance to the British crown brought disaster upon them' (27). In the section on 'Settlement,' the expansion of Upper Canada under Simcoe is related, but no mention made of the people Simcoe had to push out of his way to implement what is referred to as his 'ambitious immigration policy' (30). The discussion of further Canadian expansion to the West is justified according to the ancient European doctrine of *terra nullius*, through the claim that 'the west was still practically empty' (32). New Immigrants would have been especially happy to hear about the wonderful experience of the Doukhobors in Canada: 'The group consisted of 7,400 persons who had fled from religious persecution in the Russian Crimea and who sought sanctuary in the New World. The Canadian government guaranteed them religious freedom, exemption from military service, and gave them a large tract of land on which to settle' (78). Again, there is no doubt about the 'facts' as given. What was not mentioned is that these promises were never kept, and that the Doukhobors have been excluded, ridiculed, persecuted, disenfranchised, interned, and jailed ever since setting foot on Canadian soil.

But the Sons of Freedom should feel honoured to be included in the short list of peoples and religions that were included in *Our History*, namely the British, French, Scottish, German, Americans, Mennonites, Irish, French Canadians, Icelanders, Mormons, Doukhobors, and Ukrainians. The Chinese, Japanese, Negroes, and Hindus were totally excluded, perhaps because there was simply no way to put an appropriate spin on the relevant 'facts.' No mention was made of the Indians, Half-breeds, Métis, or Inuit, as separate groups that had made a 'contribution.' In the sense that the development of this genre has always been towards greater inclusiveness, *Our History* was actually somewhat behind *Canadians All*, to which it owed a great debt for its literary-bureaucratic existence as a mass-consumption pamphlet. It was innovative within its genre, however, in its presentation of the 'facts' of Canadian history in such a way that only the 'good facts' were mentioned in most cases, and if the 'bad' came out at all, they were accompanied by a justification, as a sort of epistemological chaperone. Rogue facts have a way of tripping up even the most poised and well-balanced of narratives, and the task of the Information Division of the Canadian Citizenship Branch was to ensure that those relevant to Our History were kept in good order.

Meanwhile, the bureaucrats were playing a fast-paced game of musical chairs. The Citizenship Branch was transferred to the newly created Department of Citizenship and Immigration. Louis St Laurent, the new prime minister, gave the Branch the old task of 'bring[ing] to full citizenship as many as possible of those who immigrate to this country ... as quickly as could reasonably be expected' (*DHC*, 26 Nov. 1949: 2285). Once the government had decided that responsibility for citizenship and immigration should be consolidated, 'it was considered that the minister responsible for this department should, in addition, be given the responsibility for the Indian Affairs Branch' (Louis St Laurent, *DHC*, 26 Nov. 1949: 2285). This shift in bureaucratic responsibility deserves some comment. While attention had been focused on the Immigrant throughout the first half of the twentieth century, official interest in the 'Indian problem' had picked up in 1946, with the formation of a special joint parliamentary committee to examine the operation of the Indian Act and recommend changes. Why the sudden resurgence of interest in the Indians? John A. Glen, whose Ministry of Mines and Resources had governmental responsibility for their management, expressed it in clear, numerical terms. The Indians – who would not assimilate and who were supposed to be dying out – were not only continuing to live, but *thriving*, with a population 'of 128,000, increasing at the rate of 1,500 a year' (*DHC*, 13 May 1946: 1447). The size of the 'Indian problem,' which was taken to be proportional to the size of the unassimilated Indian population, was therefore seen as increasing at an alarming rate.

The debate regarding the establishment of the Indian Act committee shows that the Indian was still being viewed as an inferior internal Other to be protected and given the gift of civilization. John Glen, again, at greater length:

> It would appear that we have reached a stage in our development as a nation when economic conditions will force us to do one of two things: (1) purchase at public expense the additional lands and additional hunting and trapping rights for an Indian population of 128,000, increasing at the rate of 1,500 a year; or, (2) decide on an educational and welfare programme that will fit and equip the Indian to enter into competition with the white man not only in hunting and trapping but in agriculture and in the industrial life of the nation. While I have no desire to indulge in oversimplification ... I feel that we have here the crux of what is usually referred to as the Indian problem. (*DHC*, 13 May 1946: 1447)

While this definition of the 'Indian problem' and its possible 'solutions' was indeed accurate, and centuries old, Glen also showed his awareness of recent developments in the history of Canadian diversity when he cast the 'Indian problem' in the same terms as the problem of the Immigrant, and opted for the same sort of solution:

> The educational and welfare programme to which I have referred cannot, in the nature of things, accomplish much overnight. Nor should it be

aimed at making the Indian into a white man. The Indian, as I see it, should retain and develop many of his native characteristics, and should ultimately assume the full rights and responsibilities of democratic citizenship. (1447)

Like the European Immigrant, the Indian was not to be totally assimilated, but allowed to preserve 'many of' his characteristics; that is, those which the canonical Canadian people and their state found to be non-problematic. From now on, he would be *citizenized rather than civilized*.

St Laurent was following this line in his attempt to bring all of those who were seen as *not quite Canadian* together under the same bureaucratic roof. This, it was hoped, would bring together the people themselves, united in their articulation with the state apparatus as *official Others*. When pressed on the creation of yet another ministry, St Laurent replied that 'the object in all these activities is to *make* Canadian citizens of those who come here as immigrants, and to *make* Canadian citizens of as many as possible of the descendants of the original inhabitants of this country' (*DHC*, 2 Dec. 1949: 2596, emphasis added). Still plagued with an excess of Undesirable internal Others who would not go away, and facing a new 'flood' of incoming Others because of insecurity over the size of Canada's population and its status as a capitalist power, St Laurent envisioned the new Canadian Citizenship Branch as a *machine for the production of citizens* out of raw human resources. Following the model of modern capitalist industry, he hoped that this machine would provide as many of its objects as possible, as quickly as possible.

The new Department of Citizenship and Immigration went to work immediately and issued its first report in 1951. Frank Foulds, the director of the Canadian Citizenship Branch, described its mandate as follows:

The functions of the Canadian Citizenship Branch are to promote unity among all racial groups; to awaken in every Canadian, regardless of race or creed, a deep conviction of the worth of the individual and the principles of democracy; and to encourage a greater consciousness among our people of the achievements of the Canadian nation and the fact that all Canadians actively share in these achievements. (Department of Citizenship and Immigration [DC & I] 1951a: 9)

Foulds had a vision of expanding the mandate of his branch beyond European Immigrants and Indians, to cover 'all racial groups' and 'every Canadian.' Its scope was thus not merely widened, but was made *open-ended*. Everyone, regardless of their 'race or creed,' became potentially subject to Citizenship discipline; everyone became part of the problem of Canadian diversity. Of course, everyone could also become part of the solution, if only they would occupy the position of citizen offered by the various levels of the Canadian state. In this fashion, the state took on a role similar to that played by Apollo and Artemis in ancient Ionian Hellenism, by embodying 'the hope of intervention from above, for *dei ex machina* to re-order and clarify difference' (duBois 1991: 119).

From Racial Assimilation to Cultural Integration

The question remained, however, as to *how* order would be restored and Canadian unity achieved. While still under the Secretary of State, the front-line workers and policy-makers at the Branch seemed to know that 'assimilation' was not a good term to use for what they hoped to do to 'newcomers,' but they did not yet have anything to use in its place. With the move to their own department, however, they found their word – *integration*:

> The varied activities of the Canadian Citizenship Branch in the interests of a more closely *integrated* Canadian population were carried out with good success.

> The officers of the Liaison Division continued to facilitate the *integration* of new residents of Canada by assisting them to take their place in established Canadian organizations and institutions. (DC & I 1951a: 7, 9; emphases added)

While the 1950 Citizenship Branch report was crucial in its official adoption of the strategy of integration, the report for 1951 also marked an important shift in the discourse on Canadian diversity: the fall of the category of race. Even before the war, as seen in the discussion of Kirkconnell's pamphleteering work, Nazi propaganda had caused many to question the use of the term. Once news of the death camps was being widely broadcast, and the horrible results of the fascist combination of racialism with capitalist (ir)rationalism became apparent, race came to be excluded from official discourse altogether. The Canadian Citizenship Branch followed this trend by altering its statement of purpose. Whereas it had previously been out to promote unity among 'all racial groups,' it now took as its mandate the promotion of unity 'among the various ethnic elements in Canada' (DC & I 1951b: 9). Other than this change of term, the rest of the sentence remained the same, as did the format and content of the report. Race was out. Ethnicity was in.

Even the technicians of the Canadian census, who had hung onto race for decades despite public opposition, now gave it up. In the 1951 census, 'Origin' – with no qualifier – was said to refer to 'the cultural group, sometimes erroneously called "racial" group, from which the person was descended.' Enumerators were told to 'first attempt to establish a person's origin by asking the language spoken by the person (if he is an immigrant), or by his paternal ancestor when he first came to this continent.' If that failed, they were to start providing possible answers which, interestingly, had been racial distinctions ten years before, by asking, 'Is your origin in the male line English, Scottish, Ukrainian, Jewish ...' Finally, if all else failed, 'if a person states that, because of mixed ancestry, he really does not know what to reply to the question on origin,' the census-taker was authorized to commit a sad but necessary act: 'you will mark the oval "Unknown"' (Canada, Dominion Bureau of Statistics 1951: question 17).

The last bastion of race was to be found in the Immigration Branch, which was under the same minister as Citizenship, but was a little behind the times, in that it continued to issue statistical tables under titles like 'Racial Origin of Immigrants by Nationality' until 1954 (DC & I 1954: 32–3, table 3). The next year, quite without fanfare, 'Nationality' was replaced by 'Country of Citizenship,' and 'Racial Origin' gave way to 'Ethnic Origin,' to produce an otherwise identical table under the title 'Ethnic Origin of Immigrants by Citizenship' (DC & I 1955: 32–3, table 5). As if by magic, forty-six racial designations, from Albanian to Ukrainian, became ethnicities.

The decline of racialism was not merely a Canadian phenomenon, but occurred throughout the Western world. Theo Goldberg has noted that 'since World War II ... the cultural conception of race has tended to eclipse all others. It has become paradigmatic' (Goldberg 1993: 71). Tzvetan Todorov marked the same historical endpoint in claiming that 'the period of classical racialism seems definitely behind us, in the wake of the widespread condemnation of Nazi Germany's policies toward Jews; thus, we can establish its chronological limits with a precision that is unusual in the history of ideas: from 1749 (Buffon) to 1945 (Hitler)' (Todorov 1993: 157). Todorov points out that, while the term 'race' might have fallen from favour, the work that it enabled would continue:

> The term 'race,' having already outlived its usefulness, will be replaced by the much more appropriate term 'culture'; declarations of superiority and inferiority, the residue of the attachment to the universalist framework, will be set aside in favour of a glorification of difference (a difference that is not valorized in itself). What will remain unchanged, on the other hand, is the rigidity of determinism (cultural rather than physical, now) and the discontinuity of humanity, compartmentalized into cultures ... (Todorov 1993: 156–7)

The first proposition of what Todorov calls 'classical' racialism is affirmation of the existence of races. This flexible proposition is vital to the survival of the Western discourse on human diversity, because race can easily be replaced by any means of differentiation of human types without disrupting the other axes of the discourse. Indeed, race itself was a replacement for civilization and humanity in a prior formation, and so could quite easily give way to culture, while preserving the other axes of the discourse: the continuity between physical-cultural type and character; the action of the group on the individual; hierarchical ordering of the differentiated types; and knowledge-based politics or, as I would put it, the prescription of a program to bring everyday life into line with the symbolic universe created by the discourse of differentiation (Todorov 1993: 91–6). In the case of the problem of Canadian diversity, the project of Canadian unity took this role under racialism, and kept it as culturalism began its rise in the period after the Second World War.

But culture, it seems, was not able to replace race without some help from ethnicity, which helped to provide the needed causal link between the physical body and the personality. The 1950 report, even though it spoke of unifying races, also noted the existence of 'voluntary organizations ... referred to as ethnic groups,' which were 'clubs, societies, and other organizations built around the memory of the countries from which the members or their families came' (DC & I 1951a: 10). The report also used the term 'ethnic group' in a broader

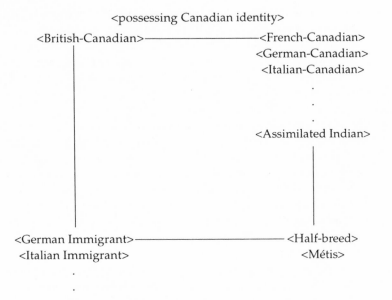

Fig. 7.1. Group identity in Canada, post-WWII

sense, noting that 'the many ethnic groups have established numerous organizations to satisfy the needs and problems peculiar to their own groups' (11). The next year, ethnicity was elevated to a central position, with the first function of the Citizenship Branch being to 'promote unity among the various ethnic elements in Canada' (1951b: 9). In its 1952 report, the Branch provided a definition of ethnic groups as 'various non-English or non-French-speaking organizations of Canada' (1952: 12). Presumably, since a separate section of that same report dealt with the Indians, they did not constitute an ethnic group. Ethnic groups were thus neither British nor French nor Indian, but were Canadian to the extent that they had assimilated and acquired, like the British and French before them, a hyphen. The semiotic square of Canadian identity that had been emerging over the post-war period can now be set out (see fig. 7.1) as a means of showing how Canadians were distinguished from non-Canadians by way of the categories of culture and ethnicity.

The representation of the hierarchies in figure 7.1 is not intended to be complete nor, by the principle of plenitude (see chapter 3), could it *ever be* complete. I have tried to capture, however, the central features of the discourse on Canadian identity and diversity at this time. The hierarchy in the <Immigrant> term was arranged according to the Great Chain of Race, and there was a 'bar' above which a group had to be placed before it could be considered for transformation into a Self group. After the Second World War, this bar was placed just below the White portion of the Chain – itself a shifting boundary – and thus excluded the Yellow, Black, and, for all practical purposes, the Red. Continental Europeans, however, could be brought over to the Self side, where they would be fitted into an appropriate place in the hierarchy within that position, which also reproduced the Great Chain of Race. This, indeed, was precisely the function of the Citizenship machine: to transform <Immigrant Xs> not possessing Canadian identity, but potentially Useful to Canadian society, into <X-Canadians> who could be seen, to some limited extent, as Selves.

By 1956, the Citizenship Branch was able to issue a clear and concise statement on 'The Integration of Immigrants in Canada,' in which the shift away from racial assimilation, begun early in the twentieth century, finally achieved explicit articulation as a government policy based on a history of respect and fair dealings:

> Canada's policy towards immigrants is naturally a reflection of the political and cultural pattern of our society. It is a society built on the ideas of individual worth and cultural difference ... The pressure of one dominant group to assimilate, that is, to absorb others is therefore impracticable as a general theory. The assimilation which does occur, is gradual and cannot be forced. (DC & I 1956: 1)

Immediately after mentioning the 'assimilation which does occur,' which is gradual and not forced, the report moved on to a discussion of integration: 'Integration, however, is used in Canada to express a theory which combines unity and diversity. The unity is sought in common principles of political philosophy and in participation in common citizenship. The diversity is maintained by reciprocal appreciation of diverse cultural contributions' (1).

In addition to explicitly formulating and justifying the shift from racial assimilation to ethnic/cultural integration of Immigrant Others, this report also ventured onto new ground. Buried within the text, and occurring only once, was a reference to 'the multicultural structure of the Canadian population' (5). The acts had been described, and the fact was now named. Although most of the work was still being done by patriotic volunteer organizations and the provinces, the post-war era saw increasing intervention of the Canadian state in providing solutions to the problem of Canadian diversity, primarily by taking on the task of what it now called 'integration' of citizens. This effort to reach out from the internment camps and RCMP surveillance systems, into the everyday lives of Canadians both canonical and problematic, was the basis for the following half-century of efforts at designing and instantiating a simulation model of the proper citizen; that is, it provided the conditions of possibility for the emergence of multiculturalism as state policy.

Chapter Eight

Unhappy Countriness:
Multiculturalism as State Policy

[W]ith a festive aura of imaginary consensus, multiculturalism implies that Canadian society offers equality of opportunity in the public sphere, regardless of private ethnic classification. Hence the usage of 'ethnic' to refer to all cultural sub-groups including 'dominant ethnics' thereby obfuscating the cultural hierarchy and redefining ethnicity until it is meaningless

– Kogila Moodley, 'Canadian Multiculturalism as Ideology,' 320

Having returned to the present, that is, to multiculturalism 'proper,' the central question set out at the start of this book can be addressed: to what extent can Canadian multiculturalism be considered as the achievement of, or a step on the way to, a post-industrial *Sittlichkeit*? As this is a complex question, involving two subquestions – of the 'achievement' and the 'step on the way' – and several subfields of multiculturalism, I will treat its elements separately. In this chapter, I will discuss the extent to which multiculturalism as state policy represents an already achieved ideal of multiculturalism that could be considered 'post-industrial' or, as I prefer, postmodern. In the final chapter, I will deal with the question of whether contemporary multiculturalism as political theory and philosophy points the way towards an ethical community of equal and mutual recognition – a *Sittlichkeit*. Since this split is clearly artificial and occurs only through the necessity of producing a linear flow of argument, I will also try, in the final chapter, to restore the question to its own state of fullness.

The 'Liberalization' of Canadian Society

Given the hegemony of British language, culture, and social and political institutions, English Canada before the 1960s was, for most purposes, a monocultural, monolingual, single-nation state, and made no apologies for being so. 'Canada is perfectly within her rights in selecting the persons whom we regard as desirable future citizens,' W.L. Mackenzie King declared in 1947. 'It is not a "fundamental human right" of any alien to enter Canada. It is a privilege' (*DHC* 1, May 1947: 2646). With its citizenship bureaucracy, the Canadian state had acknowledged the existence of non-canonical Canadian identities, but, as their surveillance, internment, and transportation during the Second World War shows, these official Others were not seen as possessing full rights of citizenship, and were allowed to exist only on the assumption that their difference would wither away. As I have tried to show in the previous chapters, this hope has always been present, and has always been in vain – *Canada has always been split*, not only in two, but in multiple fractures within fractures. What changed after the '60s was that there was a rapidly growing public *awareness* of this fragmentation, and of the fact that it would not be easily overcome. This is the contradictory position described by Hegel on the individual level as 'Unhappy Consciousness': 'This unhappy, inwardly disrupted consciousness ... must for ever have present in the one consciousness the other also; and thus is it driven out of each in turn in the very moment when it imagines it has successfully attained to a peaceful unity' (Hegel 1977: 126). The unhappy consciousness contains both Self and Other, master and slave, particular and universal, but does not know how to *reconcile* these opposites, and so suffers. In the field of ethnogenetic desire, we might name it 'Unhappy Countriness,' and see Canada in the late twentieth century as a paradigmatic case.

With the coming of the 1960s, the decade of radicalism, Canadian society began to be 'liberalized,' following an international trend towards American-style individual rights. The federal government eagerly signed on to the various declarations and proclamations, and produced its own Bill of Rights (8–9 Elizabeth II c. 44 1960). In federal language and culture policy, there were three main components to this 'reform': firstly, official bilingualism and biculturalism, which was supposed to give the Québécois nation an *official state identity*, and thereby transform it from an Other to a Self position; secondly, the policy of multiculturalism in a bilingual framework, which claimed to carry out the same transformation on the Other Ethnic Groups in a slightly different way, by offering *official recognition of possession* of identity; and, thirdly, the Indians, Inuit, and Métis were brought into official language and culture policy as 'the Aboriginal peoples,' and were granted their own set of rights. In this chapter, I will evaluate each of these areas of current state policy, with an eye to whether or not they represent a 'break with the past' (Canada 1969: 5). I will argue that, while there might now be fewer instances of violent struggle, the extension of 'rights' and 'equality' to an increasing number of mass-designed identities has not led to 'freedom,' but to further penetration of state forms into the daily lives of Canadians, through the progressive *officialization* of both Self and Other identities. I will link the genealogical work of chapters 3 through 7 with the field of Canadian diversity as it was presented in chapter 2, to argue that while Canadian multiculturalism as state policy does show signs of taking on a 'postmodern' style, it does not represent an overcoming of the history of Canadian diversity. Rather, it creatively reproduces this history by carrying out a shift from attempted control of 'modern difference' to a desire for mastery of 'postmodern *différance*.'

From Monopoly to Duopoly: The B & B Report

> Mr. Blackmore: Canada was explored, settled, and developed by two great races, two of the greatest races in the world; the French and the British people. Have these races no rights? Have their fathers no rights to see their children well provided for in this land they strove to gain for them? Have their children no rights to be well born into an environment in which they can succeed and be happy? We might sum the matter up in this simple question: Has Canada no right to remain British?
> Mr. Michaud: To remain Canadian.
> Mr. Blackmore: That is very well put. I thank the hon. member. I say, has Canada no right to remain British Canadian?
> Mr. Laurendeau: Put 'Canadian' on the record.
> Mr. Blackmore: We have finally arrived at the word which pleases everybody. Has Canada no right to remain Canadian? (*DHC*, 28 Aug. 1946: 5514; cited in Palmer 1973: 285)

Before it thought about connecting itself to what it saw as a multiplicity of cultures and ethnic groups within its territories, the Canadian state first tried to solidify and clarify its articulation with the Two

Founding Races. In theory, Canada had been a two-nation state since 1774, when the French of Quebec were granted the right to maintain certain aspects of their social, legal, and religious particularity. While this was undoubtedly a *gift* from the British, the deal struck at the time of Confederation implied that the two peoples were coming together as equals, to form, in the words of Adélard Godbout, 'the headstones of the entire edifice' of Canada (Dept. of National War Services 1940: 13). That English-Canadian nationalists had never really seen Confederation as a meeting of equals is apparent in the obstinate equation of Britishness with Canadianness in the quote that opens this section, in the policy of Limited Selective Immigration from the British Isles, and in attempts to assimilate/integrate non-British Immigrants to the English-speaking society. Whatever the BNA Act might say, or however it might have been interpreted, the Canadian state had always lived, worked, and, most importantly, *dreamed* in English.

In 1963, acknowledging yet again that it had a 'French problem,' the federal government appointed a royal commission to find a solution. The commissioners soon found themselves, like Lord Durham, 'driven to the conclusion that Canada, without being fully conscious of the fact, is passing through the greatest crisis in its history' (Royal Commission on Bilingualism and Biculturalism 1965: 13).[1] Their mandate was to 'report upon the existing state of bilingualism and biculturalism in Canada and to recommend what steps should be taken to develop the Canadian Confederation on the basis of an equal partnership between the two Founding races ...' (1). Curiously, race had resurfaced as a means of distinguishing between the two Founding groups, making the *Preliminary Report* of the Royal Commission on Bilingualism and Biculturalism sound even more like the Durham Report. But the nature of the problem of Canadian diversity had expanded considerably since the visit by the Lord and his entourage, and so the Commission was also instructed to take into account 'the contribution made by the other ethnic groups to the cultural enrichment of Canada, and the measures that should be taken to safeguard that contribution' (151).

Alerted to potential problems caused by distinguishing between 'founding races' and 'ethnic groups' during its preliminary hearings, the Commission tried to crawl out from under the heavy terminological load that had been placed upon it:

This wording, particularly the use in the English text of the word 'race,' has been a source of misunderstanding. Should it be taken to mean that the two 'races' or two 'peoples' will receive special treatment at the expense of the 'other ethnic groups'? Some understood it this way ... (xxii)

The commissioners, however, understood their terms of reference in a different way:

In our view the reference to the two 'founding races' or 'peoples who founded Confederation' is an allusion to the undisputed role played by Canadians of French and British origin in 1867, and long before Confederation. The word 'race' is used in an older meaning as referring to a national group, and carries no biological significance. (xxi)

This argument is very odd, in that it was not the biological connotation that was causing the objections, but the perpetuation of differential relations of power within the discourse on Canadian diversity. It makes sense, however, in that the Commission was following the general post-war trend of simply renaming racial distinctions as cultural, national, or ethnic, and continuing with its work.

While it accepted the necessity of struggling with the Founding races and the Other ethnic groups, the B & B Commission managed to lighten its load by shedding the Native peoples of Canada: 'We should point out here that the Commission will not examine the question of the Indians and the Eskimos. Our terms of reference contain no allusion to Canada's native populations' (xxvi). This act of exclusion highlights a subtle, but important, difference between the status of the Native peoples and the Europeans within the regime of bilingualism and biculturalism. The Other Ethnic Groups were seen as potentially making 'contributions' to the 'cultural enrichment' of Canada, but the Native peoples were to enjoy their 'preserved' cultures in solitude. For, while the Canadian state was able to consider the possibility of giving off more signs of the French race, and perhaps even displaying a touch of Ukrainian ethnicity, it could not imagine itself, under any circumstances, going Native. Indeed, despite its relative sophistication in textual construction, the Commission managed to unwittingly invoke the settlement and expansion phases of the Canadian discourse on diversity as a means of setting up a solidarity between the Other Ethnic Groups and the Two Founding Races: 'When they [the Other Ethnic Groups] arrived, their essential concern was to continue the work of *carrying civilization* into the thinly populated areas. By settling the country they helped to lay the basis for Canada's cultural growth' (xxv, emphasis added). On one side, we have the Civilized Europeans, possessed of cultures and civilizations that can be shared. On the other, the Indian, Uncivilized and, although possessed of a culture, not one of the sort that could be shared with Europeans.

In its attempt to ward off the idea that the Canadian state was offering 'special treatment' to the Two Founding Races, the Commission was deep in contradiction, since it held at the same time that 'language is the most evident expression of a culture, the one which most readily distinguishes cultural groups even for the most superficial observer' (xxx). If this is the case, a culture which was allowed to striate a space with its language would have a greater likelihood of achieving and maintaining hegemony than one that did not. Certainly, as I have shown in chapters 6 and 7, English Canada had always operated under this assumption, and there was nothing in the policy of bilingualism and biculturalism to indicate that this was changing. Indeed, at the close of its discussion of the links between language and culture, the Commission concluded that 'the vitality of the language is a necessary condition for the complete preservation of a culture' (xxxvii), and that 'the life of the two Founding cultures implies in principle the life of the two languages' (xxxviii).

After several years of research, consultations, and hearings, the Royal Commission issued a lengthy report and a series of recommendations. Access to bilingual education was to be guaranteed, and a Commissioner of Official Languages was to supervise the implementation of a federal Official Languages Act. These measures, along with several of lesser import, were called a *'new* charter for the official languages in Canada' (*B & B Report*: 1.30, emphasis added). But there was nothing 'new' about the 'fundamental duality' enshrined in this Act. It had been around for two hundred years, long enough that, rather than trying to legislate for or against it, one might begin to wonder how it *worked*. One possibility is suggested by Jean Baudrillard's comments on the 'tactical doubling of monopoly' in postmodern capitalist societies:

> In all domains, duopoly is the final stage of monopoly ... any unitary system, if it wishes to survive, must acquire a binary regulation ... It will never again be a matter of a duel or open competitive struggle, but of couples of simultaneous opposition. (Baudrillard 1983: 134).

As I have suggested, the days of the fur trade and the battles between the English and French over territory in the New World could be considered the phase of 'open competitive struggle,' while the period after the fall of Quebec would see a slow shift towards a master-slave system of strategic regulation. This peculiar situation has given rise to two more Hegelian forms that should be noted; for where could one find a better example of Stoic freedom than in the consciousness of the federalist French within Canada? From the Articles of Capitulation to official bilingualism and biculturalism, illusory freedoms and scraps of recognition have been tossed their way to be hungrily devoured. And, as for nihilistic scepticism, this can be seen in the various Québécois separatism and sovereignty movements, perhaps most profoundly in those who advise going over to the Americans – sleeping with English Canada's obviously superior rival, as a potentially self-destructive act of revenge.

While opinions on its achievements differ, there is little doubt that the process of liberalization caused the square of identity from Canadian post-war discourse to be *officialized*; that is, the semantic axis was shifted from <Canadian identity>, in the sense of Canadianness or Canadian character, to <official Canadian identity>. This implied that the state would take on the task of not only tolerating, but *itself producing*, signs of any identity deemed official. Under the regime of bilingualism and biculturalism, the British and French cultures and languages were granted this status, as races or nations, with British dominant, as the giver of the gift of equality to the French Other. The contradictory position of that which was both British and French was taken up by the French outside Quebec and the English within, for even though both of their languages and cultures were official, these hybrids could not be given a place within the fundamental duality, and thus could not possess an <official identity>. The Other Ethnic Groups, those who were neither British nor French, occupied the complementary position, where they were allowed to preserve and maintain an ethnicity, that is, a language and culture that were not official, and would not be displayed in state bureaucracies or social, economic, and political institutions. Finally, the Indians, Inuit, Métis, and Half-breeds were not considered as possessing, or lacking, any sort of official identity at all. In being excluded from the process entirely, they once again disappeared from view.

Such was the regime of official identity within the policy of bilingualism and biculturalism. While most of the old rules of the game of identity were preserved in this policy, it also contributed to an ongoing

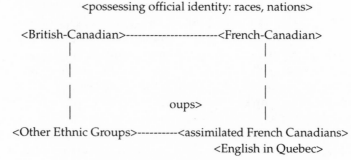

<possessing official identity: races, nations>

<British-Canadian>----------------------<French-Canadian>

oups>

<Other Ethnic Groups>----------<assimilated French Canadians>
<English in Quebec>

<lacking official identity: ethnic gr

Fig. 8.1. Official identity in Canadian bilingualism and biculturalism

evolution, by increasing the extent to which Canadians of all types were to be manufactured and scrutinized. If the Canadian Citizenship Act and its associated bureaucratic supports formed a machine for the production of citizens, the Official Languages Act added a part that specialized in the production of French-English bilingual citizens. While 'old' Canadians had previously been required only to *tolerate* signs of Otherness, they were now being told that they must *take them on themselves* in order to remain canonical. As Jean Burnet has noted, however, just as soon as [British?] Canadians 'began to accustom themselves to a new model of Canadian society ... Prime Minister Pearson and others started to speak of Canada not as bicultural but as multicultural' (Burnet 1975: 205). With the policy of 'multiculturalism in a bilingual framework,' the present of Canadian diversity began to catch up with its past, and the world of official Canadian Selfhood began to go through the same process of multiplication that had been lamented for so many years in the realm of official Otherness.

Multiculturalism in a Bilingual Framework as Strategic Simulation of Assimilation to the Other

After convincing itself once again that it 'needed' Immigrants, the Canadian state quickly abandoned official bilingualism and biculturalism in favour of what came to be known as 'multiculturalism in a bilingual framework.' In this section, I will show how this change involved certain reproductions of, and innovations in, the Canadian discourse on diversity. First, a new means of differentiating the population was found, in which all groups were granted an 'ethnocultural origin.' The state could now claim that multiculturalism was about 'equality,' since the same category was used to describe *all* Canadians. This was accompanied by a complementary – and semantically necessary – dissociation of language and culture which, I will argue, allowed the policy to be seen as both protecting the particularity of incoming Others *and* assuring canonical Canadians that these Others would be rendered into Selves. Finally, a productive confusion of assimilation and integration allowed the French colonial method of *strategic simulation of assimilation to the Other* (see chapters 4 and 7) to be recovered as the basis for handling problematic diversity within state policy. The work of this section, then, is first to show how multiculturalism in a bilingual framework creatively reproduced the post-war policy discourse, and second, to prepare for a discussion of the extent to which this creative reproduction can be seen as a 'break with' or 'overcoming of' the history of Canadian diversity.

In the 1966 *White Paper on Immigration* (Dept. of Manpower and Immigration 1966), the Canadian state clearly signalled its desire for an increased population to manage. Assuming that there was 'little dissent from the proposition that Canada still needs immigrants' (5), the *White Paper* invoked some favourite tropes from previous centuries and millennia:

> Canada is an under-populated country by most standards of measurement. It must appear *almost barren* of people to many of the countries of Africa and Asia with their *teeming millions* ... Many Canadians are attracted to the theory that [we should] *fill up our empty spaces* as rapidly as possible with any and all immigrants willing to cast their lot with us ...
> (7, emphasis added)

But, despite the wishes of 'many Canadians,' the government was not going to play at dice. The question, as always, was 'what number and kind of immigrants should be sought in the years ahead, and from what sources' (5).

This statement has a curious ring, since the consideration of 'sources' was supposed to have ended with a 'colour blind' immigration policy announced four years earlier. According to Ellen Fairclough, then Minister of Citizenship and Immigration, the new regime would ensure that 'any suitably qualified person, from any part of the world,' could be considered for immigration to Canada 'entirely on his own merit, without regard to his race, colour, national origin or the country from which he comes' (*DHC*, 19 Jan. 1962: 9). It should not be surprising that the policy did not live up to the pronouncement, as this path had been followed many times before: by Frank Oliver in present-ing the 1910 Immigration Act (*DHC*, 21 March 1910: 5505); and by Clif-ford Sifton, in his policy of the late 1800s: 'We have not been disposed to exclude foreigners of any nationality who seemed likely to become successful agriculturalists' (Sifton to Laurier, 1901, cited in Knowles 1997: 62). In 1962, as in 1910 and 1901, the Minister was simply not tell-ing the whole truth. And little could she afford to do so. Every time the Canadian government had set out to acquire Foreign bodies, it had encountered a nativist reaction from existing Canadians, which, though it may have been correlated with internal class warfare, exter-nal national warfare, or simply fear of incoming Otherness, always placed responsibility for Canada's problems on the incoming or already arrived Other. This happened before WWI, after WWII, and could reasonably be expected to occur again in the 1960s and '70s.

A similar state of dreary repetition had been reached with regard to the 'Indian problem' and its attempted solution through various Indian Acts. Leslie and Maguire note that 'for one hundred and forty years, essentially the same policy has been "rediscovered" and redefined to serve government objectives. However, it has only sustained failure in accomplishing what it set out to do ...' (1978: 191–2). In its 1969 *White Paper*, the Canadian government announced that it was going to disrupt this continuity by washing its hands of the 'Indian problem' and thereby make a 'break with the past' (Canada 1969: 5). It only ended up repro-ducing this past, of course, but this time using much of the same rhetoric as had been employed in the End of History in immigration policy: 'The Government believes that its policies must lead to the full, free, and non-discriminatory participation of the Indian people in Canadian society' (5). Ottawa planned to offload responsibility for the Indians to the provinces (9) and dismantle the Department of Indian Affairs (10). After several hundred years of abusive tutelage and failed attempts at extermination, assimilation, and integration, the Indians were now offered the gift of a 'framework within which, in an atmosphere of free-dom,' they could, 'with other Canadians, work out their own destiny' (13). Of course, there would be a 'transitional period,' but the govern-ment hoped to implement this 'solution' within five years (13).

Unfortunately for the Canadian state, a large number of Indians rec-ognized what was going on immediately. They had never wanted to become Canadian, *still* did not want to become Canadian, and saw this move, in Howard Cardinal's words, as 'a thinly disguised programme of extermination through assimilation' (Cardinal 1969: 1):

> Before the Canadian government tries to feed us hypocritical policy state-
> ments, more empty promises, more forked tonguistics, our people want,
> our people, the Indians, demand just settlement of all our treaty and
> aboriginal rights. Fulfillment of Indian right by the queen's government
> must come before there can be any future co-operation between the Indi-
> ans and the government. We demand nothing more. We expect nothing
> less. (28)

Something had to be done to solve the 'problems' of the French, the Immigrant, and the Indian once and for all. This something was called 'multiculturalism.'

As a state policy, multiculturalism emerged out of volume 4 of the *B & B Report*, which was entitled *The Cultural Contribution of the Other Ethnic Groups* (see Burnet 1975; Kallen 1982: 52–6; Lewycky 1992: 372–5). In presenting its report, the Commission cited its terms of reference as a justification for limiting its study to 'the part played by these groups in the country's history and the contribution they make to Canadian life' (*B & B Report*: 4.xxv). This is immediately recognizable as the sort of treatment given by Woodsworth and Kirkconnell, and perpetuated by the Department of Citizenship and Immigration in pamphlets like *Our History* (1961; first published in 1948) and *Notes on the Canadian Family Tree* (1960). The Commissioners picked up on this limited acknowledgment of particularity and relevance, and put it to good use in their denial of the existence of a 'third force' in Canadian politics. All that the Other Ethnic Groups had in common, according to the writers of the *B & B Report*, was their Otherness:

> In approaching our subject this way we are not implying the existence in
> Canada of a 'third force,' made up of all those of ethnic origin other than
> British or French. It should be remembered that the census lists some 30
> different ethnic origin categories and still does not list them all, and that
> there are great differences in numbers, concentration, time of arrival, and
> degree of group awareness among the different cultural groups. (*B & B
> Report*: 4.435)

With the help of the Canadian census and a rich horde of academic studies,[2] the common ground of the Other Ethnic Groups was skilfully delimited so as to allow them all to be *managed* under one policy, while being denied the right to commonly *resist* this policy.

The official adoption of multiculturalism was announced in Pierre Trudeau's famous speech to the House of Commons on the day the *White Paper on Multiculturalism* was released. Always a master of political oratory, Trudeau began with a joyous revelation: 'Mr. Speaker, I am happy this morning to be able to reveal to the House that the government has accepted all those recommendations of the Royal Commission on Bilingualism and Biculturalism which are contained in Volume IV of its reports *directed to federal departments and agencies'* (*DHC*, 8 Oct. 1971: 8545, emphasis added). This was a very creative reading of the *White Paper*, which clearly showed a reluctance to commit state resources to a new regime of ethnocultural identification. Out of the Commission's sixteen recommendations, seven were dismissed as superfluous, five were said to be out of federal jurisdiction, three were relegated to a 'research program,' and only one, suggesting increased funding for linguistic assimilation, was to be implemented (Sessional Paper 283–4/101B, *DHC*, 8 Oct. 1971, Appendix: 8583–4). Despite all of the fanfare regarding this 'new' policy, there was, by the government's own estimation, very little for it to do, other than place a different label on programs that had been in place since the 1940s.

But this did not stop Pierre Trudeau, who immediately began to erect a scaffolding of high-sounding rhetoric over the emptiness of his announcement, making use of the well-worn planks of *liberté, égalité, fraternité*: 'The individual's freedom would be hampered if he were locked for life within a particular cultural compartment by the accident of birth or language. No citizen or group of citizens is other than Canadian, and all should be treated fairly' (8545). This line was picked up and enhanced by later multiculturalism policy documents. Liberty: multiculturalism 'entrenches the idea of *freedom* of choice, which is a basic tenet of our democracy' (*MCBC*: 19). Equality: 'recognizing multiculturalism to be a central feature of Canadian citizenship ... acknowledges the essential *equality* of all our people ...' (19). Community: 'multiculturalism has evolved as a *powerful bonding agent* for Canadians ... It helps unite us and identify us' (9). This claim to have implemented the goals of the French Revolution allowed Canadian multiculturalism to be portrayed as something different from 'those distasteful, sometimes shameful, and always heart-breaking injustices in Canadian history which left members of various minority groups frustrated or humiliated or outraged' (5). That is, multiculturalism as state policy was presented as *an overcoming of the history of Canadian diversity*. This is a claim that is easily evaluated, with reference to the key features of the discourse on Canadian diversity that I have used throughout this book, and indeed derived from the official state discourse in the first instance: the means of differentiation of human types; the hierarchization and problematization of the differentiated system of types; and the modes of solution adopted to solve the problem.

Multiculturalism is certainly not an overcoming of the history of Canadian diversity in the sense that it has ceased to classify human beings based on signs of difference from a canonical type. Having moved through humanity and civilization, to race, culture, and ethnicity, differentiation within Canadian multiculturalism as state policy is accomplished with the help of yet another category: ethnocultural origin. In order to understand what this term means, I will turn to the glossary in *Multiculturalism: Building the Canadian Mosaic (MCBCM)*. To begin at the highest level of abstraction:

> MULTICULTURALISM: Recognition of the diverse cultures of a plural society based on three principles: we all have an ethnic origin (equality); all our cultures deserve respect (dignity); and cultural pluralism needs official support (community). (*MCBCM*: 87)

If 'we all have an ethnic origin,' then it would be important to know just what an 'ethnic origin' is. The text obliges:

> ETHNOCULTURAL/ETHNIC ORIGIN: Cultural, national, or racial origin of a person. Every Canadian has an ethnic origin. (The use of the word 'ethnic' as a noun e.g. 'an ethnic' or 'the ethnics' is generally a slang term and is sometimes considered derogatory. 'Ethnic' as an adjective is generally acceptable.) (87)

As long as one uses the correct grammatical construct, it is generally acceptable to mark out differences between human types based on their presumed 'cultural, national, or racial origin.' But what does this mean? Neither 'cultural origin' nor 'national origin' is seen as a key term in need of definition, and so we are left to assume that these origins would be detected, in the traditional Herodotan way, through such signs as skin colour, clothing, mode of government, and so on.

Racial origin, however, *is* seen as worthy of a definition, through its root word, *race:*

> RACE: Working term to describe ethnic origin of peoples defined on the basis of certain common physical features. Examples are Whites or Caucasians, South Asians, Blacks, Chinese or South East Asians. (87)

A strange, frustrating, but definitely *working* circularity occurs here: ethnic origin is defined as dependent upon cultural, national, and racial origin, and race is said to depend upon ethnic origin! Of course, this 'confusion' is very informative, as it provides evidence of the arbitrary nature of these categories. It also exposes the Canadian state's attempt to find an 'acceptable' language in which to express the will to problematic categorization of Others that, despite much protestation to the contrary, continues to permeate Canadian society and state policy.

Thus, while the exact nature of the categories has shifted, and the weird and wonderful diversity of types is found *inside* rather than *outside* the safely striated space of civilization, there is a definite line of descent from Herodotus to Linnaeus to J.S. Woodsworth, and on to Canadian multiculturalism as state policy. *Notes on the Canadian Family Tree*, first published in 1960 by the Canadian Citizenship Branch, describes itself as 'an attempt to provide factual information on many of the ethnic groups that comprise the Canadian population' (1960: i). This goal will be familiar to readers of *Strangers within Our Gates*, who will recognize immediately the table of contents arranged according to national/ethnic types, and the ensuing enumeration of history, characteristics, and contributions to Canada. ('The Japanese are very fond of picnics,' we are told on page 83.) The groups are presented in alphabetical order, following Kirkconnell's egalitarian innovation in *Canadians All* (1941), and number twenty-three in the first edition. This edition is also of interest because it did not include either the British or the French, 'groups on which ... much material is available in other forms' (i). This omission of the two Founding races from the Canadian family tree may at first seem odd, but makes sense when one realizes that it is not the Invisible Self groups that are being described here: it is the familiar, but still strange and problematic, diversity of Visible, audible, and olfactory Others.

A new edition of the *Canadian Family Tree* was produced for the 1967 centennial of Confederation. Like the immigration logbooks of the late 1800s, which showed a steady increase in the number of categories of

Immigrant Otherness, the new edition of the *Family Tree* was able to display forty-seven types of Canadian, including the French and the British, broken down into the Wales/Ireland/Scotland/England subgroups. The alphabetical arrangement remained unchanged, as did the narrative form of history, characteristics, and contributions. By the 1979 edition, seventy-eight groups were listed, bringing the number of categories of contributing cultures more or less in line with the number of Immigrant ethnicities. The form of the *Canadian Family Tree* can thus be traced, in a creative evolution, from Woodsworth's *Strangers within Our Gates* to the stable pattern reached in 1979 and used ever since. This stability can be attributed to the achievement of a substantive rhetoric of presentation adequate to the political rhetoric of multiculturalism: alphabetization replaced arrangement by the Great Chain of Race, signifying equality; all of the same signs of difference were noted, but the basis for the comparison, the canonical English-Canadian Self, was not; the Invisible Self groups were listed along with the Visible Others, covering for the silent basis of differentiation, and furthering the notion that all Canadians were Immigrants; and, finally, consistent and unabashed xenophilia replaced an equally unbalanced xenophobia, giving the impression that tolerance, harmony, and mutual love reigned from sea to sea.

In the face of such perfection of form, one must, to be fair, consider the possibility that one is not in the presence of art, but of an earnest and authentic change of heart on the part of canonical Canadians and their state. Although the will to categorize was obviously still strong, perhaps Canadians had finally come to consider their Others, though different, to be equal. At the very least, while human types were still being differentiated according to assigned ethnocultural characteristics, and the assumption that individuals designated as members of these groups would display the assigned characteristics had not changed, it did seem that the Great Chain of Race, or the hierarchical ordering of these types, had really been abandoned. Unfortunately, we need only set our sights a little to the west of Ottawa to see that this was not the case. The Year of Official Multiculturalism was also the centennial of British Columbia's entry into Confederation, and the celebration gave rise to *Strangers Entertained: A History of the Ethnic Groups of British Columbia* (Norris 1971). This volume featured Ken Adachi writing on the Japanese, and Rosemary Brown on the Negroes, and, except for the chapter on Native Indians, followed a rule whereby the section on each group had been written by someone who could be considered a member of that group. However, despite all of this attention to rhetoric of presentation, the table of contents was arranged according to the Great Chain of Race, from Americans, British and French, through the European continent from northwest to southeast, then to the Chinese and Japanese, finally ending with the Negroes. The hierarchy of the White, Yellow, Black, and Red races was preserved, with the exception of the Native Indians, who were placed first. The value of this honour was dubious, however, as the sections on the Two Founding Races were full of heroic stories of Discovery and Colonization. Whatever was going on in Ottawa, British Columbians had yet to understand, or perhaps even read, the past thirty years of Citizenship propaganda, and did not even know how to cover the tracks of racism when producing a celebratory pamphlet on ethnocultural contributions.

Despite the claims of a new era, repeated incessantly since the 1960s, and supposedly legislated in the Multiculturalism Act of 1988, the ethnocultural hierarchy has still not been eliminated from official Canadian discourse even at the federal level. In the 1991 census, state-sponsored social science was still reproducing the ancient European scheme – and ignoring fifty-year-old innovations in mass communication of state policy – by presenting its table of 'Population by Ethnic Origin and Sex' in the order that would be given by the Great Chain of Race: British and French are followed by Western, Northern, Eastern, and Southern European; next come West Asian, East Asian, and Latin and Central America; then Black, Aboriginal, and, finally, Multiple Origins (StatsCan 1993: Table 1A). This 'information' finds its way, of course, into a myriad of other sources, and is sometimes reproduced by writers whose critical position on issues of ethnicity would suggest that they would not be happy with this connection (e.g., Hiller 1996: 232). This continuation of the tradition of differentiation and hierarchization by the Great Chain of Race suggests that multiculturalism as state policy represents a creative reproduction, rather than an overcoming, of the history of Canadian diversity with regard to this crucial axis of the discourse.

The same can be said for the currently preferred mode of solving the problem created by the work of differentiation. *Integration*, the method of difference management that emerged out of the Nationalities Branch and the Department of Citizenship and Immigration, was taken over by multiculturalism as a 'social policy for handling diversity' because it 'works better than assimilation or other models' (*MCWR*: 9). Before integration could move on from its quiet existence in state policy documents and departmental reports, however, an innovation was required. Under the regime of bilingualism and biculturalism, federal policy was based on the assumption of a strong link between language and culture. Many statements on this subject can be found in the *B & B Report*. For example:

> ... language is at the core of the intellectual and emotional life of every individual. (*B & B Report*: 1.xxix)

> ... language is the most evident expression of a culture. In terms of our mandate, this means that the problems of bilingualism and biculturalism are inseparably linked. (1.xxx)

> Culture and the language that serves as its vehicle cannot be dissociated. (4.13)

Thus, when the French were granted 'official' equality with the English, it was assumed that the business of the state would have to be conducted in both languages – it was assumed that the state would have to *become French*. The Canadian state was now poised to give the gift of equality to the Other Ethnic Groups, but was apparently not ready to become Ukrainian, Sikh, Chinese ... Pierre Trudeau announced the solution of this problem, however, by showing that language and culture could indeed be dissociated – and even had the temerity to imply that the members of the B & B Commission supported him in this move:

> It was the view of the Royal Commission, shared by the government, and, I am sure, by all Canadians, that there cannot be one cultural policy for Canadians of British and French origin, another for the original peoples, and yet a third for all others. For *although there are two official languages, there is no official culture*, nor does any ethnic group take precedence over any other. (*DHC*, 8 Oct. 1971: 8545, emphasis added)

While the *B & B Report* held that culture could only be present through language, Trudeau's speech marked the dawn of a new policy era by dissociating these two aspects of modern identity formation.

Trudeau's dissociation of language and culture not only appears to negate the fundamental premise of several centuries of Eurocolonial and Canadian governmental action, but also contradicts some of the most influential analyses of the rise of modern nation-states. Benedict Anderson has noted how what he calls 'national print languages' were 'of central ideological and political importance' to early European nationalism (Anderson 1991: 67), and E.J. Hobsbawm has argued that national languages – though they were 'almost always semi-artificial constructs' – were crucial to what he calls the 'popular proto-national-ism' of the modern nation (1990: 54). In a discussion of the current Canadian context, Charles Taylor also assumes the existence of a 'lan-guage/culture that we need for our identity' (1993: 52), and notes that 'English Canadian spokespersons have taken refuge in the crassly phi-listine contention that language is just a medium of communication' (56). Bracketing the question of whether language 'really is' intimately connected with culture and nation, I will focus upon the possibilities that were opened up by their dissociation within the Canadian dis-course on diversity.

First, since no culture was acknowledged to possess an official state articulation, despite there being two official languages, the dissociation of language and culture allowed the Other Ethnic Groups to be granted a form of limited state articulation through *simple recognition of their existence*. This gift was granted by making use of the law of indi-vidual identification – an individual is his group – and the mass-democratic notion that one individual can adequately 'represent' a large number of other individuals. Its medium was the ethnocultural organizations, emergent forms that, from the Second World War on, had been identified by the Canadian state as possible pathways to the bodies of Immigrant Others (see chapter 7). The canonical case here is the Ukrainian-Canadian identity, whose trajectory displays the full series of transformations under state supervision, from its creation as the 'frowzy Galician' of the early twentieth century, its repression as a haven for Communists during the Second World War, its multiplica-tion in the years up to 1970 as a large and cohesive group seeking more power in Canadian society, and finally its incorporation as the 'earliest proponent of the multicultural movement' (Lupul 1993: 12).

How did the official policy of integration of ethnocultural groups differ from the previous mode of assimilation of races? Why did it 'work better than assimilation or other models' (*MCWR*: 9)? The fol-lowing definitions are given in the Glossary of Key Terms included with *Multiculturalism: Building the Canadian Mosaic:*

ASSIMILATION: A process, clearly distinct from integration, of eliminating distinctive group characteristics; this may be encouraged as a formal policy (e.g. American 'melting pot').

INTEGRATION: A process, clearly distinct from assimilation, by which groups and/or individuals become able to participate fully in the political, economic, social, and cultural life of the country. (*MCBCM*: 87)

In these definitions, assimilation and integration are presented as a binary oppositional pair, each defined as not the other. It is interesting to note that while a clear distinction between the two is claimed, the means by which one might make such a distinction are not provided. Certainly, in both cases a separation between Self and Other groups is assumed. In assimilation, this appears in the assumption of 'distinctive group characteristics' that need to be 'eliminated.' In integration, it appears in the assumption that *unintegrated* groups and individuals are unable to 'participate fully in the political, economic, social, and cultural life of the country.' Each method is thus based upon the transformation of a problematic Other into a non-problematic – 'eliminated' or 'participating' – Self. Where integration and assimilation differ is in the *means* by which this transformation is to be effected. Since integration is defined negatively with regard to assimilation, in which distinctive group characteristics are eliminated, one must assume that, in integration, distinctive group characteristics are left in place. Yet, at the same time, integrated groups are to become able to 'participate fully.'

How do they achieve this? Under assimilation it's obvious – they give up their Otherness and take on signs of Selfhood. Under integration it's a little more subtle – they are supposed to take on Selfhood without giving up Otherness. The trajectory followed by groups subjected to integration traces what I will call a *line of capture*, which takes them from absolute external Other (1), to conditional external Other (2), to conditional internal Self (3).[3] Inscribed on a 'time-based' semiotic square of Canadian identity, the line would appear as in figure 8.2. Prior to the Galician/Ukrainian-Canadian transition – and before integration was explicitly theorized – this line had been followed by two other identities: the Useless Savage became the Useful Indian, who was transformed into the integrated Aboriginal person; the subject of the King of France in Quebec became an inhabitant of the British colony of Quebec, and eventually a federalist French Canadian. Once they

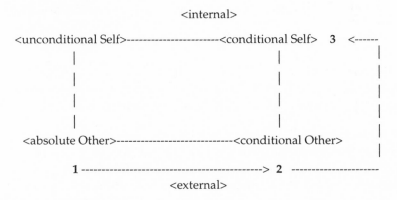

Fig. 8.2. Line of capture

reach the 'final' stage, integrated identities occupy a paradoxical position as simultaneously both Us and Them, both problematically 'distinctive' and canonically 'participating.' In each case, a desire to appear 'liberal' runs up against a prohibition against entry into the inner sanctum of unconditional Selfhood, and leads to a proliferation in ethnocultural complexity.

An examination of the role assigned to the 'bilingual framework' of Canadian multiculturalism can further clarify the current official position on the links between language and culture, and can allow us to see how multiculturalism as state policy is an implementation of what I have called, in the previous chapter, a *constrained emergence theory of identity*. The dissociation of language and culture enabled the claim that even though two *languages* were officially Canadian, this did not grant a superior position to the *cultures* associated with them. Dissociation also allowed the claim that even though a given language might *not* possess an official state connection, the culture associated with it could still be considered as one of many which were 'Canadian,' through its official *recognition*. In a list of 'common questions' about the policy, *Multiculturalism: What Is It Really About?* includes 'How do we make sure that immigrants integrate and become Canadians?' (*MCWR*: 16). The answer is that 'the strategy [of integration] emphasizes language training and helping immigrants learn about Canadian values' (16). If there is no link between language and culture, what would be the point of emphasizing language training? Why, in order to become a citizen, must immigrants 'show that they have learned some English or French' (17)? And, if there is 'no official culture,' what could possibly be considered a 'Canadian value'?

These inconsistencies in the policy seem to indicate that the Canadian state does not follow Trudeau's theory in its practice; that, in fact, *language and culture have not been dissociated.* With the policy of multiculturalism in a bilingual framework, 'minorities' can appear to enjoy the freedom to maintain certain aspects of their own identities, and to 'contribute' these to the Canadian 'mix.' This would be the realm of *emergence.* But, through the use of the official languages in their everyday lives, canonical Canadians are told that they can expect the 'integration' of these Others into one of the two dominant systems of striation – whether they are called 'cultures,' 'nations,' 'races,' or 'societies' – to proceed at a steady pace. This would be the realm of *constraint.* The question of whether either of these expectations is 'realistic' or 'objectively verifiable' is of less importance than their coexistence within the policy of multiculturalism in a bilingual framework. Based upon this strategic contradiction *within the discourse itself,* and the reproduction of a hierarchy of problematized human types upon which it depends, I would suggest that integration within multiculturalism in a bilingual framework is best seen as a creative reproduction of the colonial method of strategic simulation of assimilation to the Other, and not as an overcoming or break with this past.

Throughout this discussion, the term 'recognition' has appeared in various contexts. The final moment of multiculturalism as state policy that must be addressed is its use of this highly loaded term. As I have noted, the theory of recognition has an important place in modern political philosophy, in general, and in Canadian multiculturalist philosophy, in particular. But the official discourse is not faithful to this lineage. Rather, recognition appears as an incantation whose mere utterance is supposed to ward off antagonisms within Canadian society. For example, the Canadian Multiculturalism Act of 1988 sets out the government's commitment to:

3.(1)(a) *recognize and promote the understanding* that multiculturalism reflects the cultural and racial diversity of Canadian society;
3.(1)(b) *recognize and promote the understanding* that multiculturalism is a fundamental characteristic of Canadian heritage and identity;
...

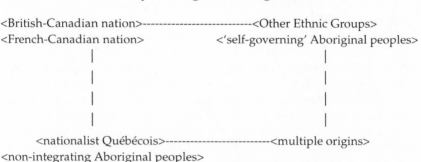

Fig. 8.3. Official recognition of identity in multiculturalism as state policy

3.(1)(d) *recognize the existence* of communities whose members share a common origin and their historic contribution to Canadian society, and enhance their development ...

The crucial point here, which will be developed further in the final chapter, is that the state does not recognize the value or equality of all 'communities'; rather, it merely recognizes their *'existence.'* That is, an acknowledgment of multiculturalism as fact, as a 'fundamental characteristic of Canadian heritage and identity,' is conflated with multiculturalism as act of reciprocal recognition, to achieve, once again, a very productive confusion.

Through this innovation, a new semiotics of Canadian identity began to emerge. Along with the dissociation of language and culture, and the replacement of race and nation with ethnocultural origin, it allowed the semantic axis to be shifted from *possession* of official identity (i.e., national language and culture) to official *recognition* of possession of identity, whether official or not. It is crucial to note that this gift of recognition has not led to any increase in 'equality.' In possessing the crucial connection of their languages with the state apparatus (Kymlicka 1995: 80), and in possessing the right to give gifts to Others, the English and French societies still occupy the dominant poles of the axis of official recognition, with English above all in the position of mastery over the French. This strategic duopoly is counterbalanced by the Other Ethnic Groups, arranged in a complex and ever-changing hierarchy. As was the case with the transfer of the Platonic hierarchy into Christianity, and then into the realm of science, the Great Chain of Race has been shifted from the realm of official Otherness into official Selfhood, through the limited recognition of some races as ethnic groups, and others as Aboriginal peoples on the way to 'full participation in Canadian society.'

While this system of inclusion might appear 'complete,' several identities can still be found within the territories claimed by the Canadian state whose existence is not officially recognized. Nationalist Québécois who have had enough of the Canadian federation immediately come to mind, as do Aboriginal people who continue to display no interest in receiving the gift of integration into a Eurocolonial society. The newest – and most interesting – identity of all, though, is the one created by those who have responded to the census and immigration officers by specifying a multiple identity that cannot be resolved by the differentiation system of the ethnocultural economy. In 1986, when it finally became possible to do so, 28 per cent of Canadians occupied this position, making it the largest 'ethnic group' of all (StatsCan 1989: vii). Is this tribe of hybrids just another census artifact, or is it possible that ethnoculture – like humanity, race, and civilization before it – is already losing its ability to differentiate the Canadian population?

Multiculturalism: Modern or Postmodern?

In cultural studies, literary theory, and educational debates, multiculturalism and postmodernism often appear together as correlates or in variously theorized cause and effect relationships.[4] This trend can also be seen in writers who directly address Canadian multiculturalism as state policy. In *The Canadian Postmodern: A Study of Contemporary English-Canadian Fiction*, Linda Hutcheon argues that 'the postmodern "different" is starting to replace the humanist "universal" as a prime cultural value. This is good news for Canadians who are not of Anglo or French origin' (1988: ix). Reginald Bibby has also noted the decline of universals, but does not celebrate it: 'Relativism has slain moral consensus,' he laments. 'It has stripped us of our ethical and moral guidelines, leaving us with no authoritative instruments with which to measure social life' (1990: 14). Taking a more cautious position, Janet McLellan and Anthony Richmond suggest that 'multicultural Canada is a model of the macroprocess of globalization' and, following Anthony Giddens, warn that 'we must minimize the dangers and maximize the opportunities that radical or postmodernity offers us' (McLellan and Richmond 1994: 679).

The Canadian government does seem to 'value' the presence of an ethnocultural diversity, and its move towards recognition of difference could be seen as 'postmodern' in the sense that it displays an awareness of the limits of the modern nation-state. Although he is consistently dismissive of 'half baked neo-Nietzschean theories ... deriving frequently from Foucault or Derrida' (1992: 70), even Charles Taylor has noted a kind of fear that is 'perhaps definitive of the modern age, the fear that the very things that define our break with earlier "traditional" societies – our affirmation of freedom, equality, radical new beginnings, control over nature, democratic self-rule – will somehow be carried beyond feasible limits and will undo us' (1993: 60). Fear of this undoing, it would seem, is what has spawned multiculturalism as state policy, which is one of the most prominent signs of the replacement of 'the humanist universal by the postmodern different' in Canadian society. In this section, I will provide an interpretation of this shift in the Canadian discourse on diversity, with specific reference to the question of whether it might be considered as an overcoming of, or an improvement upon, the role previously played by the state form.

Before proceeding, it will be necessary to discuss the resonances of some rather overworked terms. 'Postmodern' poses a real challenge, since neither the major writers usually cast as 'postmodernists,' nor those who cast them as such, seem to be happy with this term and its cognates. Yet I believe that these words mark shifts that are important to the interpretation of contemporary societies, and so do not wish to abandon them entirely. Zygmunt Bauman has put forward what I consider to be a very useful definition of postmodernity: 'The term postmodernity renders accurately the defining traits of the social condition that emerged throughout the affluent countries of Europe and of European descent in the course of the twentieth century, and took its present shape in the second half of that century' (Bauman 1992: 187). A key idea here is that postmodernity refers to a *social condition*, an environment, or 'habitat' (192), for embodied subjectivity. Bauman continues:

> The term is accurate as it draws attention to the continuity and discontinuity as two faces of the intricate relationship between the present social condition and the formation that preceded and gestated it ... *modernity* – the social formation that emerged in the same part of the world in the

course of the seventeenth century, and took its final shape ... during the nineteenth century. (187)

The key features of the postmodern social condition are, for Bauman, 'institutionalized pluralism, variety, contingency and ambivalence,' all of which have been 'turned out by modern society in ever-increasing volumes' (187). Postmodernity, then, 'makes sense' only with reference to modernity, in relation to which it does not represent a simple 'break' or 'end' or 'overcoming.' Rather, says Bauman, 'postmodernity may be interpreted as a fully developed modernity taking a full measure of the anticipated consequences of its historical work ... – *modernity for itself*' (187).

With moder*nity* and postmoder*nity* defined as social conditions, moder*nism* and postmoder*nism* can be reserved for reference to styles of cultural production – fictions, state policies, philosophies, everyday lives – that might serve to heighten the influence of modern or post-modern tendencies, respectively, within a given social formation. Post-modernism as a style has been associated with 'parody,' that is, as 'repetition with critical distance that allows ironic signaling of differ-ence at the very heart of similarity' (Hutcheon 1988: 26). While I am aware that there are debates about whether it is 'proper' – or even 'pos-sible' – to pin down postmodernism as a style, this definition seems to capture a certain tendency in cultural production, and also works well with Bauman's notion of postmodernity as 'modernity for itself.'

If postmodernity is about the uneven rise of a 'consciousness' of the failures of modernity, a given social formation could be expected to simultaneously display signs of modern, postmodern – and, of course, premodern – conditions and styles. For my purposes, the most impor-tant site of this struggle for and with awareness is occurring among states, nations, and individuals. According to modern European thought, nation-states were created when a people – sharing a single common language, culture, economy, and polity – were articulated with a bureaucratic apparatus to form a distinct society. As E.J. Hob-sbawm has pointed out, states were expected to expand (1990: 30–1), and the greatness of a people was thought to be given in the ongoing continuity and growth of its state apparatus. Thus 'the Spartan song – "We are what you were; we will be what you are" – is, in its simplicity, the abridged hymn of every *patrie*' (Renan 1990: 19). Renan's theory of the nation as a 'large-scale solidarity' (19) has been taken up by Bene-dict Anderson in his widely read *Imagined Communities* (1991). According to Anderson, those who consider themselves to be of a nation participate in an origin myth, and imagine themselves as an entity with an existence. Thus the state became, to use Nietzsche's term, one of the New Idols of the modern age.

But, as many commentators have begun to point out, the homogeneity of the state people was always already a simulation. Nation-states around the globe are therefore undergoing various forms of more or less brutal *desimulation*, as groups not 'in' the nation, but within the purview of the state, seek to striate their own spaces. This is happening in every historically possible way: decolonization within the overseas Eurocolonial domain, where a relatively 'pure' European population did not achieve numerical hegemony, as in Central America and Africa; claims of sovereignty by minorities within the New World states where a relative European hegemony has been achieved (e.g., Aboriginal peoples within Canada, and Hawaiian and Puerto Rican nationalisms within the United States); and, finally, ongoing desimulation within the European ecumene itself, most notably with the disintegration of the Soviet Union, but also in Great Britain, France, and Spain. This global phenomenon has been named as 'ethnic nationalism,' whose 'fundamental appeal ... is as a rationale for ethnic majority rule, for keeping one's enemies in their place or for overturning some legacy of cultural subordination' (Ignatieff 1993: 9) It has, for obvious reasons, become a subject of much concern to the established nationstates.

These states, as adaptive agents, have tried to hang on to their hegemony by erecting *new simulations*. In Canada, this has involved changing the meaning of key terms in the discourse of European nationalism. As I have shown above, culture, which was always seen as essentially intertwined with modern nation-statehood, has been redefined so that a 'people' can apparently acquire its benefits without becoming a 'nation' with a state articulation. But even this innovation might not be enough for the future. Cultures as compartments into which individuals might be placed, or made ready for state articulation, are themselves eroding. In Canada, the British ethnocultural group has been steadily losing its majority status since the turn of the twentieth century, and the largest ethnocultural group in Canada today is the tribe of multiple origins – not an ethnocultural group at all. As the graph in figure 8.4 shows, *the categories are emptying out, all by themselves*. Ethnocultural identity is flowing onto the floor, disappearing through the cracks, and seeking the sea from whence it came. This

Most frequently reported ethnic origins other than British or French, Canada, 1986

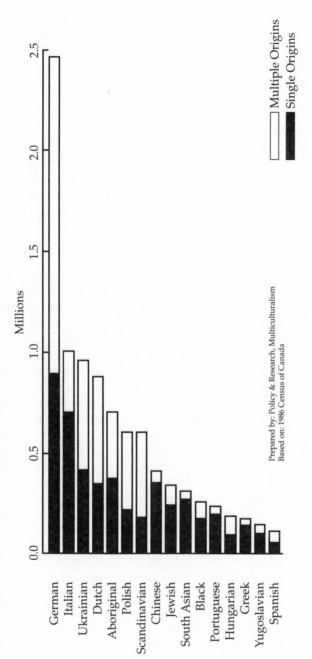

Prepared by: Policy & Research, Multiculturalism
Based on: 1986 Census of Canada

☐ Multiple Origins
■ Single Origins

Fig. 8.4. Multiple origins in Canada, 1986 census

simultaneous and contradictory rise in both ethno-nationalism and hybridity means that the modern form of articulation between state and nation – as people, culture, Us as opposed to Them – is becoming more and more difficult for the existing nation-states to sustain. New methods of articulation are required if they are to maintain their hegemony and avoid breaking apart into smaller and smaller units of organization.

While it definitely reproduces ancient and modern forms, as I have pointed out in the previous sections, Canadian multiculturalism as state policy can also be seen as an attempt to evolve a new form of state articulation appropriate to a social condition of postmodernity. Whereas the modern nation-state relied upon coercive exclusion, the postmodern nations-state proceeds primarily by seductive incorporation in its (impossible) quest for infinite striation. Instead of trying to transform its Others through assimilation, the postmodern nations-state leaves them as they are and articulates them with regimes of rational-bureaucratic discipline, through their identifications with designed positions in the ethnocultural economy. When discussing the *B & B Report*, I suggested that Baudrillard's analysis of strategic duopoly might be applicable to the world of official Canadian language and culture at that time. This model seems to work well enough in the context of 'bi' culture and language, but what can be made of the shift to a system of bilingualism in a multicultural framework? Baudrillard again, on the 0/1 binary scansion that permeates postmodern social forms: 'This is the nucleus of the simulation processes which dominate us. It can be organized as a play of unstable variations, from polyvalence to tautology, without threatening the strategic bipolar form: it is the divine form of simulation' (1983: 135). Multiculturalism in a bilingual framework: polyvalence (recognition of the Other Ethnic Groups as ethnicities) and tautology (everyone has an ethnicity) integrated with an essential duality (English and French societies, languages, and cultures). Duopoly of language and culture; monopoly of state over language, culture, and self-identification. It all seems to work so *well*.

The transition from modern to postmodern forms of discipline has been accompanied by a shift of focus from management of difference to control of *différance*. In his essay of the same name, Derrida writes that *différance* 'would be said to designate a constitutive, productive, and originary causality, the process of scission and division which would produce or constitute different things or differences' (1982: 9).[5]

As is well known, Derrida intends this term to play upon both time, in the sense of 'deferring,' and space, in the sense of 'differing.' In the context of the discourse on Canadian diversity, I would suggest that *différance* produces difference spatially through the operation of a given means of differentiation – humanity, civilization, race, culture, ethnicity, ethnocultural origin – and temporally, as that force which leads to the decline of one means of differentiation and the rise of another. In the specific case of Canadian multiculturalism, the will to the management of spatial *différance* shows up as an insistence upon using British social and political forms, and the English and French languages, as a 'framework' or 'context' or – within the terminology I have been using – as a *constraint* upon the emergence of a Canadian identity. It can also be seen in the preservation and promotion of 'frozen' identities in the form given by Western political anthropology, that is, as unvarying cultural compartments into which individuals might be placed in preparation for state articulation as 'one of the people(s).'

Out of a differentiated population in which each individual is assigned – and may or may not identify with – a preserved and promoted ethnocultural origin that resists the play of *différance*, a further means of differentiation can emerge: that of the *citizen*. Inasmuch as *everyone* is supposed to be a citizen, this appears, not as a category of differentiation, but as a *meta-category of universal similarity.* Canadian multiculturalism as state policy, I would suggest, operates to construct a meta-category of this sort. Whereas the modern nation-state *simulated a unity and dissimulated its multiplicity,* the postmodern nations-state *dissimulates its unity and simulates a multiplicity.* This is to say that there is, and always has been, a great deal of Canadian unity. Canadians both canonical and problematic are being subjected to increasingly powerful normalizing forces in almost every aspect of their lives, so that the only kind of diversity left is on the level of what has been referred to as 'symbolic ethnicity' (Gans 1979) – which, as Will Kymlicka notes, is 'almost entirely lacking in any real institutionalized corporate existence' (1995: 98).[6]

Yet, for those who identify with, and desire the continuation of, an English Canada, the problem of What It Means to Be Canadian is that 'we' (English Canadians) don't know who 'we' are, indeed are *prevented* from knowing, because there are too many of 'them' around, countering 'our' music with 'their' noise, overpowering 'our' perfume with their stench, continually Swamping 'our' carefully tilled cultural fields. As we have seen, these feelings have given rise to various forms of nativism and racism throughout Canada's history, and there are no signs of their disappearance in the near future. Slavoj Zizek sees this kind of resentment as the product of a battle over possession of what he calls the 'national Thing': 'What is at stake in ethnic tensions is always the possession of the national Thing: the "other" wants to steal our enjoyment (by ruining our "way of life") and/or it has access to some secret, perverse enjoyment' (Zizek 1991a: 165). Thus, it may be that what the official Canadian finds most disturbing about the Others is that they seem to possess, without any effort at all, what he so shamefully lacks: a set of typical characteristics, an identity ... a Self.

The project of creating good Canadians was hampered from the outset, and is still plagued, by this lack of a clear idea of just what and how a good Canadian is. If 'we' could only make 'them' like 'us,' the problem of national unity would be solved. But 'we' can't do this, because 'we' don't know who 'we' are. It's a circle, a beautiful and perfect *circulation*, and there seems to be no hope of getting out of it. This circling about a goal, while never quite attaining it, is reminiscent of the Lacanian notion of the quest for the *objet petit a*:

> Is the Freudian [national] Thing a kind of 'fatal attractor,' perturbing the regular functioning of the psychic apparatus, preventing it from establishing an equilibrium? Is not the very form of the 'strange attractor' a kind of physical metaphor for the Lacanian *objet petit a*? ... The art of the theory of chaos consists in allowing us to see the very form of chaos, in allowing us to see a pattern where ordinarily we see nothing but a formless disorder. (Zizek 1991a: 38)

To understand the absent English-Canadian identity as a fatal attractor, we must explicate the Lacanian categories of need, demand, and desire. For Lacan, following Freud, need relates only to biological necessities such as hunger or thirst, which can be satisfied by the attainment of a required object: 'The wild animal emerges from its hole *querens quem devoret*, and when he has found what he has to eat, he is satisfied, he digests it' (Lacan 1981: 165). But this is a special case that does not admit of generalization to the human condition, for individuals in society are required to *demand* (ask for) what they think they need from an Other. It is here, in the perpetual disjunction between need and its expression that desire arises: 'the function of desire is a last residuum of the effect of the signifier in the subject' (Lacan 1981:

154). Since the result of demand never quite meets the need, satisfaction is impossible and desire is fundamentally insatiable.

If the function of desire is not to achieve satisfaction, then what *is* it for? In one sense, desire is that which allows human beings to confirm or refute their theories about the attitudes of the Other towards them. Those who at least make an attempt to respond to our demand thereby verify that we exist and matter: this is why Lacan insists that the subject is constituted in the Other. But there is more than this to the role of desire in Lacanian theory, and to get at its further significance we must consider the category of drive (*Trieb*), which Lacan claims to take directly from Freud, along with its division into four subcomponents: *Drang* (impulse); *Quelle* (the source); *Objekt* (the object, or goal); *Ziel* (the aim). Lacan says that 'the use of the function of the drive has for me no other purpose than to put in question what is meant by satisfaction' (Lacan 1981: 166). In a trick reminiscent of the flow of desire itself, he shifts the ground from satisfaction to pleasure, or *enjoyment*. This move is nicely summarized by Zizek in the following passage: 'Lacan's point is that the real purpose of the drive is not its goal (full satisfaction) but its aim: the drive's ultimate aim is simply to reproduce itself as drive, to return to its circular path, to continue its path to and from the goal. The real source of enjoyment is the repetitive movement of this closed circuit' (Zizek 1991: 5)

This endless, circular, movement is tellingly represented in the most highly evolved form of the Mosaic metaphor, which I call the National Jewel (fig. 1.2). If we see the centre of this spheroid as the place of the impossible object of Canadian identity, then the triangular identity-types arrayed around it take on an order they would not otherwise appear to have – we are led to the intriguing possibility that *the circulation itself is the identity*. Through its existence as a coveted but unobtainable simulation model, the National Jewel serves double duty: to naturalize Canadian diversity; but also to give substance to an impossible, but unifying, quest for unity. As Zizek has argued, 'the ideal leveling of all social differences, the production of the citizen, the subject of democracy, is possible only through an allegiance to some particular national Cause' (Zizek 1991: 165). The Canadian government seems to be 'breaking the rules' of nation-building by trying to create a national Thing that has no particular ethnic affiliation – that allows for variety in the colour of its component triangles. However, we can see this is not the case if we note, at least on the level of multiculturalism policy, that what is emerging is not a nation-state but a *nations*-state, in which all ethnicities, in general, and therefore no ethnicity, in particular, can seek their enjoyment in the simultaneous possession and loss of a simulacrum of identity. If Canadian multiculturalism is to be seen as a technology of governance, then this technology must also be seen as perversely constraining/seducing individual bodies into becoming, that is orbiting about, *nothing at all.*

Insofar as it seems to acknowledge current social conditions of fragmentation and nihilism in its practice, multiculturalism as state policy is most certainly 'liberal' and 'postmodern.' However, as a continuation and heightening of the hegemony of the state form, it is just as certainly not an overcoming of the modern will to rational-bureaucratic microcontrol and domination. It is best cast, therefore, as a *hypermodern* disciplinary regime that seeks to maintain a precarious articulation between the Canadian state, two dominant nations and cultures, and a variety of other nations and cultures clipped back as ethnicities or national minorities. Through its articulation with these designed mass identities, the state acquires access to the bodies and souls of individuals who identify with them, and thereby maintains its ability to striate the spaces it claims as its own. While classical liberalism might be updated so that this situation appears as 'freedom,' I will argue in the final chapter that the history of Canadian diversity cannot be 'overcome,' or even adequately understood, as long as the radical potential of multiculturalism is submerged in this quest by an orphaned state to discover its 'lost' nations.

Chapter Nine

A Revaluation of Canadian Multiculturalism

In the central chapters of this book, I have tried to show that relations of power appropriate to the 'deficient' Hegelian forms of recognition, particularly the struggle to the death and the master-slave dialectic, have been the rule and norm, rather than the exception, in Canadian history. I have also produced evidence to support the claim that those forms of local autonomy and emergent identity which do exist have survived only through determined *resistance* to a statist dream of a perfectly striated space of social order. In this sense, the history of Canadian diversity has seen a proliferation of the very problem that various state forms have set out to solve, a proliferation brought on precisely through the action of the solutions themselves. In the previous chapter, I addressed the central question of this analysis, by arguing that multiculturalism as state policy does not represent a break with the history of Canadian diversity as I have outlined it. Rather, I suggested that it simply marks a shift from the modern nation-state, which simulated a unity and dissimulated its multiplicity, to the postmodern nations-state, which dissimulates its unity and simulates a multiplicity.

In this concluding chapter, I will once again address the question set out at the beginning of the book: can contemporary multiculturalism be seen as the achievement of, or a step on the way to, a 'post-industrial *Sittlichkeit*?' Here I will consider multiculturalism, as a recognition-based theory of liberal pluralism, whose leading advocates have been Charles Taylor and Will Kymlicka. This theory – along with the state policy which it 'ratifies and explains' (Kymlicka 1995: 127)[1] – has been presented as an advance by its proponents, in that it respects the partcularity of ethnocultural identifications by offering what are called 'differentiated citizenship rights.' I will argue, however, that it bestows these rights as a monological *gift*, and places limits on them precisely where they threaten to achieve what multiculturalism is supposed to be about – that is, *equal reciprocal recognition* between *all* of the peoples whom a history of violent conquest has cast within the purview of the Canadian state. I will also argue that this limitation is a necessary support for the fantasy of fullness that propels the Canadian discourse on diversity, as it helps to protect multiculturalism, as fact, act, and social ideal, from the consequences of multiculturalism as radical imaginary. As a final gesture, I will suggest how this fantasy might be traversed, and how some of the radical potential of multiculturalism might be let loose. But first, I will turn to the question of equality – and the related issues of how rights and freedoms are allocated within the ethnocultural hierarchy of Canadian multiculturalism – as it is handled in the work of Will Kymlicka.

A Critique of Kymlicka's Liberal Theory of Minority Rights

The beginning of this new paradigm in Canadian – and international – scholarship can be located in 1979, when Charles Taylor argued that the classical liberal individual had 'arrived at freedom by setting aside all external obstacles and impingements,' and for this reason was 'characterless, and hence without defined purpose, however much this is hidden by such seemingly positive terms as "rationality" or "creativity"' (cited in Kymlicka 1989: 47). Will Kymlicka responded to this critique in his *Liberalism, Community and Culture* (1989), arguing that 'the liberal view is sensitive to the way our individual lives and our moral deliberations are related to, and situated in, a shared social context' (2). He thus helped to pave the way for a political philosophy that could be seen as recognizing diversity through granting differentiated group rights, without sacrificing the goals of personal freedom and equality upon which the liberal individual founded his identity.[2]

Taylor soon adopted Kymlicka's theoretical intervention, and began to argue that achieving recognition of difference and preserving Canada's 'multinational society' meant that the model of 'procedural' liberalism had to be abandoned: 'There is a form of the politics of equal respect, as enshrined in a liberalism of rights, that is inhospitable to difference, because (a) it insists on uniform application of the rules defining these rights, without exception, and (b) it is suspicious of collective goals' (1992: 60). In the place of this model, Taylor offered up a 'non-procedural' liberalism that would guarantee certain rights to all, but would also distinguish 'these fundamental rights from the broad range of immunities and presumptions that have sprung up in modern cultures of judicial review' (61). Kymlicka advanced this position in his *Multicultural Citizenship* (1995), where he not only provided support for the theory of non-procedural liberalism, but also took on the task of specifying how it might be *implemented* in practical contexts. In this way, he began to construct a bridge between political philosophy and state policy that is of particular relevance to the Canadian case.

In *Multicultural Citizenship*, Kymlicka argues that 'we need to supplement traditional human rights principles with a theory of minority rights' (5), and sets out to show that 'minority rights are not only consistent with individual freedom, but can actually promote it' (75). This is so because 'for meaningful individual choice to be possible, individuals need not only access to information, the capacity to selectively evaluate it, and freedom of expression and association. They also need access to a societal culture' (84). Kymlicka defines 'societal culture' as 'a culture which provides its members with meaningful ways of life across the full range of human activities, including social, educational, religious, recreational, and economic life, encompassing both public and private spheres. These cultures tend to be territorially concentrated, and based on a shared language' (76). He goes on to suggest that 'for a culture to survive and develop in the modern world, given the pressures towards the creation of a single common culture in each country, it must be a societal culture' (80).

This definition at first appears inconsistent with the dissociation of language and culture carried out by the state policy of multiculturalism in a bilingual framework. Indeed, Kymlicka claims that the term 'multicultural' is 'vague' and 'obscures important distinctions' between various sorts of cultural pluralism (6). He wants to set apart 'multi-nation' states, where 'cultural diversity arises from incorporation of previously self-governing, territorially concentrated cultures into a larger state,' and 'polyethnic' states, where 'cultural diversity arises from individual and familial immigration' (6). Canada, he argues, is both multi-national and polyethnic, and thus contains both 'national minorities,' like the Québécois and Aboriginal peoples, and 'ethnic groups' composed of 'immigrants who have left their national community to enter another society' (19). It also, of course, contains a 'majority' (121), a 'we' that would have done the 'incorporation' of cultures and immigrants, and would now 'need to supplement traditional human rights with a theory of minority rights' (5).

The division of the population into a national majority – or, in Canada's case, major*ities* – national minorities, and ethnic groups is crucial to the kinds of rights that Kymlicka feels should be granted to each group of citizens. The most important of these, given his definition of the prerequisites of identity and freedom, would be the right to one's own societal culture. On this point, however, he equivocates. In chapter 5, he presents a sustained argument in which he claims to have 'tried to show that liberals should recognize the importance of people's membership in *their own* societal culture, because of the role it plays in enabling meaningful individual choice and in supporting self-identity' (105, emphasis added). At the beginning of the next chapter, however, he claims to have 'argued that access to *a* societal culture is essential for individual freedom' (107, emphasis added). It soon becomes apparent that Kymlicka is in fact advocating a return to the *B & B Report* regime of a strong association between language and culture, but *only for certain groups*. Some will be allowed to have 'their own' societal culture, while others will only be allowed access to 'a' societal culture – that of the 'majority.'

Kymlicka provides a historical justification for his ideas regarding which groups are to be granted their own societal culture by drawing a distinction between Colonizers, Colonized, and Immigrants. 'English-speaking colonists throughout the British Empire, Spanish colonists in Puerto Rico, and French colonists in Quebec ... had no expectation of integrating into another culture, but rather aimed to reproduce their original society in a new land' (15). He notes, quite accurately, that 'this is an essential feature of colonization' (15). As part of this 'reproduction,' the European colonizers 'invaded and conquered' the existing nations (11), converting them into Colonized 'national minorities.' As can be seen in the quote above, Kymlicka separates Colonizers from Immigrants based on what he presumes to be the 'expectations' of each. While Kymlicka never says whether Colonizers possess a liberal-theoretical 'right' to a societal culture they have obtained through violent means, he does say that Immigrants do *not* have such a right, 'immigration being one way of waiving' it (96). Thus, Kymlicka: 'In general ... I believe that national minorities do have societal cultures, and immigrant groups do not' (101). While these distinctions are undoubtedly historically accurate and honest, some liberals might balk at what appears to be a theoretical justification for, and validation of, what I have called the power law of sign flow. Certainly, his formula begs the question of whether an invading force could provide itself with a liberal justification for exterminating an existing societal culture – say that of the Canadian or American 'majority' – by claiming that it 'expected' to reproduce its own. This possibility becomes particularly intriguing if one begins to think about a liberal acceptance of violent internal *decolonization* by national minorities expecting to reassert the hegemony of their societal cultures.

While its justification may be questionable, Kymlicka's theory of minority rights clearly sets out the privileges that are to be granted to two of the three categories, namely, national minority (Colonized) and ethnic group (Immigrant). In the Canadian case, he notes that 'Indian homelands were overrun by French settlers, who were then conquered by the English' (12). This historical fact places the Québécois and the Aboriginal peoples in the position of national minorities. Their occupation of this position, supplanted by theoretical arguments based on principles of equality and diversity, gives them access to the 'opportunity to maintain themselves as a distinct culture, if they so choose' (113), and to a limited form of autonomy by way of 'self-government' and 'external protections.' In the case of the Québécois, Kymlicka is of the opinion that something akin to the existing Canadian federation is adequate to the needs of this national minority. He claims that 'Quebec ensures self-government for the Quebecois' (29), and that 'the right to preserve and promote their culture [is] affirmed in the existing system of federalism' (45). Thus, when applied in practice, his theoretical position leads to little deviation from the status quo established in 1867.

The BNA Act does not meet the needs of the Aboriginal peoples, however, since 'federalism can only serve as a mechanism for self-government if the national minority forms a majority in one of the federal subunits,' and 'this is not true of most indigenous peoples in North America' (29). For the Aboriginal peoples, 'self-government claims typically take the form of devolving political power to a political unit substantially controlled by the members of the national minority, and substantially corresponding to their historical homeland or territory' (30). As an illustration, Kymlicka gives the example of the creation of Nunavut Nunavut Act, 40–41–42 Elizabeth II c. 28). Yet, however much this new 'territory' might represent an advance over the past – and I truly hope that it will not simply be another Manitoba[3] – the form of 'self-government' granted to the Inuit is all too familiar. First of all, while the Inuit generally refer to Nunavut as a Homeland, the Canadian government has established a 'territory of Canada, to be known as Nunavut' (Nunavut Act, Article 3). Nunavut is to have a legislature (12), which will have a wide range of powers, including 'the administration of justice' (23.1e), taxation (j), some aspects of land use and sale (i, r, s), education (m), and cultural and linguistic affairs (m, n). But it is not without clauses that are distinctly colonial in tenor. The territory is to have a 'Commissioner,' appointed by the Governor in Council, who will take instructions from Ottawa (6.2) and sit in the legislative assembly, though s/he will not be elected. The Commissioner, it seems, is to play the role assigned to Governors within the British Empire. This is most apparent in the powers reserved by the Canadian state:

> 28. (1) A copy of every law made by the Legislature shall be transmitted to the Governor in Council within thirty days after its enactment ...
> (2) The Governor in Council may disallow any law made by the Legislature or any provision of any such law at any time within one year after its enactment.

Ottawa also reserves for itself the right to appoint the judges of the superior courts in the territory (31). Whatever powers the people and legislature of Nunavut have been granted, their use will be closely scrutinized by a colonial administration centred in Ottawa, where ultimate power still resides. In eliding this critical issue, multiculturalism as liberal pluralism again seems to provide no clear advance on, and more importantly offers no critique of, the reproduction of colonial relations by the Canadian state.

With the category of Immigrant, we enter the realm of what Kymlicka refers to as 'polyethnic rights,' which are 'intended to help ethnic groups and religious minorities express their cultural particularity and pride without it hampering their success in the economic and political institutions of the dominant society' (31). Unlike the rights granted to national minorities, 'polyethnic rights are usually intended to promote integration into the larger society, not self-government' (31). The practical implications are clearest here, since Kymlicka directly refers to 'the Canadian government's "multiculturalism" policy' as 'promoting polyethnicity rather than assimilation for immigrants' (17). Indeed, in a summary that encapsulates his suggested treatment of both national minorities and ethnic groups, Kymlicka explicitly endorses current Canadian state policy in its broadest outlines. 'Canada, with its policy of "multiculturalism in a bilingual framework" and its recognition of

Aboriginal rights to self-government, is one of the few countries which has officially recognized and endorsed both polyethnicity and multi-nationality' (22).

Curiously, the text is not so clear in setting out the rights that would be granted to the third category – that of majority (Colonizer). The first problem is that Kymlicka tends to avoid naming the majority in his discussions of actual nation-states. In the Canadian case, he notes that 'Indian homelands were overrun by French settlers, who were then conquered by the English' (12). From this statement, and from the discussion about Colonization, one would assume that the societal culture that has become known as Canada would be English. This assumption is further justified by a reference to 'the majority Anglophone society in both the United States and Canada' (22). Here, Kymlicka notes that 'national groups, as I am using that term, are not defined by race or descent' (22), but presumably – observing the reference to Anglophone – by language. However, on the next page, Kymlicka writes that 'in talking about national minorities ... I am not talking about racial or descent groups, but about cultural groups' (23). It would seem that national *majorities*, for Kymlicka, are defined through language, while national *minorities* are distinguished by culture, and neither are defined by race or descent. Following this interpretation of what appears to be a somewhat open question in Kymlicka's text, I will refer to the 'national majority' of Canada as 'English-Canadian' in my discussion.

Unfortunately, the rights to be granted to Canada's majority are even more difficult to discover than its name and the means by which it can be delimited. The index contains only 8 references to 'English Canadians,' none of which leads to a discussion of what rights they are to be granted. This is scanty treatment when compared to the 29 entries for 'French-Canadian' and 'Québécois,' and 57 for 'Aboriginal peoples (Canada)' and 'indigenous peoples.' Kymlicka does note, though, that 'in a democratic society, the majority nation will always have its language and societal culture supported, and will have the legislative power to protect its interests in culture-affecting decisions' (113). Presumably, it would also have the legislative power to affect the interests of other nations and ethnic groups, and so would have a very powerful 'right' that one might wish to see explicitly theorized. But *Multicultural Citizenship* does not oblige here. Instead, there is a constant reference to a passively voiced 'we' that will decide what gifts to give to 'them': 'I will discuss whether immigrant groups *should be given* the rights and resources necessary to sustain a distinct societal culture' (76). 'If people have a deep bond with their own culture ... *should we not allow* immigrants to re-create their own societal cultures?' (95). '*We should aim at ensuring* that all national groups have the opportunity to maintain themselves as a distinct societal culture' (113). By remaining implicit, this 'we' forms a silent, Invisible Self group that chooses to give, or not to give, gifts of recognition and self-government to noisy, Visible Others.

This is not to suggest, of course, that those who do not consider themselves to be English-Canadian cannot *read* Kymlicka's text, but that when they do, they will find themselves constructed as a 'them' to the text's implicit 'us.' They will also find that, despite being 'recognized,' they are once again to be placed in an inferior position in a hierarchy of human types differentiated by what is presumed to be their 'origin,' and the place assigned to them in a Eurocentric history of colonization and the play of power. Of course, this is all justified for *liberals*, in terms of *liberal* theory, but those who do not identify with this tradition will be sure to notice that, rather than critically addressing the colonial remainder in the history of Canadian diversity, this brand of multiculturalism rather perversely finds pride in its reproduction. In this sense, again, it is deeply rooted in the history of Canadian diversity, and does not take us beyond 'actually existing' multiculturalism as state policy.

Charles Taylor and the Limits of Recognition

A second – and potentially more radical – moment in multiculturalism as non-procedural liberal pluralism can be found in the concept of recognition. In chapter 2, I introduced Charles Taylor's argument that recognition can lead to 'reconciliation' on two levels: that of the individual and his or her people; and of a multiplicity of peoples and their state. We are now in a position to evaluate this claim, both from the point of view of the history of Canadian diversity, and immanently, from within the confines of Taylor's discourse itself. As far as the possibility of achieving a unity *sometime in the future* is concerned, this appears in Hegelian terms as a dialectical movement, meaning a sublation of stages leading to a higher unity. But, as I have shown in the previous chapters, in Canada we have not undergone a dialectical process, but rather a series of struggles to the death alongside a mass of interlocking contradictions, coexisting rather than sublated. We cannot anticipate immanent union with Absolute Spirit, but rather must expect a profusion of subject-positions, a complex system of master-slave relations, as well as numerous positions of Stoic and Sceptical consciousness. If there is no dialectic in progress, it seems quite unlikely that there will ever be an *Aufhebung*. With regard to the second possibility, that of *recovering* a unity from the *past*, it is difficult to see that a Canada has ever existed; therefore it would seem that there is simply *nothing to be recovered*.

I want to be as fair as possible and assume that Taylor is not really depending upon the Canadian Folk Spirit to save the day. But there are other problems. His prescription is also immanently inadequate given its Hegelian genesis, since the recognition that Taylor speaks of is not equal, reciprocal, and freely given, but a partial and grudgingly bestowed *gift* from a canonical Self group to a series of problematic Others. This can be seen in his ambivalent stance (present also in state policy, as analysed in the previous chapter) regarding recognition of the Other versus recognition of the *difference* of the Other – what in Hegel would be recognition (*Anerkennen*) versus 'mere' cognition (*Erkennen*). Cognition of difference is always already with us as self-identified members of groups. By itself, it allows us only to know the Other as Other, that is, as a thing to be assimilated, exterminated, toler-ated, or whatever. Recognition is something different. It is a certain sort of *response* to cognition of the Other. As Taylor notes, 'truly recog-nizing difference' involves 'recognizing the *equal value* of different ways of being' (1991: 51).

But Taylor finds it hard to move from the position of mere cognition. It bothers him that those advocating a 'politics of recognition' demand that 'we all *recognize* the equal value of different cultures; that we not only let them survive, but acknowledge their *worth*' (1992: 64). This dif-ficulty is based on two points which Taylor is unwilling to grant. First, while he emphasizes the positive contribution that recognition makes to identity formation, he is less willing to acknowledge the damage that can be done through its absence. Indeed, when he comes to speak about how the process of recognition can *fail*, he is always careful to put the claims in the mouths of others. This is apparent when he writes about the concept of 'misrecognition' as it is used in identity politics. 'The demand for recognition in these ... cases [minority groups, femi-nism, multiculturalism] is given urgency by the *supposed* links between recognition and identity ...' (1992: 25, emphasis added). In *The Malaise of Modernity*, Taylor writes that 'equal recognition is not just the appropriate mode for a healthy democratic society. Its refusal can inflict damage on those who are denied it, *according to a widespread modern view'* (1991: 49, emphasis added). Taylor goes on to acknowledge that 'refusal' of recognition, or 'non-recognition,' can be a 'form of repression,' but again he hedges by suggesting that the importance of this refusal may be 'exaggerated' (50). Taylor himself is one of those who believes very strongly in the 'links between recognition and identity.' So why does he degrade this link to the status of a 'widely held' 'supposition' and 'exaggeration'? It seems that he wants to play a dual game: when considering how the process of recognition can *succeed* in producing a unified identity, he wants to give it all the force he can. However, he does not approve of those who make use of actual historical failures of recognition to support a politics of difference that might be threatening to a precious, but fragile, Canadian unity.

A further problem for Taylor is that 'mere difference can't itself be the ground of equal value' (1992: 51). Rather, the judgment of equal worth that leads to recognition must be an *empirical* question: 'On examination, either we will find something of great value in culture C, or we will not. But it makes no more sense to demand that we do so than it does to demand that we find the earth round or flat, the temperature of the air hot or cold' (69). That is, 'if the judgment of equal value is to register something independent of our own wills and desires, *it cannot be dictated by a principle of ethics'* (69, emphasis added). Here Taylor leaves Hegel far behind, and again seems to be working against his own position, in arriving at a theory of ethical community which wishes to free itself of a principle of ethics.

But again I want to be fair. In his more recent work, Taylor has acknowledged that recognition of oneself in the people or the state cannot be expected to occur transparently, that dialogue and negotiation are required. Presumably, this would apply to his own reluctance to acknowledge the equal worth of Others without some 'objective' basis for the judgment. Also, as can be seen from the quotes above, he does not always reduce the question of judgment to epistemology, but at times shows an awareness of its axiological component. 'To come together on a mutual recognition of difference – that is, of the equal value of different identities – requires that we … share … some standards of value on which the identities concerned check out as equal' (1991: 52). Now, the difficult question is: since such standards clearly do not exist – or there would be no problem of diversity – how are they to be produced?

There are several options available. The 'standard' can be blithely ethnocentric, with those who do not 'check out as equal' being subjected to various forms of discipline by the state people (e.g., extermination, transportation, rejection, deportation). Here a standard is created and maintained by elimination of difference, as has been the case throughout most of Canadian history. Another possibility is that the ethnocentricity of the standard can be dissimulated, by openly welcoming 'all races and ethnicities' to be judged by a disguised universal standard silently employed by the state people. This would be management by strategic simulation of assimilation of difference, as found in Canadian multiculturalism as state policy. A third way of producing a universal standard has been described by Slavoj Zizek in his recent criticism of multiculturalism in the *New Left Review*. The multiculturalist can 'empty his own position of all positive content,' yet 'retain this position as the privileged empty point of universality from which one is able to appreciate (and depreciate) properly other particular cultures' (Zizek 1997a: 44). Habermas's 'civic nationalism' would belong in this category, I think.

But where would Taylor fit in? Clearly he does not wish to perpetuate modern methods of violent exclusion. Sometimes, though, it seems that he does lean towards strategic simulation of assimilation to the Other, as can be seen in the contradictory status of the 'we' that must share standards of worth. To achieve a 'non-disguised' universal, this 'we' would have to include 'everyone' who lives within the purview of the state in question. However, when Taylor talks about giving the gift of recognition, he often employs a different, less universal 'we,' which is called upon to give certain gifts, but is reluctant to do so. For example, in a discussion of an early essay of Kymlicka's, he writes: 'In certain circumstances, with disadvantaged populations, the integrity of the culture may require that *we* accord *them* more resources or rights than others' (1992: 41 n.16, emphasis added). Or, in the passage cited above, Taylor is uncomfortable with the 'demand' that '*we* not only let *them* [cultures] survive, but acknowledge their worth' (1992: 64, emphasis added). Who is this we – which is so reminiscent of Kymlicka's – that is confronted by demands from feminists and minority groups? And why does it not have to make such demands itself? Its identity can perhaps be found in Taylor's frequent references to 'Western liberal society' and 'Atlantic civilization.' This is, of course, none other than the we of Western political anthropology, which has achieved hegemony by way of its position in the ethnocultural hierarchy and its 'special' articulation as the state people.[4] This is the ethnocultural residue or stain, the little bit of the Real in Taylor's discourse. It is not always apparent, and sometimes he tries to explicitly ward it off. But it always returns as a distinction between the 'we' who must give gifts, and the 'they' who are demanding them.

It must be noted, however, that the presence of this residue means that Taylor's 'true position' is not 'the void of universality.' In fact, his true position cannot be encompassed by any of the above categories, as it takes a hermeneutic line of flight from both subjectivism and relativism. 'Real judgments of worth suppose a fused horizon of standards ... they suppose that we have been transformed by the study of the Other, so that we are not simply judging by our original familiar standards' (1992: 70). That is, in the ideal case, the 'we' of 'North Atlantic civilization' in its particularity would undergo some sort of 'transformation' through an encounter with its Others in *their* particularity. As a result of this process, it would become part of a larger 'we' including not only the state people but, to some extent, all of those peoples within the purview of the state. This is how 'we' would create a shared standard of value, and thereby recover the lost ethical community, the Canadian who finds herself in her Canada. Stripped of its Hegelian residue, this could be the most radical moment in Taylor's work, and it would be interesting to see it taken further.

Taylor goes at least part of the way in realizing the potential of this idea through his concept of 'deep diversity.' While his goal is obviously a unified community, he expects that this cannot be achieved via the 'tight, uniform, nineteenth century nations,' but requires an 'innovative path' (1993: 200). Anyone with a knowledge of Canadian history would be compelled to ask: how deep is this diversity to be? In *Reconciling the Solitudes*, when he allows himself to 'dream in colours,' Taylor comes up with the following vision of a Canada that has 'survived the crisis' and reached a higher stage in its development:

> It would unquestionably be dual in one important respect. There would be two major societies, each defined by its own dominant language. But each of these societies within itself would be more and more diverse. First, each would be more and more ethnically varied and, in different ways, multicultural; second, each would have significant minorities of the other official language; third, each would contain aboriginal communities with substantial but varying degrees of self-government. (1993: 20)

This is from a text written in 1992, and its content is easily recognizable as the status quo which had by then existed for about twenty years. Taylor's dream thus might seem rather black and white, or perhaps even radio; to many, it is no dream at all, but a nightmare. Jean Morriset is quite clear in his denunciation of what he calls the 'mythology ... of the right of all Canadians to assimilation by sublimation or, to multiculturalism' (Morriset 1998: 123). 'Although our [half-breed] ancestors had been conquered by a superior military,' Howard Adams has written, 'in the long run it was the weapon of a political culture that kept us perpetually in a state of subjugation and exploitation' (1995: 8). Karl Peter has noted that 'Canada has been horsetrading for the preservation of an obsolete political structure, for an empty political shell derived from colonial conquests whose internal contradictions led to the mutual retardation of all for the benefit of the few' (1981: 67). Himani Bannerji sees multiculturalism as part of a tradition in which 'Europeans continue the same solidarity of ruling and repression, blended with competitive manipulations, that they practised from the dawn of their conquests and state formations' (1996: 107). Seeing no such Euro-solidarity, Québécois nationalists argue that 'multiculturalism ... was a means to *avoid recognizing* the country's biculturalism and admitting the political consequences of Quebec's specificity' (Dufour 1990: 79, emphasis added).

Multiculturalism as a means to avoid recognizing the history of Canadian diversity: this seems to go directly to the heart of Taylor's refusal to talk about non- and mis-recognition in his own voice. It also helps us to understand why he often speaks of a 'self-occlusion of the politics of recognition' via its 'displacement' onto issues of equality, justice, and oppression (1993: 192). That is, it might explain his tendency to reduce demands for justice, autonomy, and the reform of existing social structures to a call for recognition. In ignoring or reducing these voices, in accusing them of 'false consciousness' or 'bad faith,' it seems that Taylor is not playing the game as he says it should be played – he is not taking these identities for 'what they really are.' The only reason he can afford to do this, of course, is that the 'we' of 'North Atlantic civilization' with which he identifies is in a position of mastery as the state people. Thus, as much as he might wish to transcend it, Taylor remains within the unequal form of recognition found in the master-slave relation. Although English Canada has risked itself to get to this position, it is now unable to take a further risk, that of unconditionally recognizing its Others as human subjects; that is, as beings who would *not only receive but also give* the gift of recognition. Paradoxically, but crucially, *English Canada renounces the value of equal recognition* by its Others.

This renunciation has had two effects. First, as Hegel points out, it leaves the master empty, unsure of his own existence. This is precisely what continues to happen to English Canada, which famously lacks a positive identity, and has been enslaved by its own history of mastery and failed identifications. Second, it means that Taylor's community must fail to achieve the reciprocal recognition necessary to render it 'ethical' in the Hegelian sense in which he intends it. As long as the state people refuses to acknowledge the worth of its Others as such, these Others will be incapable of providing recognition. It seems to me that Taylor's multiculturalist ideal here runs up against a liberalism – no matter how plural or non-procedural – in which recognition cannot move beyond the limits set by the necessity of maintaining a hegemonic articulation between a single nation and the state. This sort of arrangement is appropriate to Empires, not to 'free' peoples. But, let us not forget, that Canada is in fact an Empire formed through violent conquest – though this has been kept very quiet, supported first by a fantasy of voluntary 'confederation,' and now by one of voluntary 'multiculturalism.'

From Deep Diversity to Radical Imaginary

As a parting gesture, I would like to make a few tentative suggestions regarding how my reading of the history of Canadian diversity might contribute to the emergence of a more critical and radical multiculturalism. First and foremost, multiculturalism as theory and philosophy must address some hard questions that have so far been ignored. To give the most pertinent example, it must become cognizant of its application within the system of states, and begin to address the ongoing failure of state-sponsored rational-bureaucratic action to solve the problem of diversity. At the very least, it would be interesting to see an explicit theorization of, and justification for, the role of the state in multiculturalism. Without addressing this issue, we are left with an implicit reproduction of the Hegelian idea that the state somehow 'inherently' occupies a pole of universality, that it can and will provide an appropriate ground for a dialogue between ethnic groups, regions, and so on. This theory of the state must not be a projection of abstract possibilities which any 'right-thinking modern liberal' would recognize, but must show an awareness of the actual role of the state form in the history of Canadian diveristy and of the latest developments in social and political theory.

This is not to say that the state form is inherently evil or by definition the sole purview of the capitalist European male. Obviously, any form can be more or less successfully bent to any use. It is to claim, however, that the Canadian state *is presently* articulated, through a history of violent relations of power, more strongly with a set of British institutions, customs, and language, than it is with any other. It is to claim that, even as this state claims to be 'nothing in particular,' through allowing choice in food, festivals, and hats, it hangs on to its particularity using the same methods of violence to maintain a centralized and hierarchical system of mass-representative 'politics.' To ask for the radical possibilities of multiculturalism to be explored is also not to ignore the argument that the full deployment of Western liberal democracy is 'yet to come.' It is to wonder, though, how long certain groups must wait. In Canada, some have been hanging on for centuries while being constantly reassured in precisely this way. Is it finally time to ask if there is not something about mass, state-centralized, non-participatory forms of democracy that limits the possibilities of their extension? The crucial question, it seems to me, is: if the current forms of social and political organization are 'not necessarily' connected to any particular culture or ethnicity, then why is there such resistance to putting them at risk? Why can they not be taken from the realm of constraint and subjected to the free play of emergence? Why can democracy not be extended *now*, rather than later?

To answer this question requires an awareness of the fantasmatic structure of Canadian multiculturalism as a nation-building project. We must note its unwillingness to accept that there is no Canada to recover from the past, and none to come in the future. We must see this incompleteness as a feature constitutive of all identities, and realize that the only reason any nation has ever *appeared* complete is because it was able to use a state to establish this 'fact' through hegemonic striation of a particular set of spaces. Multiculturalism must traverse this complex fantasy of fullness and harmony associated with the nation(s)-state, and allow itself to discover that the history of Canadian diversity in fact *does* contain what is necessary for its own overcoming. Here I am not referring to the myth of harmonious coexistence, but to those aspects of this history that have been most vigorously excluded and repressed. To move on, Canadian multiculturalism must begin to identify with these symptoms of its malady. It must (i) openly admit and orient to the impossibility of full identity; (ii) affirm the value of difference and the Other as such; and (iii) recognize the necessity of a negotiation of *all* universal horizons, including that of the nation(s)-state. I will now try to describe what is involved in each of these affirmations, which, taken together, would constitute a revaluation of Canadian multiculturalism.

As Canadian history clearly teaches, no amount or kind of rational-bureaucratic intervention in everyday life can be expected to yield a critical mass of 'correct' person-types. Affirmation of the impossibility of identity is, first and foremost, affirmation of the impossibility of any *removable* impediment to unity. It is, as such, the end of problematic diversity and of attempts to solve this problem through management techniques. Further, if no person-type can be 'correct,' then it is senseless to try to order person-types in a *hierarchy* of correctness, be it the Great Chain of Race or the Immigration Points System. Indeed, it has never been much of an achievement to 'include everyone' when this 'everyone' has been carefully selected to pose as little challenge as possible to the existing (attempt at) order.

This is where the affirmation of difference as such becomes important. This position must be contrasted to what I have called strategic simulation of assimilation to the Other, in which limited forms of difference are allowed to exist only so long as is necessary for their transformation into similarity. To affirm difference as such is to have no need of tolerance, which appears only as a defence against what is repulsive. One must ask: what is it, precisely, that is so frightening about the ethnocultural Other? Is it really his outlandish customs and costumes? Or is it rather the claim he necessarily makes, through his simple presence, to engagement as another human being? Is it that the Other calls the Self to a *response* which may vary in content from extermination to acceptance, but which is invariant in its necessary *ethical* form? In the context of a society trying to become more 'liberal,' this call takes the form of a requirement to treat the Other as though he were a Self. But this requirement is not easy to meet, especially within the confines of a paternalistic state. Everything else is done for me, the Good Canadian says, so surely the state can take on this onerous task, as well? Indeed it can, and it has. But only at a cost, for engagement with the Other is necessary to both individual and group identifications, which rely upon difference in order to know their own limits and specificity. The encounter with the Other is valuable precisely to the extent that it *demands* the modification of the Self's own structures, that it demands change and thereby helps to ward off decadence. If traversal of the fantasy requires identification with the symptom, and if the symptom of the problem of Canadian diversity is the existence of the Other, then English Canada must identify with its Others, must affirm that both are 'one,' or at least situated similarly, in an impossible quest for identity amidst the endless play of *différance*.

If all identities are similarly dependent upon identification, there is no rational justification for privileging one identification over another. Yet, from the earliest 'free' emergence theories up to the present day, English Canada has tried to shield from negotiation a set of institutions that are supposed to be both 'for everyone' and 'particularly Canadian' at the same time. However, what has been protected has been a set of colonial institutions that attempt to destroy or co-opt all other forms, and have thus served only to *constrain* the development of what has been, and might be, particularly 'Canadian.' Everywhere and always, there has been a strong resistance to the necessity of negotiating *all* universal horizons, even within the most elaborate and up-to-date theories of non-procedural liberal pluralism.

Fortunately, this is not all that the history of Canadian diversity has to offer to a multiculturalism of the future. With a radicalization of what I have called the free emergence theories of the early twentieth century, particularly Canadian forms could be explored and given their place. But first, mass-democratic liberal capitalist institutions derived from the modern European model of the nation-state must be taken out of the realm of constraint. Instead of being wielded as a tool to build a pre-designed nation, the Canadian state's role would be to create a space of free play. It would be seen, not as the guardian of a perfect yet fragile order, but as providing a minimal field of structure out of which almost *anything* might emerge, and where even this minimal role would not have essential content, but would itself be subject to ongoing revision. Not a static, solidified order, but a dynamic and fluid chaos.

Now, there are many who will react immediately and violently to this suggestion: what about our precious Canadian unity? What about the National Jewel? Will it not be stolen or smashed if we do not stand on guard, every moment of every day? Surely the Others are as jealous of our ethnocultural enjoyment as we are of theirs! The answer is yes, the jewel will be put at risk, but, if I am right, this is precisely what must be done. The project of Canadian unity must be abandoned, so

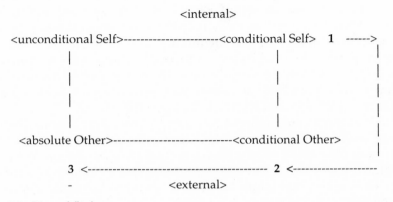

Fig. 9.1. Line of flight

that the problem of Canadian diversity can be *dissolved*. As a palliative to aid the ingestion of this strong medicine, I would point out that, like multiculturalism as liberal pluralism, this is only an acknowledgment in theory of a trend that can already be observed in history. In chapter 8, I pointed out how the standard trajectory for 'new' identifications in the system of Canadian diversity has tended to follow a line of capture that takes them from full exclusion to partial inclusion. But the line of capture can also be followed in reverse, in which case it constitutes a *line of flight* (see fig. 9.1) out to the margins of the Empire. If we abandon the tomes of Our History, if we shift our gaze from those who have 'built' Canada to those who have opposed or fled from it, a long and determined tradition of creative flight comes into view. Certainly the *coureurs de bois* were operating in an environment in which, at first, every move would have to be invented. Day-to-day life at Hudson's Bay Company trading posts, to the extent that it was not, and could not be, in accord with directives from London, was also full of invention and risk. In both of these cases, lines of flight from Empire led to the emergence of extremely interesting new modes of social organization.

Of course, this sort of creativity is not only a thing of the past. The signifier 'Québécois' is a supple point of identification which has survived the centuries by intelligent adaptation to the English-Canadian environment, tracking the singularities of culture, society, polity, and economy as they have arisen. By abandoning first the (dubious) position of unconditional Self (member of a Founding Race), then that of conditional articulation as a French Canadian, and by refusing to join the ranks of the Multiple Origins, the Québécois nationalist opts for a line of flight that becomes easier to follow the more often it is taken. We might also note that many Aboriginal people are still fleeing the Canadian state – not physically now, but semiotically – by refusing the position of integrated Aboriginal Canadian in favour of membership in a historically located and identified nation.[5] It would seem that the English-Canadian citizen is, and has always been, *surrounded* by identities which take a line of flight from state forms, and this is precisely what makes him so insecure. And well it should. To the extent that Canadian multiculturalism treats these emergent identifications as competitive aberrations to be eliminated, absorbed, or merely recognized in their difference, it robs itself of its own particularity, of precisely what it needs to achieve its dream of identity and unity. Such is the contradictory unhappiness in which English Canada is mired. It has yet to realize that, like all neurotics, it has nothing to lose but its own affliction.

In affirming difference as such, recognizing the impossibility of identity, and accepting the necessity of an ongoing negotiation of all universal horizons, Canada could start to move from multiculturalism as deep diversity – as 'more well-managed difference' within an authoritarian and hierarchical capitalist state form – to multiculturalism as radical imaginary, as *différance*, de-territorialization, more-than-life. But, of course, this would be to say yes to a force which could dig so deep that it might even undermine the foundation of the state people itself. I think this is why the affirmations I have mentioned tend to appear only in their domesticated form as official toleration of citizen diversity. They point the way to a reciprocal renunciation of recognition by non-canonical identities that would leave behind the state peoples and their system of states; that is, they threaten the further achievement of the community of equals English Canada always claims to desire, but without guaranteeing anything ... not even the sources of its own Self.

Notes

1: Introduction

1 The term 'dividing practices' comes from Michel Foucault, who has used it to characterize what he set out to study in the 'second part' of his work, namely, during the period in which he investigated the differentiation of 'the mad and the sane, the sick and the healthy, the criminals and the "good boys"' (Foucault 1982: 208).
2 I will use the term 'Self' to refer to a group constructed as possessing propriety, normality, and validity, the existence of which does not pose a public problem of diversity. The term 'Other' will be used with reference to those groups constructed as 'not-Self,' which are seen as improper and problematic by those who identify with the Self group, and against whom various actions may be taken to change or eliminate their presumed problematic qualities.
3 See Young 1995: 6-19 for an interesting and helpful discussion of modern European ideas regarding hybridity, fertility, and the differentiation of human types by way of species and race.
4 Far be it from me, of course, to suggest that anyone who *wants* a hybrid identity articulated with a state form 'should not' have it, or that it is 'better' to be displaced, contained, or exterminated than it is to be incorporated as a hybrid or newly pure identity. I am simply pointing out that hybrid identities, like those that are supposed to be more 'stable,' can be used in this way.

2: The Field of Canadian Diversity

1 I do not want to leave unaddressed the question of whether Foucault's

notion of discourse is compatible with Bourdieu's. In *The Archaeology of Knowledge* (1972), Foucault argues that belief in pre-existing forms of continuity – such as that claimed for the tradition of Canadian multiculturalism/diversity – must be suspended. The goal of the researcher is to seek out the rules which allow such claims of continuity to be made, to investigate what is unsaid and taken for granted by hegemonic narratives. Once this is done, Foucault suggests that 'an entire field is set free. A vast field, but one that can be defined nonetheless' (26–7). The term "field" (*champs*) is used here in a way that suggests a similarity with Bourdieu's insistence that a field is an analytic construct created through certain methodological choices.

2 Here the word 'original' should not be given any essentialist connotation, and should be read as referring to an 'emergence' in the sense given this term in Foucault's 'Nietzsche, Genealogy, History' (1985).

3 Some readers of previous drafts of this text have been surprised by its 'failure' to repeat the common wisdom regarding the relationship between Canada and the United States. I think that this 'omission' is methodologically justified by the limitations here described, and politically interesting in that it could be taken as the sort of reciprocal denial of recognition associated, in Hegel, with the movement from slavery to freedom. Of course, inasmuch as the American discourse is of marginal concern to the Canadian, references to it do appear from time to time.

4 See Bourdieu 1977: 72 for a discussion of the notion of the 'structured structuring structure.'

5 Buchignani's involvement in this project strikes me as somewhat surprising, since in his other work he displays a critical distance from, and sometimes contempt for, the state policy discourse that is perpetuated by this text.

6 Curiously, Ward seems to be of the opinion that anti-Orientalism in British Columbia stopped after the 1940s.

7 Taylor's work will be given only a cursory treatment here, but will be addressed in greater depth in chapter 8.

8 As Jacques Derrida has noted, 'the rigorous and subtle corridors through which the dialectic of master and slave passes are well known. They cannot be summarized without being mistreated' (1978: 254).

9 Obviously, an adequate account of the changing meaning and role of the state in Hegel's works would require far more space than can be allotted here, and would involve close comparisons between its role in the *System of Ethical Life*, the *Phenomenology*, and the *Philosophy of Right*. My remarks are made with this limitation in mind.

10 Here two final methodological concerns must be addressed. First, the dialectic of recognition is played out in Hegel in a binary form at the level of
individual self-consciousness, and leads to the emergence of an intersubjec-
tivity. But I want to ask: is the same process at work at the level of these
emergent intersubjectivities themselves? That is, does it make sense to
apply Hegel's individual dialectic of 'anthropogenetic desire' to peoples, to
posit an analytic category of 'ethnogenetic desire'? This would be a desire
of each ethnic group to negate-incorporate-assimilate its others, which
would resist, leading to the various modes imagined in Hegel's dialectic of
recognition. It seems to me that Charles Taylor implicitly assumes that such
a move is valid, though he never mentions or justifies it. I think it has value,
since with this notion we can fruitfully examine the claim that 'recognition'
can help to solve the problems posed by 'identity politics' with reference to
particular historical contexts. Second, Hegel's historical and sociological
insights must be rescued from his theodicy. Instead of sublated stages in the
rationalization and actualization of World Spirit, we must think of multiple
coexisting modes: contradictions preserved, intensified, with no resolution;
'stages' leaped many at a time; and 'regression' from what Hegel would see
as a higher stage to a lower happening all the time. We need to use genealogy rather than teleology.

3: European Antecedents to the Problem of Canadian Diversity

1 I am not claiming here that individuals do not identify with races, nations,
and cultures, nor am I suggesting that 'guesses' that one might make about
the attributes of an individual based on 'visible' signs are *necessarily* wrong.
I am claiming, however, that these guesses *may* be wrong, and that there is
no necessary or conclusive link between other-ascribed group characteristics and individual identifications or personality traits. I am also taking this
stance because I believe that *attempting* to guess is at best an imposition, at
worst the beginning of a round of violence; and, finally, I believe that whatever predictive power these other-ascriptions might have had is dwindling,
in contexts like that of Canada in the 1990s, as multiple rather than single
'origin' individuals become the norm.

2 The extent to which Plato marked a change may be a contentious issue, but
I mention it only out of respect for duBois's argument. It is not a central
issue for my analysis since, as will become apparent, what matters for me is
the presence, and not the origin, of polarity, analogy, and contradiction
within a hierarchical system.

3 Anthony Smith might serve as an exemplar of this approach. According to

him, *'ethnie* (ethnic communities) may ... be defined as named human populations with shared ancestry myths, histories and cultures, having an association with a specific territory and a sense of solidarity' (Smith 1986: 32).

4 See Gregory Vlastos's comments on slavery in Plato's Utopia, in 'Does Slavery Exist in Plato's *Republic*?' (Vlastos 1981: 140–6).

5 I should point out that in presenting material from the texts of Plato and Aristotle, I make no claim to be offering a definitive or final 'philosophical' reading, nor do I claim to be 'doing philosophy' at all. My aim, on the contrary, is to simply indicate how these texts might be seen as contributing to the European discourse on diversity, by pointing out how they construct and manage problematic human difference. Emma Dench has argued that 'Herodotus makes panhellenic sentiments come to the fore against the background of the Persian wars,' and that the idea of Greek supremacy gained momentum after that (1995: 50). Following Lovejoy's (1936) reading of the relation between Plato and Aristotle on the hierarchical order of beings, Page duBois argues that a 'new philosophical discourse' emerged in the fourth century B.C. This discourse was 'centred on questions of hierarchy, of mind over body, man over woman, "human" over foreigner, over slave ... The terms in which Plato articulated his problematic have defined Western philosophical discourse ever since' (1991: 152). My reading is in line with this body of scholarship.

6 Debate and practice on the European frontier proceeded as though uninformed by the orders of several popes. Paul III, for example, declared in 1537 that the Savages were not to be treated as 'dumb brutes created for our service' but 'as truly men ... capable of understanding the Catholic faith' (papal bull, *Sublimus Deus Sic Dilexit*, 1537, cited in Dickason 1984: 32).

4: Two 'Canadian' Solutions to the Problem of Diversity

1 Throughout this section, I will use the term 'Savage' only as it pertains to a discursive category appropriate to the European discourse on diversity as it was brought to the 'New World.' I do not believe that there is, or ever was, a referent for this term, and do not intend it to apply to any person or peoples who live, or have lived, in what is now known within the dominant British-Canadian culture as 'North America.'

2 This term plays on the distinction between massacre societies and sacrifice societies made in Todorov's *Conquest of America* (1984: 143), where the Spanish and Aztecs are respectively cast in these roles.

3 An allusion to the quote from Virgil in chapter 2.

4 Trigger (1985: 36) gives several more examples.

5 Trigger, who is usually more balanced, falls into the trap of assigning blame for French attempts at extermination on the 'recalcitrant Mohawks' and the 'reluctant Oneidas' (1985: 284). Eccles, who writes in the grand old style of historical glorification, suggests that Frontenac was 'forced' to burn Onondaga villages (1966: 78). Charlevoix refers to the campaign against the Iroquois as a 'holy war' (1870: 3.95).

6 Chapter 4 of Quinn's *New American World* (1979), an excellent compendium of primary sources, provides countless examples in dozens of thinkers and Explorers.

7 In 1790 a Mr Harry Miller told Pulling that he had 'sent eight of his men ... in pursuit of some Indians who had the preceding summer taken away some of his Salmon-netts – Traps & many other things then & at different times before' (Marshall 1989: 123). Despite the fact that Miller could not have known who was stealing his equipment, and that even if it had been Beothuck, his men could not have known if any people they found were those who had stolen the gear, they set out 'fully resolved to kill everyone we saw both Big & small to be revenged on them for killing Thomas Rowsell the summer before' (123). A classic use of the law of individual–group identification: anyone who looks like 'them' must be 'them'; the one stands for the many and the many for the one, justifying the random slaughter of the Other.

5: Repetition and Failure in British North America

1 Six ships destined for South Carolina were forced to land in Boston, where it was discovered that they did not have adequate supplies to reach their destination. The people were kept in Massachusetts, 'bound by contract to English masters,' and prevented from leaving the colony to look for lost relatives without first obtaining a pass (Arsenault 1966: 152). 'Virginia flatly refused to receive the 1200 Acadians deported there. They were detained for some time at Williamsburg, where an epidemic broke out, killing off hundreds of them' (156). In Georgia, the British North American view of the Acadians was made most explicit, as they were 'put to work on the plantations with the Negro slaves' (157).

2 'Six hundred and eighty-six houses, eleven mills and two churches were set on fire in the two parishes of Grand-Pré and Rivère aux Canards alone' (Arsenault 1966: 147). Many Acadians, however, had friends and relatives amongst the Native inhabitants of the region, and so were able to flee into the woods: 'Governor Lawrence decided to get rid of them by putting a bounty on scalps. In a proclamation dated May 14, 1756, he guaranteed

30 pounds for the scalp of every male Indian over 16, and 25 pounds for scalps of younger males or for any female or child brought back alive. A number of English soldiers, however, confused Indian and Acadian scalps. They had the legal excuse that officially all Acadians had been deported from Nova Scotia' (162–3).

3 Scholars differ as to precisely when the term 'race' was first used with the connotations it has today, but by the end of the eighteenth century, the word was becoming current in Europe. Petty used it as early as 1677, and Francois Bernier in 1684 (Todorov 1993: 99). Theo Goldberg has argued that 'the *concept* of race enters European social consciousness more or less explicitly in the fifteenth century' (Goldberg 1993: 21, emphasis added), while duBois is of the opinion that the concept did not come into play until the late 1700 (duBois 1991: 92, note 1). Whatever its origin and development in the various European languages and intellectual communities, there is little doubt that differentiation by race was on the rise, adding natural-historical credibility to the Great Chain of Being.

6: The Dominion of Canada and the Proliferation of Immigrant Otherness

1 The BNA Act begins: 'Whereas the Provinces of Canada, Nova Scotia, and New Brunswick have *expressed their Desire to be federally united* into One Dominion under the Crown of the United Kingdom of Great Britain ...' (*RSC* [1970], Appendix 9: 257; emphasis added). From their earliest attempts to wrest control of the Northwest away from the Hudson's Bay Company, the Canadians represented themselves as the bearers of a gift of unity and civilization. For example, they petitioned the British government to 'unite Rupert's Land and the North-Western territory with this Dominion, and to grant to the Parliament of Canada authority to legislate for their future welfare and good government' (*RSC* [1970], Appendix 9: 264). It is now commonplace to read that Manitoba '*entered* confederation' (*MCBCM*: 15) or that '*Riel asked* that the Red River area be made a province ...' (Buchignani and Engel 1983: 49). I would also refer the reader to the discussion of what I call 'Our History' in chapter 6.

2 Section 1 provided for immigration offices only in London 'and elsewhere in the United Kingdom,' and also 'on the Continent of Europe.' Not all, however, were welcome. Masters of ships arriving at Canadian ports were required to report on any passengers who were 'lunatic, idiotic, deaf or dumb, blind or infirm, stating also whether they are accompanied by relatives able to support them' (sect. 9.1). 'Pauper immigrants' were also prohibited from landing (section 16), and the established practice of using

medical quarantine stations to filter out diseased bodies was continued (section 1).

3 Throughout the 1880s, the writers of the *Statistical Yearbook of Canada* cautioned that it was only possible 'to form a general idea of the numbers that yearly settle in each province,' on account of much unofficial travel across the American border, British Columbia not distinguishing between visitors and settlers, and so on (*CSY* [1888]: 66). In the twentieth century, the Canadian classic seems to be Ryder 1955.

4 In 1899, during Sifton's tenure, the Canadian government sent out 886,000 maps and pamphlets. These were printed in 'Bohemian, German, Swedish, French and English, Danish, the Scandinavian language, Icelandic and Hungarian,' and sent to Great Britain, the European continent, and the United States (*JHC* [1900], v. 35, App. 1: 349).

5 Although Canadian nativism has not been well studied, Howard Palmer's *Patterns of Prejudice: A History of Nativism in Alberta* (Palmer 1982a) deals in depth with these, and other, nativist reactions in Alberta and provides references to further sources.

6 See Ward 1978: 53–76 for a full discussion of the riot and the events leading up to and following it.

7 This statement anticipates and foreshadows evidence that will be presented in chapter 8.

8 In the interest of maintaining a focus on the problem of Canadian diversity, rather than on Woodsworth's place within history, I should point out that it is not my intention to challenge the view, expressed by Marilyn Barber in the Introduction to the 1972 edition of the book, that Woodsworth possessed 'an inquiring mind with a deep interest in people and their welfare' (viii). Rather, I hope to show that Woodsworth, like his less inquiring and compassionate contemporaries, was reproducing and heightening the problem of Canadian diversity in his attempts to define and solve it through rational-bureaucratic means.

9 That 'northern, eastern and southern Europe' were seen as 'remote and little known' regions also serves to highlight the arbitrary character of the assignation of problematic difference. Individuals whose genetic stock derives from these regions are now cast much more often as 'invisible selves' than 'visible others.'

10 'In Africa the people are unstable, indifferent to suffering, and easily aroused to ferocity by the sight of blood or under great fear. They exhibit certain qualities which are associated with their descendants in this country, namely aversion to silence and solitude, love of rhythm, excitability, and lack of reserve. All travelers speak of their impulsiveness, strong sex-

ual passion, and lack of will power ... The very qualities of intelligence and manliness which are essential for citizenship in a democracy were systematically expunged from the negro race through two hundred years of slavery' (158).

11 For more on the Black as unmentionable, excluded Other in Canadian history, see James Walker's *A History of Blacks in Canada*. Walker suggests that the exclusion of the Black experience from Canadian history might have something to do with the fact that it challenges the belief that British Canada has only been home to freed American slaves, having never owned any of its own. 'But from the early nineteenth century,' Walker writes, 'there was never a time when blacks were not held as slaves in Canada. Slavery is thus a very real part of our history, yet the fact that slavery ever existed here has been one of our best-kept historical secrets' (Walker 1980: 19).

12 For more on the Canadian social gospel movement, whose relation to immigration and assimilation has yet to be fully explored, see Allen 1971, Antonides 1985, and Fraser 1988.

13 While it was only with this Act that the legal means were set in place to deport people from Canada, it seems that the practice had been going on illegally for quite some time. In his 1877 Report to the Select Standing Committee on Immigration and Colonization, the Secretary of the Department of Agriculture, Mr Lowe, let it be known that his department had a 'rule' about these things: 'The rule of the Department is that immigrants who have not been over one year in the country, are, in some measure, under the care of the Department; and if it has been found, after they have come to the country, that, from illness or bodily infirmity, they have been unable to get their living, they have been sent back, as the simplest and cheapest mode of dealing with them' (*SPHC* [1877], App. 6: 40). Other parts of Lowe's evidence are cited by Barbara Roberts, who encountered it in the Immigration archives, at page 5 of her book, *Whence They Came: Deportation from Canada 1900–1935*. She offers up many insightful comments on the role and function of deportation in Canada over this period.

14 For further description and comment on the *Komogata Maru* incident, see Ward 1978: 87–3; and Ferguson 1975).

15 The intent of this Order, and those like it, was confirmed by J.A. Calder in the House of Commons: '[A]n order in Council is in existence prohibiting the entry of skilled and unskilled labour from Asia; at least skilled and unskilled labour is not permitted to enter our British Columbia ports, which means that, in so far as this class is concerned, we are excluding it' (*DHC*, 29 April 1919: 1874).

7: The Rise of the Mosaic Metaphor

1 This is only a logical contradiction, however, if one takes both terms to exist on the same level, as being of the same logical type. Certainly a unity can, and often does, emerge out of a diversity as a distinct, but interconnected, logical type at a different level. See Wilden 1980 for this distinction in general, and Angus 1997 (138–40, 144) for its application in the particular context of a national unity emerging out of an ethnocultural diversity.

2 J.M. Gibbon appears to have been the first to ascribe this priority to Hayward's usage, in the Peface to his *Canadian Mosaic* (Gibbon 1938: viii–ix).

3 Later in the twentieth century, both the Canadian state and some Canadian philosophers of multiculturalism would challenge the assumption of a strong link between language and culture. These issues will be discussed in the chapter on multiculturalism as state policy. I should point out now, however, that the question of the 'objective' ability of language to assimilate Others is not what is of importance to my analysis. Rather, I only claim that England *hoped* that linguistic assimilation was possible, and that it played a role of constraint in his *theory* of seductive assimilation.

4 Even the much-vaunted separation of the courts and the police disappeared in 1940, when Order in Coucil 2363 (4 June 1940) redefined 'Justice of the Peace' to include 'a police magistrate' and 'every commissioned officer of the Royal Canadian Mounted Police.' This allowed the police to issue their own search warrants, and thereby bypass even the minimal protection that the courts offer against the arbitrary exercise of their authority.

5 Alderman Jake Penner of Winnipeg was one of those interned. Joseph Zuken, who was present for Penner's appeal, says that it was dismissed 'without any evidence produced against him' (Repka and Repka 1982: 15). How could a duly elected representative of the People be an Enemy Alien? He was an anti-fascist communist, one of several hundred rounded up and interned during the war. *Dangerous Patriots* (Repka and Repka 1982) gives a number of first-hand accounts from Second World War political internees, most of whom were feared as communists.

6 See Ken Adachi's (1976) *The Enemy That Never Was* for a critique of the Japanese internment.

7 'In constructive diplomacy as in bone ailments, there are two main methods. The first method is the most spectacular, prompt, and popular. It is the equivalent of a surgical intervention. It often requires other operations to follow. It is rapid, drastic and aggressive. One attacks the foreign element which has entered the body politic. In the realm of diplomacy it takes the

form of threat and direct action. It is a regrettable wartime technique extended to the realm of the civilian' (section VI-1).

8 Kirkconnell's readers need not have felt *too* badly about their lingering habits of Racial thought, however, as the author himself, or at very least his editor, was guilty of committing 'the most dangerous error that can delude the human brain' many times in the same pamphlet. On the bottom of page 19, there is a photograph of what appears to me, trained in discourse of difference emerging out of the 1960s, as a group of White men eating. Underneath the photograph is the caption: 'The lumber camps have long been the meeting ground of the races.' Similar 'errors' are made on page 47, and on page 21, where the title 'Racial Origins' heads a list including 'French Canadians,' 'German Canadians,' and many others that Kirkconnell had explicitly – and rather mockingly – declared *not* to be races.

9 This announcement was also a continuation of another Canadian tradition, that of bypassing Parliament in setting immigration 'levels' and 'sources.' Order in Council 2071 of 28 May 1946 had created the category of 'sponsored' immigration, which was to allow Canadians to bring in relatives from Continental Europe who had been displaced by the war. Under this order, post-war immigration had already increased from 12,000 in 1944 to 64,000 in 1947. Order in Council 1734 of 1 May 1947 extended the 'terms of admissibility' of the already admissible classes of British and Americans and also, for the first time, openly welcomed 'persons who are suitable for employment in the primary industries' (cited in *DHC*, 1 May 1947: 2645).

10 See, for example, *A Look at Canada* (1996), produced by the Integration Branch of the Department of Citizenship and Immigration as a study guide for citizenship exams. *MCBC* is another good example, as noted in the Introduction, but pretty much any government pamphlet on immigration, citizenship, or naturalization will do.

8: Unhappy Countriness: Multiculturalism as State Policy

1 Subsequent references will refer to the 'B & B Commission' and the 'B & B Prelim. Report.'

2 Volume 4 of the *B & B Report* boasts a six-page academic bibliography, many entries in which were funded by the Royal Commission itself.

3 Here I am playing upon Deleuze and Guattari's characterization of the state form as an 'apparatus of capture,' and providing what seems like an appropriate complement to their notion of 'line of flight' (Deleuze and Guattari 1987: 137, 424–73).

4 For an overview of the theoretical arguments and positions, see Poster 1992.

5   In providing a 'definition,' I do not propose to exhaust or fully circumscribe the resonances of this term as it is used within Derrida's texts – such a project would be foolish indeed – but rather to produce enough limitation to allow it to be used 'successfully' in the context of this dissertation.

6   For Kymlicka, of course, this does not represent a 'problem,' for, as I have shown, he believes that immigrants have 'waived their right' to such an existence by not coming to Canada as Colonizers.

9: A Revaluation of Canadian Multiculturalism

1   It is interesting to note how relations between state policy, academic analysis, and popular culture have changed and remained the same since the 1940s. During the earliest days of multiculturalism, academics led with theory, the state implemented policy behind a blaze of propaganda, and the population largely resisted or ignored them both. The people are still resisting and ignoring, and there are still strong correlations between the leading philosophy of multiculturalism and state policy, but now the philosophers appear to be following rather than leading. Will Kymlicka has written that, 'like Jay Sigler, I believe that providing a liberal defence of minority rights "does not create a mandate for a vast change. It merely ratifies and explains changes that have taken place in the absence of theory"' (1995: 127). In a similar vein, Ian Angus has noted that 'the practice of multiculturalism in English Canada has proceeded further in its everyday, institutional, and policy contexts than it has as social and political philosophy' (1997: 137). Indeed, it is possible that some of the most interesting possibilities of multiculturalism have been obscured or left unexplored precisely because contemporary theory has been following the lead of the state policy discourse.

2   This intervention in the 'communitarian-liberal' debate is crucial to Kymlicka's position. He is trying to ward off the argument, as one commentator has put it, that 'the democratic way conflicts with any rigid idea of, or absolute right to, cultural survival' (Rockefeller 1992: 92). In the form to which Kymlicka particularly objects, the communitarian argument holds that the nation provides 'too vast a scale across which to cultivate the shared self-understanding necessary to community in the ... constitutive sense' (Sandel 1984: 93). Obviously, if he is to argue for the mutual coexistence of majorities, national minorities, and ethnicities within a single state, Kymlicka must defend some conception of a greater common – but changeable – notion of the good life, which he does explicitly on page 91 of *Multicultural Citizenship*. A similar stance against communitarianism has been taken by Chantal Mouffe, who also advocates building a political society out of a

number of identities that are not mutually exclusive, but oriented to a changing common cause of radical democracy. 'The communitarian insistence on a substantive notion of the common good and shared moral values is incompatible with the pluralism that is constitutive of modern democracy ...' (Mouffe 1993b: 83). Interestingly, communitarian and radical-democratic theorists each accuse the other of being anti-democratic.

3 Nunavut looks like something quite stunning and unprecedented, a nation-state giving away some of its territory without bloodshed – at least, among the generations involved – and, to some extent, it is. The Inuit are clearly not being 'given' the means to create what Kymlicka would call a societal culture. But they may be being given enough to one day create, perhaps *take*, one. Another Red River? Let us hope so!

4 In Quebec, it would be the Québécois subject that occupies this position; in the rest of Canada, it would be the English-Canadian, as British-Canadian – a category so 'normal' that it does not really exist. One must always locate the state nation in relation to other nations; that is, it is a differential identity like all others.

5 These examples show that taking a line of flight does not lead to something like what is called 'freedom' in Enlightenment thought, but that what comes after position 3 is entirely contingent. Taking an ethnocultural line of flight can lead to recapture by a different state apparatus, a marginal ('nomadic') lifestyle, or even to the acquisition of a 'sovereign' position as unconditional self within a new nation-state.

Bibliography

Adachi, K. (1976). *The Enemy That Never Was: A History of the Japanese Canadians*. Toronto: McClelland and Stewart.

Adams, H. (1995). *A Tortured People: The Politics of Colonization*. Penticton, BC: Thetus Books.

– (1989). *Prison of Grass: Canada from a Native Point of View*. Saskatoon: Fifth House Publishers.

Akins, T.B. (1972). *Papers Relating to the Acadian French 1714–1755*. Cottonport, LA: Polyanthos.

– (1849). *A Sketch of the Rise and Progress of the Church of England in the British North American Provinces*. Halifax: W. Cunnabell.

Allen, R. (1971). *The Social Passion: Religion and Social Reform in Canada 1914–28*. Toronto: University of Toronto Press.

Anderson, B. (1991). *Imagined Communities*. London: Verso.

Anderson, J.T.M. (1918). *The Education of the New Canadian: A Treatise on Canada's Greatest Educational Problem*. Toronto: J.M. Dent.

Angus, I. (1997). *A Border Within: National Identity, Cultural Plurality, and Wilderness*. Montreal and Kingston: McGill-Queen's University Press.

– ed. (1988a). *Ethnicity in a Technological Age*. Edmonton: Canadian Institute of Ukrainian Studies.

– (1988b). 'Oral Tradition as Resistance.' In *Continuity and Change: The Cultural Life of Alberta's First Ukrainians*. Ed. M. Lupul. Edmonton: Canadian Institute of Ukrainian Studies.

Angus Reid Group. (1991). *Multiculturalism and Canadians: Attitude Survey 1991*. Hull: Multiculturalism and Citizenship Canada.

Antonides, H. (1985). *Stones for Bread: The Social Gospel and Its Contemporary Legacy.* Jordan Station, ON: Paideia Press.

Aristotle. (1981). *Politics.* Harmondsworth: Penguin.

Arsenault, B. (1966). *History of the Acadians.* Montreal: Le Conseil de la vie française en Amérique.

Augustine, Saint. (1972). *Concerning the City of God against the Pagans.* Harmondsworth: Penguin.

Avery, D. (1995). *Reluctant Host: Canada's Response to Immigrant Workers, 1896–1994.* Toronto: McClelland and Stewart.

– (1979). *Dangerous Foreigners: European Immigrant Workers and Labour Radicalism in Canada 1896–1932.* Toronto: McClelland and Stewart.

Bannerji, H. (1996). 'On the Dark Side of the Nation: Politics of Multiculturalism and the State of "Canada."' *Journal of Canadian Studies* 31(3): 103–28.

– ed. (1993). *Returning the Gaze.* Toronto: Sister Vision Press.

Bartholomaeus. (1975). *On the Properties of Things: John Trevista's Translation of Bartholomaeus Anglicus De Proprietatabus Rerum.* Vol. 2. Oxford: Clarendon Press.

Bartlett, R. (1990). *Indian Reserves and Aboriginal Lands in Canada.* Saskatoon: University of Saskatchewan Native Law Centre.

Baudrillard, J. (1983). *Simulations.* New York: Semiotext(e).

Bauman, Z. (1992). *Intimations of Postmodernity.* London: Routledge.

– (1987). *Legislators and Interpreters.* New York: Cornell University Press.

Berger, T. (1991). *A Long and Terrible Shadow.* Vancouver: Douglas and McIntyre.

Bergeron, L. (1975). *The History of Quebec: A Patriote's Handbook.* Toronto: NC Press.

Bhabha, H. (1994). *The Location of Culture.* London: Routledge.

– ed. (1991). *Nation and Narration.* London: Routledge.

Bibby, R. (1990). *Mosaic Madness.* Toronto: Stoddart.

Biggar, H.P., ed. (1925). *The Works of Samuel de Champlain.* Toronto: The Champlain Society.

– ed. (1911). *The Precursors of Jacques Cartier.* Ottawa: Government Printing Bureau.

Bissoondath, N. (1994). *Selling Illusions: The Cult of Multiculturalism in Canada.* Toronto: Penguin.

Bourdieu, P. (1992). *An Invitation to Reflexive Sociology.* Chicago: University of Chicago Press.

– (1990). *In Other Words: Essays towards a Reflexive Sociology.* Stanford: Stanford University Press.

– (1988). 'Vive La Crise.' *Theory and Society* 17: 773–8.

– (1984). *Distinction.* Chicago: University of Chicago Press.

– (1977). *Outline of a Theory of Practice*. Cambridge, MA: Harvard University Press.

Brotz, H. (1980). 'Multiculturalism in Canada: A Muddle.' *Canadian Public Policy* 6(1): 41–6.

Brown, J. (1980). *Strangers in Blood: Fur Trade Company Families in Indian Country*. Vancouver: University of British Columbia Press.

Brown, J., and J. Peterson, eds. (1985). *The New Peoples: Being and Becoming Métis in North America*. Lincoln: University of Nebraska Press.

Bryce, G. (1968). *The Remarkable History of the Hudson's Bay Company*. New York: Burt Franklin.

Buchignani, N. (1982). 'Canadian Ethnic Research and Multiculturalism.' *Journal of Canadian Studies* 17(1): 16–34.

Buchignani, N., and J. Engel. (1983). *Cultures in Canada: Strength in Diversity*. Edmonton: Weigl Educational Publishers Inc.

Burnet, J. (1975). 'The Policy of Multiculturalism within a Bilingual Framework: An Interpretation.' In *Education of Immigrant Students: Issues and Answers*. Ed. A. Wolfgang. Toronto: OISE.

Butler, J. (1990). *Gender Trouble*. London: Routledge.

– (1987). *Subjects of Desire: Hegelian Reflections in Twentieth-Century France*. New York: Columbia University Press.

Canada. (1969). *Statement of the Government of Canada on Indian Policy, 1969*. Ottawa: Queen's Printer.

– (1891). *Indian Treaties and Surrenders from 1680 to 1890*. Ottawa: Queen's Printer.

– (1876). *Description of the Country between Lake Superior and the Pacific Ocean, on the Line of the Canadian Pacific Railway*. Ottawa: Government of Canada. In History of the Canadian Northwest Microfilm Series, Reel 5, PNW 362.

– (1858). *Report on the Exploration of the Country between Lake Superior and the Red River Settlement*. Toronto: John Lovell. In History of the Canadian Northwest Microfilm Series, Reel 5, PNW 361.

Canada. Dept. of Agriculture. (1886–1905). *The Statistical Year-Book of Canada*. Ottawa: Government of Canada.

Canada. Dept. of Citizenship and Immigration. (1952–65). *Report*. Issued annually. Ottawa: King's Printer.

– (1951a). *Report of the Department of Citizenship and Immigration for the Fiscal Year Ended March 31, 1950*. Ottawa: King's Printer.

– (1951b). *Report of the Department of Citizenship and Immigration for the Fiscal Year Ended March 31, 1951*. Ottawa: King's Printer.

Canada. Dept. of Citizenship and Immigration. Canadian Citizenship Branch. (1961). *Our History*. Ottawa: Queen's Printer.

– (1960). *Notes on the Canadian Family Tree*. Ottawa: Queen's Printer.

Canada. Dept. of Citizenship and Immigration. Integration Branch. (1996). *A Look at Canada*. Ottawa: Queen's Printer.

Canada. Dept. of Employment and Immigration. (1991). *Guidelines for the Immigrant Investor Program*. Ottawa: Supply and Services Canada.

– (1985). *The Revised Selection Criteria for Independent Immigrants*. Ottawa: Supply and Services Canada.

Canada. Dept. of Manpower and Immigration. (1966). *White Paper on Immigration*. Ottawa: Minister of Government Services.

Canada. Dept. of National War Services. (1940). *A Call to Canadian Unity*. Ottawa: Director of Public Information.

Canada. Dept. of the Secretary of State. (1987). *Multiculturalism: Being Canadian*. Ottawa: Supply and Services Canada.

Canada. Dept. of the Secretary of State. (1946–9). *Report*. Ottawa: King's Printer.

Canada. Dept. of the Secretary of State. Canadian Citizenship Branch. (1967). *The Canadian Family Tree*. Ottawa: Queen's Printer.

Canada. Dept. of the Secretary of State. Multiculturalism Directorate. (1979). *The Canadian Family Tree: Canada's Peoples*. Ottawa: Queen's Printer.

Canada. Dominion Bureau of Statistics. (1951). *Ninth Census of Canada, 1951: Instructions for Enumerators*. Ottawa: King's Printer.

– (1936). *Seventh Census of Canada, 1931: Summary (v. 1)*. Ottawa: King's Printer.

Canada. House of Commons. Special Committee on the Participation of Visible Minorities in Canadian Society. (1984). *Equality Now! Report of the Special Committee on Visible Minorities in Canadian Society*. Ottawa: Supply and Services Canada.

Canada. Ministry of State for Multiculturalism and Citizenship (1991). *Multiculturalism: What Is It Really About?* Ottawa: Supply and Services Canada.

Canada. Parliament. (1865). *Parliamentary Debates on the Subject of the Confederation of the British North American Provinces*. Quebec: Hunter, Rose & Co.

Canada. Privy Council (1939). *Defence of Canada Regulations*. Ottawa: King's Printer.

Canada. Royal Commission on Bilingualism and Biculturalism. (1973). *Bilingualism and Biculturalism: An Abridged version of the Royal Commission Report*. Ed. R. Innis. Toronto: McClelland and Stewart.

– (1969). *Report*. Ottawa: Supply and Services Canada.

– (1965). *Preliminary Report*. Ottawa: Supply and Services Canada.

Canada. Standing Committee on Multiculturalism. (1987). *Multiculturalism: Building the Canadian Mosaic*. Ottawa: Supply and Services Canada.

Canada. Statistics Canada. (1996). *Canadian Economic Observer Historical Statisti-*

cal Supplement, 1995/1996. Ottawa: Minister of Industry, Statistics Canada Catalogue no. 11–010–XPB.

– (1993). *Ethnic Origin: 1991 Census of Canada*. Ottawa: Industry, Science, and Technology Canada. Statistics Canada Catalogue no. 93–315.

– (1989). *Ethnicity, Immigration, and Citizenship: 1986 Census of Canada*. Ottawa: Minister of Supply and Services. Statistics Canada Catalogue no. 93-109.

– (1906–). *The Canada Year Book*. Ottawa: Statistics Canada.

– (1887). *Census of Manitoba, 1885–6*. Statistics Canada Catalogue no. 98–1886F.

Canadian Club of Vancouver. (1907). *Addresses Delivered before the Canadian Club of Vancouver*. Vancouver: Canadian Club of Vancouver.

Canadian Historical Publishing Co. (1888). *The New West: Wealth and Growth*. Winnipeg: Canadian Historical Publishing Co. In History of the Canadian Northwest Microfilm Series, Reel 12, PNW 440.

Cardinal, H. (1969). *The Unjust Society*. Edmonton: M.G. Hurtig Ltd.

Castoriadis, C. (1987). *The Imaginary Institution of Society*. Baltimore: Johns Hopkins University Press.

Cell, G. (1982). *Newfoundland Discovered: English Attempts at Colonization, 1610–1630*. London: Hakluyt Society.

Chapais, T. (1964). *The Great Intendant*. Toronto: University of Toronto Press.

Charlevoix, P.F.X. (1870). *History and General Description of New France*. Trans. J. Shea. Chicago: Loyola University Press.

Clark, W., ed. (1904). *Empire Club Speeches*. Toronto: William Briggs.

Clifton, R., and L. Roberts. (1982). 'Exploring the Ideology of Canadian Multiculturalism.' *Canadian Public Policy* 8(1): 88–94.

Cockloft, J. (1960). *Cursory Observations Made in Quebec, 1811*. Toronto: Oxford University Press.

Columbus, C. (1961). *Four Voyages to the New World*. New York: Corinth Books.

Connor, R. (1909). *The Foreigner*. Toronto: The Westminster Company.

Conseil de la vie française en Amérique. (1967). *Nothing More, Nothing Less: A French-Canadian View of Bilingualism and Biculturalism*. Toronto and Montreal: Holt Rinehart.

Cook, R. (1993). *The Voyages of Jacques Cartier*. Toronto: University of Toronto Press.

– (1985). *The Regenerators: Social Criticism in Late Victorian English Canada*. Toronto: University of Toronto Press.

Cumming, P., and N. Mickenburg. Eds. (1972). *Native Rights in Canada*. Toronto: Indian-Eskimo Association of Canada / General Publishing.

Dawson, Rev. A.M. (1870). *Our Strength and Their Strength: The North West Territory*. Ottawa: Times Office.

Deleuze, G., and F. Guattari. (1987). *A Thousand Plateaus: Capitalism and Schizophrenia*. London: Athlone.

– (1986). *Nomadology: The War Machine*. New York: Semiotext(e).

Dench, E. (1995). *From Barbarians to New Men: Greek, Roman, and Modern Perceptions of Peoples of the Central Apennines*. Oxford: Clarendon.

Derrida, J. (1982). 'Différance.' In *Margins of Philosophy*. Chicago: University of Chicago Press.

– (1978). *Writing and Difference*. London: Routledge.

– (1976). *Of Grammatology*. Cambridge: Polity Press.

Dickason, O. (1984). *The Myth of the Savage and the Beginnings of French Colonialism in the Americas*. Edmonton: University of Alberta Press.

Dreisziger, N.F. (1988). 'The Rise of a Bureaucracy for Multiculturalism: The Origins of the Nationalities Branch, 1939–1941.' In *On Guard for Thee: War, Ethnicity, and the Canadian State, 1939–1945*. Ottawa: Ministry of Supply and Services.

Driedger, L. (1996). *Multi-Ethnic Canada: Identities and Inequalities*. Toronto: Oxford University Press.

duBois, P. (1991). *Centaurs and Amazons: Women and the Pre-History of the Great Chain of Being*. Ann Arbor: University of Michigan Press.

Dufour, C. (1990). *A Canadian Challenge / Le Défi québécois*. Lantzville, BC: Oolichan Books.

Dyck, N. (1991). *What Is the Indian Problem: Tutelage and Resistance in Canadian Indian Administration*. St John's: ISER.

Eccles, W.J. (1966). *The Ordeal of New France*. Montreal: Canadian Broadcasting Service.

Elliot, J.L., and A. Fleras. (1992). *Unequal Relations: An Introduction of Race and Ethnic Dynamics in Canada*. Scarborough, ON: Prentice Hall.

England, R. (1980). *Living, Learning, Remembering: Memoirs of Robert England*. Vancouver: Centre for Continuing Education.

– (1929). *The Central European Immigrant in Canada*. Toronto: Macmillan.

Ferguson, T. (1975). *A White Mans' Country: An Exercise in Canadian Prejudice*. Toronto: Doubleday.

Fisher, R. (1988). 'The Image of the Indian.' In *Out of the Background*. Ed. K. Coates, K. Fisher, and R. Fisher. Toronto: Copp Clark.

Foster, K. (1926). *Our Canadian Mosaic*. Toronto: YWCA.

Foucault, M. (1985). 'Nietzsche, Genealogy, History.' In *The Foucault Reader*. Ed. P. Rabinow. New York: Pantheon Books.

– (1982). 'The Subject and Power.' In *Michel Foucault: Beyond Structuralism and Hermeneutics*. Ed. H.L. Dreyfus and P. Rabinow. Sussex: The Harvester Press.

- (1980). *Power/Knowledge: Selected Interviews and Other Writings 1972–1977*. Ed. C. Gordon. New York: Pantheon Books.
- (1979). *Discipline and Punish: The Birth of the Modern Prison*. Hammondsworth: Penguin.
- (1978). *The History of Sexuality, Volume I*. New York: Vintage.
- (1972). *The Archaeology of Knowledge*. New York: Random House.
- (1970). *The Order of Things*. New York: Random House.
Francis, D., and T. Morantz. (1983). *Partners in Furs: A History of the Fur Trade in Eastern James Bay 1600–1870*. Kingston and Montreal: McGill-Queen's University Press.
Fraser, B.J. (1988). *The Social Uplifters: Presbyterian Progressives and the Social Gospel in Canada, 1875–1915*. Waterloo, ON: Wilfrid Laurier University Press.
Friedman, J.B. (1981). *The Monstrous Races in Medieval Art and Thought*. Cambridge, MA: Harvard University Press.
Gagnon, S. (1982). *Quebec and Its Historians 1840 to 1920*. Montreal: Harvest House.
Gans, H. (1979). 'Symbolic Ethnicity: The Future of Ethnic Groups and Cultures in America.' *Ethnic and Racial Studies* 2(1): 1–20.
Geertz, C. (1986). 'Distinguished Lecture: Anti Anti-Relativism.' *American Anthropologist* 86(2): 263–78.
Gellner, E. (1983). *Nations and Nationalism*. Oxford: Basil Blackwell.
Georges, P. (1994). *Barbarian Asia and the Greek Experience: From the Archaic Period to the Age of Xenophon*. Baltimore: Johns Hopkins University Press.
Gibbon, J.M. (1938). *Canadian Mosaic: The Making of a Northern Nation*. Toronto: McClelland and Stewart.
Goldberg, T. (1993). *Racist Culture: Philosophy and the Politics of Meaning*. Oxford and Cambridge: Blackwell.
Gosse, R., et al. (1994). *Continuing Poundmaker and Riel's Quest*. Saskatoon: Purich Publishing.
Great Britain. Parliament. House of Commons. (1857). *Report from the Select Committee on the Hudson's Bay Company*. CIHM 48795.
Green, V. (1996). *A New History of Christianity*. New York: Continuum.
Gregorovich, J.B. (1983). *Ukrainian Canadians in Canada's Wars: Materials for Ukrainian Canadian History, Volume I*. Toronto: Ukrainian Canadian Research Foundation.
Greimas, A.J. (1987). *On Meaning*. London: Pinter.
Griffiths, N.E.S. (1969). *The Acadian Deportation: Deliberate Perfidy or Cruel Necessity?* Toronto: Copp Clark.
Gusfield, J. (1981). *The Culture of Public Problems: Drinking-Driving and the Symbolic Order*. Chicago: University of Chicago Press.

Haarhoff, T.J. (1948). *The Stranger at the Gate: Aspects of Exclusiveness and Co-operation in Ancient Greece and Rome, with Some Reference to Modern Times.* Oxford: Basil Blackwell.

Habermas, J. (1996). 'Labour and Interaction: Remarks on Hegel's Jena *Philosophy of Mind.*' In *Hegel's Dialectic of Desire and Recognition.* Ed. J. O'Neill. Albany: SUNY Press.

– (1991). *Moral Consciousness and Communicative Action.* Cambridge, MA: MIT Press.

– (1989). *The Theory of Communicative Action.* Boston: Beacon Press.

Hall, D.J. (1981). *Clifford Sifton, Volume One: The Young Napoleon 1861–1900.* Vancouver: University of British Columbia Press.

Hall, E. (1989). *Inventing the Barbarian: Greek Self-Definition through Tragedy.* Oxford: Clarendon Press.

Hall, S. (1991). 'Cultural Identity and Diaspora.' In *Colonial Discourse and Post-Colonial Theory: A Reader.* London: Harvester Wheatsheaf.

– (1987). 'Minimal Selves.' In *Identity: The Real Me.* London: ICA.

Halli, S., et al., eds. (1990). *Ethnic Demography: Canadian Immigrant, Racial, and Cultural Variations.* Ottawa: Carleton University Press.

Hawkes, A. (1919). *The Birthright: A Search for the Canadian Canadian and the Larger Loyalty.* Toronto: J.M. Dent.

Hayward, V. (1922). *Romantic Canada.* Toronto: Macmillan.

Hegel, G.W.F. (1983). 'The Jena Lectures on the Philosophy of Spirit.' In *Hegel and the Human Spirit.* Trans. L. Rauch. Detroit: Wayne State University Press.

– (1979). *System of Ethical Life and First Philosophy of Spirit.* Ed. and trans. T.M. Knox and H.S. Harris. Albany: SUNY Press.

– (1977). *Phenomenology of Spirit.* Trans. A.V. Miller. Oxford: Oxford University Press.

– (1956). *The Philosophy of Spirit.* Trans. J. Sibree. New York: Dover Publications.

– (1952). *Philosophy of Right.* Trans. T.M. Knox. Oxford: Clarendon Press.

Henderson, W.B. (1980). *Canada's Indian Reserves: Pre-Confederation.* Ottawa: Ministry of Indian Affairs and Northern Development.

Herodotus. (1954). *The Histories.* Harmondsworth: Penguin.

Hiller, H. (1996). *Canadian Society: A Macro Analysis.* Scarborough, ON: Prentice Hall.

Hillgarth, J.N. (1986). *Christianity and Paganism, 350–750: The Conversion of Western Europe.* Philadelphia: University of Philadelphia Press.

Hind, H.Y. (1859). *Northwest Territory: Reports of Progress; Together with a Preliminary and General Report on the Assiniboine and Saskatchewan Exploring Expedi-*

tion. Toronto: John Lovell, by order of the Legislative Assembly of the Province of Canada.

Hippocrates. (1923). 'Airs, Waters, Places.' In *Hippocrates*. Vol. 1. Harvard, MA: Harvard University Press.

Hobsbawm, E.J. (1990). *Nations and Nationalism since 1780*. New York: Cambridge Press.

Hodgen, M. (1964). *Early Anthropology in the Sixteenth and Seventeenth Centuries*. Philadelphia: University of Pennsylvania Press.

Honneth, A. (1995). *The Struggle for Recognition*. Cambridge: Polity Press.

Hopkins, J.C. (1912). *The Story of Our Country*. Toronto: John C. Winston Co.

– ed. (1911). *Empire Club Speeches*. Toronto: Saturday Night Press.

– ed. (1910). *Empire Club Speeches*. Toronto: Warwick Bros. & Rutter.

Howley, J.P. (1974). *The Beothucks or Red Indians: The Aboriginal Inhabitants of Newfoundland*. Toronto: Coles Publishing Co.

Hryniuk, S., and L. Luciuk. (1993). *Multiculturalism and Ukrainian Canadians*. Polyphony Series, volume 13. Toronto: University of Toronto Press.

Hudson's Bay Record Society. (1965). *Letters from Hudson Bay 1703–40*. Ed. K.G. Davies. London: Hudson's Bay Record Society (v. 25).

– (1957). *Copy Booke of Letters Commissions Instructions Outward, 1688–1696*. London: Hudson's Bay Record Society (v. 20).

– (1951). *Cumberland and Hudson House Journals 1775–82*. London: Hudson's Bay Record Society (v. 14).

– (1948). *Copy-Book of Letters Outward &c, 1680–1687*. London: Hudson's Bay Record Society (v. 11).

– (1946). *Minutes of the Hudson's Bay Company 1679–1684*. London: Hudson's Bay Record Society (v. 9).

Humphreys, S.C. (1978). *Anthropology and the Greeks*. London: Routledge.

Hutcheon, L. (1988). *The Canadian Postmodern: A Study of Contemporary English-Canadian Fiction*. Toronto: Oxford University Press.

Ignatieff, M. (1993). *Blood and Belonging*. Toronto: Penguin.

Jaenen, C.J. (1991). 'French Sovereignty and Native Nationhood during the French Régime.' In *Sweet Promises: A Reader on Indian-White Relations in Canada*. Ed. J.R. Miller. Toronto: University of Toronto Press.

Jenson, J. (1993). 'Naming Nations: Making Nationalist Claims in Canadian Public Discourse.' *Canadian Review of Sociology and Anthropology* 30(3): 337–58.

Kallen, E. (1982). 'Multiculturalism: Ideology, Policy, and Reality.' *Journal of Canadian Studies* 17(1): 51–63.

Kelly, E. (1974). *Murder for Fun*. Cobalt, ON: Highway Book Shop.

Kingsford, W. (1968 [1887]). *The History of Canada*. Vol. 3. New York: AMS Press.

Kirkconnell, W. (1967). *A Slice of Canada: Memoirs*. Wolfville, NS: published for Acadia University by University of Toronto Press.

– (1943). 'Our Communists and the New Canadians.' Address delivered before the Canadian Club of Toronto, 1 Feb. 1943. Toronto: Southam Press.

– (1941). *Canadians All: A Primer of Canadian National Unity*. Ottawa: Director of Public Information.

Knowles, V. (1997). *Strangers at Our Gates: Canadian Immigration and Immigration Policy, 1540–1997*. Toronto: Dundurn Press.

Kojeve, A. (1969). *Introduction to the Reading of Hegel*. New York: Basic Books.

Kymlicka, W. (1995). *Multicultural Citizenship: A Liberal Theory of Minority Rights*. Oxford: Clarendon Press.

– (1989). *Liberalism, Community and Culture*. Oxford: Clarendon Press.

Lacan, J. (1981). *The Four Fundamental Concepts of Psycho-analysis*. New York: Norton.

– (1968). *Speech and Language in Psychoanalysis*. Baltimore: Johns Hopkins University Press.

Laclau, E. (1996). *Emancipations*. London: Verso.

– (1990). *New Reflections on the Revolution of Our Time*. London: Verso.

Laclau, E., and C. Mouffe. (1985). *Hegemony and Socialist Strategy*. London: Verso.

Laclau, E., and L. Zac. (1994). 'Minding the Gap: The Subject of Politics.' In *The Making of Political Identities*. Ed. E. Laclau. London: Verso.

Lacombe, D. (1996). 'Reforming Foucault: A Critique of the Social Control Thesis.' *British Journal of Sociology*. 47(2): 332–52.

Lahontan, Baron de. (1940). *The Oakes Collection: New Documents by Lahontan, concerning Canada and Newfoundland*. Ottawa: J.O. Patenaude, Printer to the King's Most Excellent Majesty.

– (1703). *New Voyages to North America*. London: H. Bonwicke. CIHM 37429.

Légaré, E.I. (1995). 'Canadian Multiculturalism and Aboriginal People: Negotiating a Place in the Nation.' *Identities* 1(4): 347–66.

Lehmann, H. (1986). *The German Canadians 1750–1937: Immigration, Settlement and Culture*. St John's: Jesperson Press.

Lescarbot, M. (1907 [1618]). *The History of New France*. Toronto: The Champlain Society.

Leslie, J., and R. Maguire, eds. (1978). *The Historical Development of the Indian Act*. 2nd ed. Ottawa: Ministry of Indian Affairs and Northern Development.

Lewycky, L. (1992). 'Multiculturalism in the 1990s and into the 21st Century: Beyond Ideology and Utopia.' In *Deconstructing a Nation: Immigration, Multiculturalism, and Racism in 90's Canada*. Ed. V. Satzewich. Halifax: Fernwood.

Li, P. (1990). *Race and Ethnic Relations in Canada*. Toronto: Oxford University Press.

Long, T. (1986). *Barbarians in Greek Comedy*. Carbondale and Edwardsville: Southern Illinois University Press.

Lovejoy, A.O. (1936). *The Great Chain of Being: A Study of the History of an Idea*. Cambridge, MA: Harvard University Press.

Lower, A.M. (1946). *Colony to Nation: A History of Canada*. Don Mills, ON: Longmans Canada.

Lucas, C. (1912). *Lord Durham's Report on the Affairs of British North America*. New York: Augustus M. Kelly.

Luciuk, L., ed. (1994). *Righting an Injustice: The Debate over Redress for Canada's First National Internment Operations*. Toronto: Justinian Press.

Lupul, M. (1993). 'A Question of Identity: Canada's Ukrainians and Multiculturalism.' *Polyphony* 13: 8–13.

Lyotard, J.-F. (1984). *The Postmodern Condition*. Minneapolis: University of Minnesota Press.

MacBeth, R.G. (1912). *Our Task in Canada*. Toronto: Westminster Co.

Major, R.H., ed. (1961). *Christopher Columbus: Four Voyages to the New World, Letters and Selected Documents*. New York: Corinth Books.

Marshall, I. (1996). *A History and Ethnography of the Beothuk*. Montreal and Kingston: McGill-Queen's University Press.

– (1989). *Reports and Letters by George Christopher Pulling, relating to the Beothuk Indians of Newfoundland*. St John's: Breakwater Press.

Maseres, F. (1772). *Collection of Several Commissions and Other Public Proclamations Proceeding from His Majesty* ... London: W. & J. Richards.

McLean, D. (1987). *Home from the Hill: A History of the Métis in Western Canada*. Regina: Gabriel Dumont Institute.

McLellan, J., and A. Richmond. (1994). 'Multiculturalism in Crisis: A Postmodern Perspective on Canada.' *Ethnic and Racial Studies* 17(4): 662–83.

Mealing, S.R., ed. (1963). *The Jesuit Relations and Allied Documents: A Selection*. Toronto: McClelland and Stewart.

Melnycky, P. (1983). 'The Internment of Ukrainians in Canada.' In *Loyalties in Conflict: Ukrainians in Canada during the Great War*. Ed. Frances Swyripa and J.H. Thompson. Edmonton: Canadian Institute of Ukrainian Studies.

Miller, J.R., ed. (1991). *Sweet Promises: A Reader on Indian-White Relations in Canada*. Toronto: University of Toronto Press.

– (1989). *Skyscrapers Hide the Heavens: A History of Indian-White Relations in Canada*. Toronto: University of Toronto Press.

Millot, B. (1988). 'Symbol, Desire, and Power.' *Theory, Culture and Society* 5: 675–94.

Minh-ha, Trinh T. (1991). *When the Moon Waxes Red*. New York: Routledge.

Moodley, K. (1983). 'Canadian Multiculturalism as Ideology.' *Ethnic and Racial Studies* 6(3): 320–31.

Morriset, J. (1998). 'The Native Path and Its Trance-Cultural Connections.' In *Multiculturalism in a World of Leaking Boundaries*. Ed. D. Haselbach. Münster: LIT.

Mouffe, C. (1993a). 'Feminism, Citizenship, and Radical Democratic Politics.' In *Social Postmodernism*. Ed. L. Nicholson and S. Seidman. Cambridge: Cambridge University Press.

– (1993b). *The Return of the Political*. London: Verso.

Neilsen, G., and J. Jackson. (1991). 'Cultural Studies, a Sociological Poetics: Institutions of the Canadian Imaginary.' *Canadian Review of Sociology and Anthropology* 28(2): 279–98.

Newman, P. (1985). *Company of Adventurers*. Markham, ON: Viking.

Nietzsche, F. (1967a). *On the Genealogy of Morals*. New York: Random House.

– (1967b). *The Will to Power*. New York: Random House.

– (1967c). *Ecce Homo*. New York: Random House.

Nish, C. (1966). *The French Canadians 1759–1766: Conquered? Half-Conquered? Liberated?* Toronto: Copp Clark.

Norris, J., ed. (1971). *Strangers Entertained: A History of the Ethnic Groups of British Columbia*. Vancouver: British Columbia Centennial 71 Committee.

Norriss, W. (1875). *The Canadian Question*. Montreal: Lovell Printing and Publishing Co.

Nunavut Constitutional Forum. (1983). *Building Nunavut*. Ottawa: The Forum.

Nute, G.L. (1943). *Caesars of the Wilderness*. New York: D. Appleton.

– (1935). 'Radisson and Groseilliers' Contribution to Geography.' *Minnesota History* 16: 414–26.

Oliver, E.H., ed. (1914). *The Canadian Northwest: Its Early Development and Legislative Records*. Publications of the Canadian Archives, no. 9. Ottawa: Government Printing Bureau.

Onufrijchuk, R. (1988). 'Post-modern or Perednovok: Deconstructing Ethnicity.' In *Ethnicity in a Technological Age*. Ed. I. Angus. Edmonton: Canadian Institute of Ukrainian Studies.

Optima Consultants in Applied Social Research Inc. (1988). *Analysis of Thompson Lightstone Survey of Public Attitudes towards Multiculturalism*. Ottawa: Secretary of State, Multiculturalism.

Ostergard, U. (1992). 'What is National and Ethnic Identity?' In *Ethnicity in Hellenistic Egypt*. Ed. P. Bilde. Aarhus: Aarhus University Press.

Palmer, H. (1991). *Ethnicity and Politics in Canada since Confederation*. Ottawa: Canadian Historical Association.

- (1982a). *Patterns of Prejudice: A History of Nativism in Alberta*. Toronto: McClelland and Stewart.
- (1982b). 'Canadian Immigration and Ethnic History in the 1970s and 1980s.' *Journal of Canadian Studies* 17(1): 35–50.
- ed. (1975). *Immigration and the Rise of Multiculturalism*. Toronto: Copp Clark.
- (1973). 'Nativism and Ethnic Tolerance in Alberta 1920–1972.' Canadian Theses on Microfilm, no. 17136.
Parkman, F. (1915). *The Jesuits in North America in the Seventeenth Century*. New York: Scribner's.
- (1890). *The Old Regime in Canada*. Boston: Little, Brown.
Pedley, C. (1863). *The History of Newfoundland from the Earliest Times to the Year 1860*. London: Longman, Green, Roberts, and Green.
Peter, K. (1981). 'The Myth of Multiculturalism and Other Policitical Fables.' In *Ethnicity, Power, and Politics in Canada*. Ed. J. Dahlie and T. Fernando. Toronto: Methuen.
Peterson, J. (1985). 'Many Roads to Red River: Métis Genesis in the Great Lakes Region, 1680–1815.' In *The New Peoples: Being and Becoming Métis in North America*. Ed. J. Peterson and J. Brown. Winnipeg: University of Manitoba Press.
Petty, Sir W. (1967). *The Petty Papers*. New York: Augustus M. Kelley.
Plato. (1980). *The Laws*. Trans. T. Pangle. New York: Basic Books.
- (1965). *Timaeus and Critias*. Harmondsworth: Penguin.
- (1955). *The Republic*. Harmondsworth: Penguin.
Pliny. (1940). *Natural History*. London and Cambridge: Harvard University Press.
Plotinus. (1969). *The Enneads*. Trans. S. McKenna. London: Faber.
Polo, Marco. (1968). *The Travels of Marco Polo*. New York: AMS Press.
Porter, J. (1975). 'Ethnic Pluralism in Canadian Perspective.' In *Ethnicity: Theory and Experience*. Ed. N. Glazer and P. Moynihan. Cambridge, MA: Harvard University Press.
- (1969). 'Bilingualism and the Myths of Culture.' *Canadian Review of Sociology and Anthropology* 6(2): 111–19.
- (1965). *The Vertical Mosaic: An Analysis of Social Class and Power in Canada*. Toronto: University of Toronto Press.
Poster, M. (1992). 'Postmodernity and the Politics of Multiculturalism: The Lyotard-Habermas Debate over Social Theory.' *Modern Fiction Studies* 38(3): 567–80.
Purich, D. (1992). *The Inuit and Their Land*. Toronto: James Lorimer & Co.
- (1988). *The Métis*. Toronto: James Lorimer & Co.

Quinn, D.B. (1979). *New American World: A Documentary History of North America to 1612*. New York: Arno Press.

Renan, E. (1990). 'What Is a Nation?' In *Nation and Narration*. Ed. H. Bhabha. London: Routledge.

Repka, W., and K. Repka. (1982). *Dangerous Patriots: Canada's Unknown Prisoners of War*. Vancouver: New Star.

Resnick, P. (1994). *Thinking English Canada*. Toronto: Stoddart.

Rich, E.E. (1967). *The Fur Trade and the Northwest to 1857*. Toronto: McClelland and Stewart.

– (1958). *The History of the Hudson's Bay Company 1670–1870*. London: The Hudson's Bay Record Society (vols. 21–2 of series).

Rioux, M. (1971). *Quebec in Question*. Toronto: James Lewis and Samuel.

Roberts, B. (1988). *Whence They Came: Deportation from Canada 1900–1935*. Ottawa: University of Ottawa Press.

Rocher, G. (1976). 'Multiculturalism: The Doubts of a Francophone.' In Canadian Consultative Council on Multiculturalism, Conference Report, *Multiculturalism as State Policy*. Ottawa: Supply and Services Canada.

– (1969). 'Le Canada: Un pays à rebâtir?' *Canadian Review of Sociology and Anthropology* 6(2): 119–25.

Rockefeller, S. (1992). 'Comment.' In *Multiculturalism and the Politics of Recognition*. Ed. A. Gutman. Princeton: Princeton University Press.

Rorty, R. (1985). 'Habermas and Lyotard on Postmodernity.' In *Habermas and Modernity*. Ed. R. Bernstein. London: Polity Press

– (1979). *Philosophy and the Mirror of Nature*. Princeton: Princeton University Press.

Ross, A. (1972). *The Red River Settlement: Its Rise, Progress, and Current State*. Rutland, VT: Charles E. Tuttle.

Rowe, F. (1977). *Extinction: The Beothuks of Newfoundland*. Toronto: McGraw-Hill Ryerson.

Ryder, N.B. (1955). 'The Interpretation of Origin Statistics.' *Canadian Journal of Economics and Political Science* 21(4): 466–79.

Sandel, M. (1984). 'The Procedural Republic and the Unencumbered Self.' *Political Theory* 12(1): 81–96.

Sapir, E. (1912). 'The Work of the Division of Anthropology of the Dominion Government.' *Queen's Quarterly* 20(1): 60–72.

Satzewich, V., ed. (1992). *Deconstructing a Nation: Immigration, Multiculturalism and Racism in 90's Canada*. Halifax: Fernwood Publishing.

Schleifer, R. (1987). *A.J. Greimas and the Nature of Meaning*. London: Croom Helm.

Scott, J. (1992). 'Multiculturalism and the Politics of Identity.' *October* 61: 12–19.

Shortt, A., and G. Doughty, eds. (1907). *Documents Relating to the Constitutional History of Canada*. Ottawa: King's Printer.

Singh, Narinder. (1994). *Canadian Sikhs: History, Religion, and Culture of Sikhs in North America*. Ottawa: Canadian Sikhs' Studies Institute.

Smith, A.D. (1986). *The Ethnic Origins of Nations*. New York: Basil Blackwell.

Smith, D.B. (1989). 'The Dispossession of the Mississauga Indians: A Missing Chapter in the Early History of Upper Canada.' In *Historical Essays on Upper Canada: New Perspectives*. Eds. Johnson and B.G. Wilson. Ottawa: Carleton University Press.

Smith, L.A.H. (1969). 'Le Canadien and the British Constitution, 1806–1810.' In *Constitutionalism and Nationalism in Lower Canada*. Ed. R. Cook. Toronto: University of Toronto Press.

Smith, Melvin H. (1995). *Our Home or Native Land?* Victoria: Crown Western.

Smith, W.G. (1919). *A Study in Canadian Immigration*. Toronto: Ryerson.

Society for the Propagation of the Gospel in Foreign Parts. (1882). *The Results of 180 Years of Work, As Set Forth in Letters of Colonial and Missionary Bishops*. Westminster, S.W.: The Society. CIHM 64610.

Stanley, G.F.G. (1961). *The Birth of Western Canada: A History of the Riel Rebellions*. Toronto: University of Toronto Press.

– (1949). 'The Policy of "Francisation" as Applied to the Indians during the Ancien Regime.' *Revue d'Histoire de l'Amérique Française* 3(3): 333–48.

Tacitus, C. (1954). *Agricola*. Trans. H. Mattingly. Harmondsworth: Penguin.

Tajfel, H. (1978). 'Interaction and the Social World.' In *Introducing Social Psychology*. Ed. H. Tajfel and C. Fraser. Harmondsworth: Penguin.

– (1969). 'The Formation of National Attitudes: A Social-Psychological Perspective.' In *Interdisciplinary Relationships in the Social Sciences*. Ed. M. Sherif and C.W. Sherif. Chicago: Aldine.

Taylor, C. (1993). *Reconciling the Solitudes: Essays on Canadian Federalism and Nationalism*. Montreal and Kingston: McGill-Queen's University Press.

– (1992). 'The Politics of Recognition.' In *Multiculturalism and the Politics of Recognition*. Ed. A. Gutman. Princeton: Princeton University Press.

– (1991). *The Malaise of Modernity*. Concord, ON: Anansi.

– (1985a). 'Understanding and Ethnocentricity.' In *Philosophy and the Human Sciences: Philosophical Papers 2*. Cambridge: Cambridge University Press.

– (1985b). 'Interpretation and the Sciences of Man.' In *Philosophy and the Human Sciences: Philosophical Papers 2*. Cambridge: Cambridge University Press.

– (1975). *Hegel*. Cambridge: Cambridge University Press.

Thompson, J.H. (1991). *Ethnic Minorities during Two World Wars*. Ottawa: Canadian Historical Association.

Thompson, L.A. (1989). *Romans and Blacks*. Norman and London: University of Oklahoma Press.

Thwaites, R.G. (1897). *The Jesuit Relations and Allied Documents* Cleveland: Burrows Brothers.

Tobias, J.L. (1991). 'Protection, Civilization, and Assimilation: An Outline of Canada's Indian Policy.' In *Sweet Promises*. Ed. J.R. Miller. Toronto: University of Toronto Press.

Todorov, T. (1993). *On Human Diversity: Nationalism, Racism, and Exoticism in French Thought*. Cambridge, MA: Harvard University Press.

– (1984). *The Conquest of America: The Question of the Other*. New York: Harper and Row.

Trigger, B. (1985). *Natives and Newcomers: Canada's 'Heroic Age' Reconsidered*. Kingston and Montreal: McGill-Queen's University Press.

Trudel, M. (1973). *The Beginnings of New France*. Toronto: McClelland and Stewart.

Tucker, R. (1978). *The Marx-Engels Reader*. New York: Norton.

Tully, J. (1995). *Strange Multiplicity: Constitutionalism in an Age of Diversity*. Cambridge: Cambridge University Press.

Tyrrell, J.B., ed. (1931). *Documents Relating to the Early History of Hudson Bay*. Toronto: Champlain Society.

Upton, L.F.S. (1992). 'The Extermination of the Beothucks of Newfoundland.' In *Sweet Promises*. Ed. J.R. Miller. Toronto: University of Toronto Press.

Urquhart, M.C., ed., (1965). *Historical Statistics of Canada*. Toronto: Macmillan.

Vachon, R., and J. Langlais, eds. (1983). *Who Is a Québécois?* Ottawa: Tecumseh Press.

Virgil. (1962). *The Aenid*. Trans. I.R. Lind. Bloomington: Indiana University Press.

Vlastos, G. (1981). *Platonic Studies*. Princeton: Princeton University Press.

Wakefield, E.G. (1929). *A Letter from Sydney and Other Writings*. London: J.M. Dent.

Walker, J. (1980). *A History of Blacks in Canada*. Ottawa: Minister of State for Multiculturalism.

Ward, P. (1978). *White Canada Forever: Popular Attitudes and Public Policy toward Orientals in British Columbia*. Montreal: McGill-Queen's University Press.

Wardman, A. (1982). *Religion and Statecraft among the Romans*. Baltimore: Johns Hopkins University Press.

Waubageshig, ed. (1970). *The Only Good Indian*. Toronto: New Press.

Weber, M. (1946). *From Max Weber*. New York: Oxford University Press.

Whitaker, R. (1991). *Canadian Immigration Policy since Confederation*. Ottawa: Canadian Historical Association.

– (1987). *Double Standard: The Secret History of Canadian Immigration*. Toronto: Lester and Orpen Denys.

Whitbourne, R. (1971). *A Discourse and Discovery of New-Found-Land*. Amsterdam and New York: Da Capo Press.

Whittaker, M. (1984). *Jews and Christians: Graeco-Roman Views*. Cambridge: Cambridge University Press.

Wilden, A. (1980). *System and Structure: Essays in Communication and Exchange*. 2nd ed. London: Tavistock.

– (1968). *Speech and Language in Psychoanalysis*. Baltimore: Johns Hopkins University Press.

Williams, R. (1997). *Hegel's Ethics of Recognition*. Berkeley: University of California Press.

– (1992). *Recognition: Fichte and Hegel on the Other*. New York: SUNY Press.

Woodsworth, J.S. (1972a). *Strangers within Our Gates; or, Coming Canadians*. Toronto: University of Toronto Press.

– (1972b). *My Neighbour*. Toronto: University of Toronto Press.

Young, R. (1995). *Colonial Desire: Hybridity in Theory, Culture, and Race*. New York: Routledge.

Yuzyk, P. (1965). 'Canada: A Multicultural Nation.' *Canadian Slavonic Papers* 7: 25–31.

Zaslove, J. (1994). 'Constituting Modernity: The Epic Horizons of Constitutional Narratives.' *Public* 9: 62–77.

Zizek, S. (1997a). 'Multiculturalism; or, The Cultural Logic of Late Capitalism.' *New Left Review* 225: 28–52.

– (1997b). *The Plague of Fantasies*. London: Verso.

– (1991a). *Looking Awry: An Introduction to Jacques Lacan through Popular Culture*. Cambridge, MA: MIT Press.

– (1991b). *For They Know Not What They Do: Enjoyment as a Political Factor*. London: Verso.

– (1990). 'Beyond Discourse-Analysis' In *New Reflections on the Revolution of Our Times*. Ed. E. Laclau. London: Verso.

Index